THAI
PHRASEBOOK

Compiled by
LEXUS

ROUGH
GUIDES

www.roughguides.com

Credits

Thai Phrasebook	Rough Guides Reference
Compiled by: Lexus with David and Somsong Smyth	Director: Andrew Lockett
Lexus series editor: Sally Davies	Editors: Kate Berens, Ian Blenkinsop, Tom Cabot, Tracy Hopkins, Matthew Milton, Joe Staines
Layout: Nikhil Agarwal	
Pictures: Nicole Newman	

Publishing information

First edition published in 1999
This updated edition published October 2011 by
Rough Guides Ltd, 80 Strand, London, WC2R 0RL
Email: mail@roughguides.com

Distributed by the Penguin Group:
Penguin Books Ltd, 80 Strand, London, WC2R 0RL
Penguin Group (USA), 375 Hudson Street, NY 10014, USA
Penguin Group (Australia), 250 Camberwell Road, Camberwell,
Victoria 3124, Australia
Penguin Group (New Zealand), Cnr Rosedale and Airborne Roads,
Albany, Auckland, New Zealand

Rough Guides is represented in Canada by Tourmaline Editions Inc.,
662 King Street West, Suite 304, Toronto, Ontario, M5V 1M7

Printed in Singapore by Toppan Security Printing Pte. Ltd.

© Lexus Ltd, 2011
Travel tips © Paul Gray & Lucy Ridout

248 pages

A catalogue record for this book is available from the British Library.

978-1-84836-737-1

1 3 5 7 9 8 6 4 2

CONTENTS

How to use this book

The Rough Guide Thai Phrasebook is a highly practical introduction to the contemporary language. It gets straight to the point in every situation you might encounter: in bars and shops, on trains and buses, in hotels and banks, on holiday or on business. Laid out in clear A–Z style with easy-to-find, colour-coded sections, it uses key words to take you directly to the phrase you need – so if you want some help booking a room, just look up "room" in the dictionary section.

The phrasebook starts off with **Basics**, where we list some essential phrases, including words for numbers, dates and telling the time, and give guidance on pronunciation, along with a short section on the different regional accents you might come across. Then, to get you started in two-way communication, the **Scenarios** section offers dialogues in key situations such as renting a car, asking directions or booking a taxi, and includes words and phrases for when something goes wrong, from getting a flat tyre or asking to move apartments to more serious emergencies. You can listen to these and download them for free from www.roughguides.com/phrasebooks for use on your computer, MP3 player or smartphone.

Forming the main part of the guide is a double dictionary, first **English–Thai**, which gives you the essential words you'll need plus easy-to-use phonetic transliterations. Then, in the **Thai–English** dictionary, we've given the phrases you'll be likely to hear (starting with a selection of slang and colloquialisms), followed by the **Signs** section, which explains many of the signs, labels, instructions and

other basic words you'll come across in print or in public places. Scattered throughout the sections are travel tips direct from the authors of the Rough Guides guidebook series.

Finally, there's an extensive **Menu reader**. Consisting of separate food and drink sections, each starting with a list of essential terms, it's indispensable whether you're eating out, stopping for a quick drink or looking around a local food market.

เที่ยวให้สนุกนะ
têe-o hâi sa-nòok ná!
Have a good trip!

BASICS

Basic phrases

yes krúp (kâ); châi ครับ(ค่ะ) ใช่

no mâi ไม่

OK oh-kay โอเค

hello sa-wùt dee สวัสดี

hi! bpai nǎi? ไปไหน

good morning sa-wùt dee krúp (kâ) สวัสดีครับ(ค่ะ)

good evening sa-wùt dee krúp (kâ) สวัสดีครับ(ค่ะ)

good night sa-wùt dee krúp (kâ) สวัสดีครับ(ค่ะ)

goodbye lah gòrn ná ลาก่อนนะ

bye lah gòrn ลาก่อน

see you! jer gun mài ná! เจอกันใหมนะ

see you later děe-o jer gun èek เดี๋ยวเจอกันอีก

please (requesting something) kòr... ขอ ...
(offering) chern krúp (kâ) เชิญครับ(ค่ะ)

(could you) please...? chôo-ay... nòy dâi mái? ช่วย... หน่อยได้ไหม

yes please ao krúp (kâ) เอาครับ(ค่ะ)

thanks, thank you kòrp-koon ขอบคุณ

no thanks, no thank you mâi ao kòrp-koon ไม่เอาขอบคุณ

thank you very much kòrp-koon mâhk ขอบคุณมาก

don't mention it mâi bpen rai ไม่เป็นไร

how do you do? sa-wùt dee krúp (kâ) สวัสดีครับ(ค่ะ)

how are you? bpen yung-ngai bâhng? เป็นอย่างไรบ้าง

fine, thanks sa-bai dee krúp (kâ) สบายดีครับ(ค่ะ)

nice to meet you yin dee têe dâi róo-jùk gun ยินดีที่ได้รู้จักกัน

excuse me (to get past, to say sorry) kòr-tôht ขอโทษ
(to get attention) koon krúp (kâ) คุณครับ (ค่ะ)
(to say pardon?) a-rai ná? อะไรนะ

I'm sorry pǒm (chún) sěe-a jai ผม(ฉัน)เสียใจ

sorry?/pardon (me)? (didn't understand) a-rai ná krúp (ká)? อะไรนะครับ(คะ)

I see/I understand
kâo jai láir-o เข้าใจแล้ว

I don't understand
pŏm (chún) mâi kâo jai
ผม(ฉัน)ไม่เข้าใจ

do you speak English?
koon pôot pah-săh
ung-grìt bpen mái?
คุณพูดภาษาอังกฤษเป็นไหม

I don't speak Thai pŏm (chún)
pôot pah-săh tai mâi bpen
ผม(ฉัน)พูดภาษาไทยไม่เป็น

**could you speak more
slowly?** pôot cháh cháh nòy!
พูดช้า ๆ หน่อย

could you repeat that?
pôot èek tee dâi mái?
พูดอีกทีได้ไหม

**could you write it
down?** chôo-ay kĕe-un
long hâi nòy, dâi mái?
ยเขียนลงให้หน่อยได้ไหม

I'd like a... pŏm (chún) ao...
ผม(ฉัน)เอา...

I'd like to... pŏm (chún) yàhk...
ผม(ฉัน)อยาก...

can I have...? kŏr... dâi mái?
ขอ... ได้ไหม

how much is it? tâo-rài? เท่าไร

it is... bpen... เป็น...

where is it? yòo têe năi?
อยู่ที่ไหน

is it far? yòo glai mái?
อยู่ไกลไหม

Note: there are different polite particle forms for male and female speakers. Where you have krúp (kâ) or krúp (ká), the form in brackets should be used by a female speaker. Where you have pim (chún) ('I' or 'me') in a phrase, pim should be used by a male speaker and chún by a female speaker.

Dates

Dates are expressed using the pattern: wun (**day**) + ordinal number + month. Ordinal numbers are formed by placing têe in front of the cardinal number. A list of numbers is given on page 12. Thais use both the Western calendar and a Buddhist calendar. Buddha is said to have attained enlightenment in the year 543BC, so Thai dates start from that point: thus 1996 AD becomes 2539 BE (Buddhist Era).

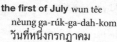

the first of July wun têe
nèung ga-rúk-ga-dah-kom
วันที่หนึ่งกรกฎาคม

the twentieth of March
wun têe yêe sìp mee-nah-kom
วันที่ยี่สิบมีนาคม

Days

Monday wun jun วันจันทร์

Tuesday wun ung-kahn
วันอังคาร

Wednesday wun póot วันพุธ

Thursday wun pá-réu-hùt
วันพฤหัส

Friday wun sùk วันศุกร์

Saturday wun săo วันเสาร์

Sunday wun ah-tít วันอาทิตย์

Months

January mók-ga-rah-kom
มกราคม

February goom-pah-pun
กุมภาพันธ์

March mee-nah-kom มีนาคม

April may-săh-yon เมษายน

May préut-sa-pah-kom
พฤษภาคม

June mí-too-nah-yon มิถุนายน

July ga-rúk-ga-dah-kom
กรกฎาคม

August sĭng-hăh-kom สิงหาคม

September gun-yah-yon
กันยายน

October dtoo-lah-kom
ตุลาคม

November préut-sa-ji-gah-yon
พฤศจิกายน

December tun-wah-kom
ธันวาคม

Time

The Thai system of telling the time seems rather complicated at
first because it uses different words for **'o'clock'** depending on
what time of day it is: **from 1 a.m. to 5 a.m.** dtee; **from 6 a.m. to
midday** mohng cháo; **from 1 p.m. to 4 p.m.** bài; **from 5 p.m. to 6
p.m.** yen; **from 7 p.m. to midnight** tôom.

Here, then, is how the hours are expressed in Thai:

1 a.m. dtee nèung ตีหนึ่ง

2 a.m. dtee sŏrng ตีสอง

3 a.m. dtee săhm ตีสาม

4 a.m. dtee sèe ตีสี่

5 a.m. dtee hâh ตีห้า

6 a.m. hòk mohng cháo
หกโมงเช้า

7 a.m. jèt mohng cháo
เจ็ดโมงเช้า or mohng cháo
โมงเช้า

8 a.m. bpàirt mohng cháo
แปดโมงเช้า or sŏrng mohng
cháo สองโมงเช้า

9 a.m. gâo mohng cháo
เก้าโมงเช้า or săhm mohng
cháo สามโมงเช้า

10 a.m. sìp mohng cháo
สิบโมงเช้า or sèe mohng cháo
สี่โมงเช้า

11 a.m. sìp èt mohng cháo
สิบเอ็ดโมงเช้า

or hâh mohng cháo ห้าโมงเช้า

midday têe-ung wun เที่ยงวัน

1 p.m. bài mohng บ่ายโมง

2 p.m. bài sŏrng mohng
บ่ายสองโมง

3 p.m. bài săhm mohng
บ่ายสามโมง

4 p.m. bài sèe mohng
บ่ายสี่โมง

5 p.m. hâh mohng yen
ห้าโมงเย็น

6 p.m. hòk mohng yen
หกโมงเย็น

7 p.m. tôom nèung ทุ่มหนึ่ง

8 p.m. sŏrng tôom สองทุ่ม

9 p.m. săhm tôom สามทุ่ม

10 p.m. sèe tôom สี่ทุ่ม

11 p.m. hâh tôom ห้าทุ่ม

midnight têe-ung keun
เที่ยงคืน

Note: There is no equivalent of **'it is...'** in Thai when stating the time; săhm tôom means both **'9 p.m.'** and **'it is 9 p.m.'**.

To say **'half-past'**, use the word krêung (half). There is no special word for **'quarter past'** or **'quarter to'** the hour; these are translated by **'fifteen minutes (past)'** and **'fifteen minutes (to)'** the hour:

11.30 a.m. sìp-èt mohng krêung
สิบเอ็ดโมงครึ่ง

3.30 p.m. bài săhm mohng
krêung บ่ายสามโมงครึ่ง

11.30 p.m. hâh tôom krêung
ห้าทุ่มครึ่ง

1.15 p.m. bài mohng síp hâh
nah-tee บ่ายโมงสิบห้านาที

1.45 p.m. èek sìp hâh nah-
tee bài sŏrng mohng
อีกสิบห้านาทีบ่ายสองโมง

Note that when expressing minutes past the hour, the word order is:
hour time   **number of minutes**   nah-tee (minutes)

2.10 p.m. bài sŏrng mohng sìp
nah-tee บ่ายสองโมงสิบนาที

8.25 p.m. sŏrng tôom yêe sìp hâh
nah-tee สองทุ่มยี่สิบห้านาที

To express minutes to the hour, the word order is as follows:
number of minutes   **hour time**   èek (further, more)

4.50 p.m. èek sìp nah-
tee hâh mohng yen
อีกสิบนาทีห้าโมงเย็น

10.55 p.m. èek hâh nah-tee hâh
tôom อีกห้านาทีห้าทุ่ม

what time is it? gèe mohng
láir-o? กี่โมงแล้ว

hour chôo-a-mohng ชั่วโมง

minute nah-tee นาที

two minutes sŏrng nah-tee
สองนาที

second wí-nah-tee วินาที

a quarter of an hour sìp hâh
nah-tee สิบห้านาที

half an hour krêung chôo-a-
mohng ครึ่งชั่วโมง

three quarters of an hour sèe
sìp hâh nah-tee สี่สิบห้านาที

Numbers

0 sŏon ๐ ศูนย์

1 nèung ๑ หนึ่ง

2 sŏrng ๒ สอง

3 săhm ๓ สาม

4 sèe ๔ สี่

5 hâh ๕ ห้า

6 hòk ๖ หก

7 jèt ๗ เจ็ด

8 bpàirt ๘ แปด

9 gâo ๙ เก้า

10 sìp ๑๐ สิบ

11 sìp-èt ๑๑ สิบเอ็ด

12 sìp-sŏrng ๑๒ สิบสอง

13 sìp-săhm ๑๓ สิบสาม

14 sìp-sèe ๑๔ สิบสี่

15 sìp-hâh ๑๕ สิบห้า

16 sìp-hòk ๑๖ สิบหก

17 sìp-jèt ๑๗ สิบเจ็ด

18 sìp-bpàirt ๑๘ สิบแปด

19 sìp-gâo ๑๙ สิบเก้า

20 yêe-sìp ๒๐ ยี่สิบ

21 yêe-sìp-èt ๒๑ ยี่สิบเอ็ด

22 yêe-sìp-sŏrng ๒๒ ยี่สิบสอง

30 săhm-sìp ๓๐ สามสิบ

31 săhm-sìp-èt ๓๑ สามสิบเอ็ด

40 sèe-sìp ๔๐ สี่สิบ

50 hâh-sìp ๕๐ ห้าสิบ

60 hòk-sìp ๖๐ หกสิบ

70 jèt-sìp ๗๐ เจ็ดสิบ

80 bpàirt-sìp ๘๐ แปดสิบ

90 gâo-sìp ๙๐ เก้าสิบ

100 nèung róy ๑๐๐ หนึ่งร้อย

101 nèung róy nèung
๑๐๑ หนึ่งร้อยหนึ่ง

102 nèung róy sŏrng
๑๐๒ หนึ่งร้อยสอง

110 nèung róy sìp
๑๑๐ หนึ่งร้อยสิบ

200 sŏrng róy ๒๐๐ สองร้อย

201 sŏrng róy nèung
๒๐๑ สองร้อยหนึ่ง

202 sŏrng róy sŏrng
๒๐๒ สองร้อยสอง

210 sŏrng róy sìp
๒๑๐ สองร้อยสิบ

1,000 nèung pun ๑๐๐๐ หนึ่งพัน

2,000 sŏrng pun ๒๐๐๐ สองพัน

10,000 nèung mèun
๑๐๐๐๐ หนึ่งหมื่น

100,000 nèung săirn
๑๐๐๐๐๐ หนึ่งแสน

1,000,000 nèung láhn
๑๐๐๐๐๐๐ หนึ่งล้าน

100,000,000 nèung róy láhn
๑๐๐๐๐๐๐๐๐ หนึ่งร้อยล้าน

Ordinals

1st têe nèung ที่หนึ่ง

2nd têe sŏrng ที่สอง

3rd têe săhm ที่สาม

4th têe sèe ที่สี่

5th têe hâh ที่ห้า

6th têe hòk ที่หก

7th têe jèt ที่เจ็ด

8th têe bpàirt ที่แปด

9th têe gâo ที่เก้า

10th têe sìp ที่สิบ

Pronunciation

Throughout this book Thai words have been written in a romanized system (see the Thai alphabet on pp.17–18) so that they can be read as though they were English, bearing in mind the notes on pronunciation below. There are, however, some sounds that are unlike anything in English. In this pronunciation guide, words containing these sounds are given in Thai script as well; ask a Thai to pronounce them for you.

Vowels

a as in alive
e as in ten
i as in sin
o as in on
u as in fun
ah as the a in rather
ai as in Thai
air as in fair
ao as in Lao
ay as in hay
ee as in see
er as in number

er-ee as in the Thai word ner-ee เนย (butter): the r is not pronounced
eu as in the Thai word meu มือ (hand): like the English exclamation 'ugh!'
ew as in few
oh as the o in no
oo as in boot
oo as in look
oy as in boy

Consonants

bp sharp p sound (don't pronounce the b). It occurs in the word bpai ไป (go)
dt sharp t sound (don't pronounce the d). It occurs in the word dtàir แต่ (but)
g as in gate
ng as in ring

When k, p and t are at the end of a word, it may sound almost as if these consonants are not being pronounced. Ask a Thai to say: lâhk ลาก (drag), lâhp ลาบ (minced meat) or lâht ลาด (cover; spread).

When a final r is followed by a vowel, the r is not pronounced: ner-ee เนย (butter).

Tones

Thai is a tonal language which means that the pitch at which a word is pronounced determines its meaning. The same combination of letters pronounced with a different tone will produce different words. In Thai there are five different tones: mid tone (no mark); high tone ´; low tone `; falling tone ^; and rising tone ˇ. For example:

mai ไมล์ (mid-tone) mile

mài ใหม่ (low tone) new

mái ไม้ (high tone) wood

mǎi ไหม (rising tone) silk

mâi ไม่ (falling tone) not

In Thai, the tone is as important a part of the word as the consonant and vowel sounds.

To help you get a clearer idea of how the tones sound, Thai script equivalents are given for the words in this section. Ask a Thai speaker to read the words for you so that you can hear the tonal differences.

Mid-tone: e.g. bpai (go). This can be thought of as normal voice pitch. The following are words pronounced with mid-tone:

mah มา come

mee มี have

bpen เป็น is

tum ทำ do

nai ใน in

High tone: e.g. rórn (hot). The voice has to be pitched slightly higher than normal. The following are words pronounced with high tones:

sái ช้าย left

rót รถ car

cháo เช้า morning

lék เล็ก little

náhm น้ำ water

Low tone: e.g. nèung (one). The voice should be pitched below the normal level:

yài ใหญ่ big

tòok ถูก cheap

jàhk จาก from

gài ไก่ chicken

bpìt ปิด closed

Falling tone: e.g. dâi (can). The best way to convey a falling tone is to speak very emphatically, but this doesn't mean that Thai words with falling tones have to be shouted. English speakers tend to find this the most difficult tone and do not let the voice fall sufficiently. The secret is to start at a fairly high pitch in order to achieve a distinct fall:

têe ที่ at

mâi ไม่ not

hâh ห้า five

mâhk มาก much

chôrp ชอบ like

Rising tone: e.g. sŏrng (two). The rising tone is like the intonation used when asking a question in English:

pŏm ผม I (said by a man)

kwăh ขวา right

kŏr... ขอ... may I...

lăi หลาย several

The relative positions of the five Thai tones can be represented graphically like this:

High Tone   Falling Tone   Mid Tone   Low Tone   Rising Tone

The Thai alphabet

Vowels

-อ	or	เ-ะ	-e
-ะ	a	เ-า	-ao
◌ั	-u-	เ-าะ	-or
◌ัว	-oo-a	เ-อ	-er
-า	-ah	เ-ีย	-ee-a
-ำ	-um	เ-ียะ	-ee-a
◌ิ	-i	เ-ือ	-eu-a
◌ี	-ee	แ-	-air
◌ึ	-eu	แ-็	-air
◌ื	-eu	แ-ะ	-air
◌ุ	-oo	โ-	-oh
◌ู	-oo	โ-ะ	-o
-เ	-ay	ใ-	-ai
เ-็	-e	ไ-	-ai
เ-ย	-er-ee	ก	g
เ-อะ	-er	ข	k

Consonants

ค	k	ย	y
ฆ	k	ฎ	d
ง	ng	ฏ	dt
จ	j	ฐ	t
ฉ	ch	ฑ	t
ช	ch	ฒ	t
ซ	s	ณ	n
ฌ	ch	ด	d

ต dt	ร r
ฏ t	ฤ reu
ฑ t	ฤๅ reu
ธ t	ล l
น n	ฦ leu
บ b	ฦๅ leu
ป bp	ว w
ผ p	ศ s
ฝ f	ษ s
พ p	ส s
ฟ f	ห h
ภ p	ฬ l
ม m	อ consonant that is not sounded
ย y	ฮ h

Bangkok Thai

Among some Bangkok speakers, when there are two consonants at the beginning of a word, the second consonant sound is often omitted:

bplah (fish) becomes bpah
gra-tee-um (garlic) becomes ga-tee-um

Sometimes, words beginning with a kw sound are pronounced as if they began with an f instead:

kwfh (right) becomes ffh
kwahm sòok (happiness) becomes fahm sòok

Other regional accents

Different dialects are spoken in the various regions of Thailand. Thais from Bangkok will probably have difficulty understanding the dialects spoken in the south, northeast and north of Thailand.

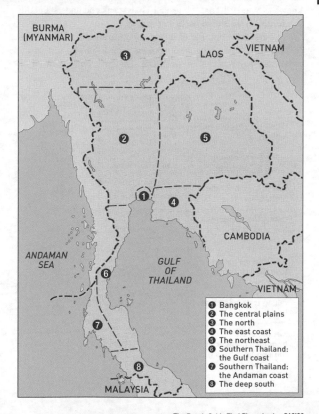

1. Bangkok
2. The central plains
3. The north
4. The east coast
5. The northeast
6. Southern Thailand: the Gulf coast
7. Southern Thailand: the Andaman coast
8. The deep south

For example, the word for **I** is chăn in central Thailand, răo in the south, kòi in the northeast and pên or pèn in the north; the word for **hello** is sa-wùt dee in central Thailand, pĕu in the south, pai-săi in the northeast and sa-wùt dee-jào in the north.

But the Thai language has been standardized and schools throughout the entire country teach the dialect of central Thailand, also known as Standard Thai. Almost all Thais speak and understand this in addition to their own particular dialect.

There are also a number of different ethnic and linguistic groups in Thailand. Other languages spoken include pa-să-i-săn in the northeast, pa-să-nĕu-a in northern Thailand and pa-să-tâi in

			central accent	
rising tone becomes high tone	หัว	head	hŏo-a	
mid tone becomes rising or low tone	ตาย	to die	dtai	
falling tone becomes high tone	ต้ม	to boil	dtôm	
falling tone becomes low tone; p becomes bp	พ่อ	father	pôr	
mid tone becomes low, high or rising tone	กิน	eat	gin	
falling tone becomes low tone	ข้าว	rice	kâo	
r at the start becomes h and k at the end becomes g	รัก	to love	rúk	

southern Thailand. It is not unusual to come across Thais who are fluent in more than one language and dialect.

The hill tribes who live in the border regions between northern Thailand, Laos and Myanmar (Burma) have their own languages, which are not related to Thai.

Using the system of pronunciation given in this book you will be able to communicate in Standard Thai, which means you'll be able to talk to almost all Thais from any part of the country (apart from the hill tribes) once you have mastered pronunciation and tones.

The chart below gives some of the main differences in accent or pronunciation that you may hear in Thailand.

south	northeast	north
hóo-a	hŏo-a	hŏo-a
dtăi	dtăi	dtăi
dtóm	dtôm	dtôm
pòr	èe-pòr	bpôr
gìn	gin	gìn
kào	kào	kâo
rúk	húg	húg

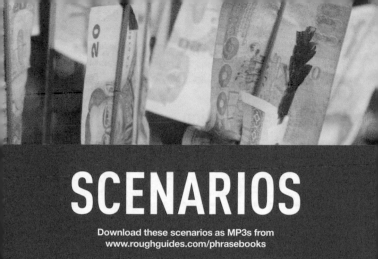

SCENARIOS

Download these scenarios as MP3s from
www.roughguides.com/phrasebooks

1. Accommodation

▶ Is there an inexpensive hotel you can recommend?
Chôo-ay náir-num rohng rairm rah-kah tòok, hâi nòy kâ?

> ▶▶ I'm sorry, they all seem to be fully booked.
> **Kŏr-tôht krúp, dtem mòt láir-o.**

▶ Can you give me the name of a good middle-range hotel?
Kŏr chêu rohng rairm têe dee bpahn glahng, dâi mái ká?

> ▶▶ Let me have a look; do you want to be in the centre?
> **Kŏr doo gòrn ná krúp, dtôrng gahn púk jai glahng meu-ung châi mái krúp?**

▶ If possible.
Tâh bpen bpai dâi.

> ▶▶ Do you mind being a little way out of town?
> **Têe púk glai nít-nòy, mâi bpen rai châi mái krúp?**

▶ Not too far out.
Mâi koo-un glai gern bpai kâ.

▶ Where is it on the map?
Yòo dtrong năi bon păirn-têe ká?

▶ Can you write the name and address down?
Kĕe-an chêu têe yòo hâi nòy dâi mái ká?

▶ I'm looking for a room in a private house.
Gum-lung hăh hôhng púk hôrng nèung, nai bâhn púk sòo-an dtoo-a kâ.

2. Banks

bank account	bun-chee ta-nah-kahn
to change money	lâirk ngern
cheque	chék
to deposit money	fàhk ngern
pin number	mǎi lâyk ra-hùt
pound	bporn
to withdraw money	tŏrn ngern

▶ Can you change this into baht?
Rúp lâirk bpen ngern bàht mái krúp?

> ▶▶ How would you like the money?
> **Dtôrng-gahn lâirk ngern bàirp nǎi ká?**

▶ Small notes.   ▶ Big notes.
Báirng yôy.   **Báirng yài.**

▶ Do you have information in English about opening an account?
Mee kôr moon gahn bpèrt bun-chee bpen pah-sǎh ung-grìt mái krúp?

> ▶▶ Yes, what sort of account do you want?
> **Mee kâ, dtôrng-gahn bpèrt bun-chee bàirp nǎi ká?**

▶ I'd like a current account.
Dtôrng-gahn bpèrt bun-chee gra-sǎir rai wun krúp.

> ▶▶ Your passport, please.
> **Kǒr doo núng-sěu dern tahng nòy kâ?**

▶ Can I use this card to draw some cash?
Chái bùt née tŏrn ngern dâi mái krúp?

> ▶▶ You have to go to the cashier's desk.
> **Dtôrng bpai têe káirt-chee-a kâ.**

▶ I want to transfer this to my account at Bangkok Bank.
Dtôrng-gahn ohn ngern kâo bun-chee ta-nah-kahn groong-tâyp krúp.

> ▶▶ OK, but we'll have to charge you for the phonecall.
> **Dâi kâ, dtàir dtôrng kít ngern kâh toh-ra-sùp ná ká.**

3. Booking a room

shower	hôrng núm fùk boo-a
telephone in the room	toh-ra-sùp nai hôrng púk
payphone in the lobby	toh-ra-sùp săh-tah-ra-ná têe lórp-bêe

▶ Do you have any rooms?
Mee hôrng púk wâhng mái krúp?

> ▶▶ For how many people?
> **Sŭm-rùp gèe kon ká?**

▶ For one/for two.
Sŭm-rùp kon dee-o/sŭm-rùp sŏrng kon.

> ▶▶ Yes, we have rooms free.
> **Mee kâ, mee hôrng wâhng.**

> ▶▶ For how many nights?
> **Ja púk gèe keun ká?**

▶ Just for one night.
Keun dee-o krúp.

▶ How much is it?
Tâo-rài krúp?

> ▶▶ 150 baht with bathroom and 100 baht without bathroom.
> **Hôrng púk mee hôrng núm róy hâh-sìp bàht, hôrng púk mâi mee hôrng núm róy bàht kâ**

▶ Does that include breakfast?
Roo-um ah-hăhn cháo dôo-ay mái krúp?

▶ Can I see a room with bathroom?
Kŏr doo hôrng púk mee hôrng núm dâi mái krúp?

▶ OK, I'll take it.
Dtòk-long ao hôrng née krúp.

▶ When do I have to check out?
Dtôrng chék-áo gèe mohng krúp?

▶ Is there anywhere I can leave luggage?
Fàhk gra-bpăo têe năi krúp?

4. Car hire

automatic	gee-a ùt-dta-noh-mút
full tank	dtem tŭng
manual	gee-a meu
rented car	rót châo

▶ I'd like to rent a car.
Kŏr châo rót nèung kun krúp.

▶▶ For how long?
Châo nahn tâo-rài ká?

▶ Two days.
Sŏrng wun.

▶ I'll take the...
Pŏm ao...

▶ Is that with unlimited mileage?
Mâi jum-gùt ra-ya tahng châi mái krúp?

▶▶ It is.
Châi kâ.

▶▶ Can I see your driving licence, please?
Kŏr doo bai kùp kèe nòy kâ?

▶▶ And your passport?
Núng-sĕu dern tahng dôo-ay kâ?

▶ Is insurance included?
Roo-um bpra-gun mái krúp?

▶▶ Yes, but you have to pay the first 1000 baht.
Roo-um kâ, dtàir dtôrng jài ngern sòo-un râirk pun bàht ayng.

▶▶ Can you leave a deposit of 1000 baht?
Wahng ngern mút jum pun bàht, dâi mái ká?

▶ And if this office is closed, where do I leave the keys?
Tâh órp-fít bpìt láir-o, keun goon-jair têe năi krúp?

▶▶ You drop them in that box.
Yòrn mun long nai glòrng nún kâ.

5. Car problems

brakes	bràyk
to break down	sĕe-a
clutch	klút
diesel	núm mun rót dee-sel
flat battery	bair-dta-rêe mòt
flat tyre	yahng bairn
petrol	núm mun

▶ Excuse me, where is the nearest petrol station?
Kŏon ká, bpúm núm mun têe glâi têe sòot yòo năi ká?

▶▶ About 5km away.
Hàhng jàhk têe nêe bpra-mahn hâh gì-loh.

▶ The car has broken down.
Rót sĕe-a.

▶▶ Can you tell me what happened?
Bòrk nòy dâi mái ká, gèrt a-rai kêun?

▶ I've got a flat tyre.
Rót yahng bairn kâ.

▶ I think the battery is flat.
Chún kít wâh bair-dta-rêe mòt.

▶▶ Can you tell me exactly where you are?
Bòrk dâi mái ká wâh kŏon gum-lung yòo têe năi?

▶ I'm about 2km outside of Khorat on the Sukhumvit Road.
Têe ta-nŏn sòo-kŏOm-wít bpra-mahn sŏrng gì-loh nôrk meu-ung koh-raht.

▶▶ What type of car? What colour?
Rót bpra-pâyt năi? Sĕe à-rai?

▶ Can you send a tow truck?
Chôo-ay sòng rót lâhk mah dâi mái ká?

6. Children

baby	dèk òrn
boy	dèk pôo-chai
child, children	dèk, lôok
(your own child or children)	
cot	têe norn sŭm-rùp dèk
formula	ah-hăhn dèk òrn
girl	dèk pôo-yĭng
highchair	gâo êe kăh sŏong sŭm-rùp dèk lék
nappies (diapers)	pâh òrm

▶ We need a babysitter for tomorrow evening.
Rao dtôrng gahn pêe lée-ung dèk prôong née dtorn yen.

▶▶ For what time?
Gèe mohng ká?

▶ From 7.30 to 11.00.
Tôom krêung tĕung hâh tôom.

▶▶ How many children? How old are they?
Mee dèk gèe kon ká? Ah-yóo tâo-rài?

▶ Two children, aged four and eighteen months.
Sŏrng kon kâ, ah-yóo sèe kòo-up láir ah-yóo sìp bpàirt deu-un.

▶ Where can I change the baby?
Bplèe-un pâh ôrm dèk dâi têe nǎi ká?

▶ Could you please warm this bottle for me?
Chôo-ay òon kòo-ut nom hâi nòy ká?

▶ Can you give us a child's portion?
Kŏr ah-hǎhn jahn lék sŭm-rùp dèk kâ?

▶ We need two child seats.
Rao dtôrng gahn têe nûng sŭm-rùp dèk sŏrng têe kâ.

▶ Is there a discount for children?
Lót rah-kah hâi dèk mái ká?

7. Communications: Internet

@, at sign	àirt
computer	korm-pew-dter
email	ee-mayl
Internet	in-dter-nèt
keyboard	kee-bòrt
mouse	máo

▶ Is there somewhere I can check my emails?
Chék ee-mayl dâi têe nǎi, ká?

▶ Do you have wifi?
Mee wai-fai mái, ká?

▶ Is there an Internet café around here?
Mee ráhn in-dter-nèt tǎir-o née mái, ká?

▶▶ Yes, there's one in the shopping centre.
Mee kâ, têe sŏon gahn káh.

▶▶ Do you want fifteen minutes, thirty minutes or one hour?
Dtôrng-gahn sìp hâh nah-tee, săhm sìp nah-tee rĕu nèung chôo-a-mohng, ká?

▶ Thirty minutes please. Can you help me log on?
Kŏr săhm sìp nah-tee, kâ. Chôo-ay lórk-orn hâi nòy kâ?

▶▶ OK, here's your password.
Dái kâ, nêe ra-hùt pàhn kŏrng kOOn.

▶ Can you change this to an English keyboard?
Chôo-ay bplèe-un kee-bòrt bpen pah-săh ung-grìt, hâi nòy ká?

▶ I'll take another quarter of an hour.
Kŏr èek sìp hâh nah-tee, kâ.

▶ Is there a printer I can use?
Mee krêu-ung bprín-dter têe chún chái dâi mái ká?

8. Communications: phones

mobile phone (cell phone)	toh-ra-sùp meu tĕu
payphone	toh-ra-sùp săh-tah-ra-ná
phone call	toh-ra-sùp
phone card	bùt toh-ra-sùp
phone charger	krêu-ung cháht toh-ra-sùp
SIM card	sim gáht toh-ra-sùp

▶ Can I call abroad from here?
Kŏr toh bpai dtàhng bpra-tâyt dâi mái ká?

▶ How do I get an outside line?
Toh òrk yang-ngai ká?

▶ What's the code to call the UK/US from here?
Jàhk têe nêe chái ra-hùt à-rai toh bpai ung-grìt/a-may-ri-gah ká?

▶ Hello, can I speak to Mrs Thanya?
Hun-lŏh, kŏr pôot gùp kOOn tan-yah nòy kâ?

zero	sŏon
one	nèung
two	sŏrng
three	săhm
four	sèe
five	hâh
six	hòk
seven	jèt
eight	bpàirt
nine	gâo

▶▶ Yes, that's me speaking.
Kâ, gum-lung pôot.

▶ Do you have a charger for this?
Koon mee krêu-ung cháht sŭm-rùp toh-ra-sùp krêu-ung née mái ká?

▶ Can I buy a SIM card for this phone?
Kŏr séu sim gáht toh-ra-sùp sŭm-rùp toh-ra-sùp krêu-ung née nòy kâ?

9. Directions

| Where? | Têe năi? |
| Which direction? | Tahng năi? |

▶ Hi, I'm looking for Yaowarat Road.
Sa-wùt dee krúp, pŏm gum-lung hăh ta-nŏn yao-wa-râht.

▶▶ Sorry, never heard of it.
Kŏr-tôht kâ, mâi ker-ee dâi yin mah gòrn ler-ee.

▶ Hi, can you tell me where Yaowarat Road is?
Sa-wùt dee krúp, bòrk nòy dâi mái wâh ta-nŏn yao-wa-râht yòo têe năi krúp?

straight ahead	dtrong bpai	past the...	pàhn... bpai
opposite	dtrong kâhm	just after	por pàhn
near	glâi	on the right	tahng kwăh
back	kâhng lǔng	on the left	tahng sái
in front of	kâhng nâh	street	ta-nŏn
further	ler-ee bpai	over there	têe nôhn
turn off	lée-o	next	tùt bpai

▶▶ I'm a stranger here too.
Chún gôr mâi châi kon têe nêe kâ.

▶ Hi, Yaowarat Road, do you know where it is?
Sa-wùt dee krúp, sǎhp mái wâh, ta-nŏn yao-wa-râht yòo têe nǎi krúp?

▶▶ Around the corner.
Lée-o dtrong hŏo-a mOOm.

▶▶ Left at the second traffic lights.
Lée-o sái têe sŭn-yahn fai têe sŏrng.

▶▶ Then it's the first street on the right.
Lŭng jàhk nún, ta-nŏn râirk tahng kwǎh keu ta-nŏn yao-wa-râht kâ.

10. Emergencies

accident	OO-bùt-dti-hàyt
ambulance	rót pa-yah-bahn
consul	sa-tǎhn gong-sǒon
embassy	sa-tǎhn tôot
fire brigade	nòo-ay dùp plerng
police	dtum-ròo-ut

▶ Help!
Chôo-ay dôo-ay!

▶ Can you help me?
Chôo-ay nòy dâi mái ká?

▶ Please come with me! It's really very urgent.
Mah gùp chún nòy kâ! Mee rêu-ung dòo-un mâhk jing jing.

▶ I've lost my keys.
Chún tum gOOn-jair hǎi.

▶ My car is not working.
Rót chún sěe-a.

▶ My purse has been stolen.
Chún dohn ka-moy-ee gra-bpăo sa-dtahng.

▶ I've been mugged.
Chún dohn jêe.

▶▶ What's your name?
Chêu a-rai krúp?

▶▶ I need to see your passport.
Kŏr doo núng-sĕu dern tahng nòy krúp.

▶ I'm sorry, all my papers have been stolen.
Kŏr-tôht kâ, àyk-ga-săhn túng-mòt dohn ka-moy-ee kâ.

11. Friends

▶ Hi, how're you doing?
Sa-wùt dee, sa-bai dee mái?

▶▶ OK, and you?
Sa-bai dee, láir-o kOOn lâ?

▶ Yeah, fine.　　　▶ Not bad.
Sa-bai dee.　　　**Gôr dee.**

▶ D'you know Pairot?
Róo-jùk pai-róht mái?

▶ And this is Suchada.
Láir nêe sòo-chah-dah.

>> ▶▶ Yeah, we know each other.
>> **Hây, róo-jùk gun láir-o.**

▶ Where do you know each other from?
Róo-jùk gun têe năi?

>> ▶▶ We met at Sukda's place.
>> **Jer gun têe bâhn sùk-dah.**

▶ That was some party, eh?
Mee bpah-dtêe rěr?

>> ▶▶ The best.
>> **Yêe-um mâhk.**

▶ Are you guys coming for a beer?
Bpai gin bee-a mái?

>> ▶▶ Cool, let's go.
>> **Dee, bpai gun tèr.**

>> ▶▶ No, I'm meeting Alisa.
>> **Mâi bpai ná, děe-o bpai jer a-lí-să.**

▶ See you at Sukda's place tonight.
Keun née jer gun têe bâhn sùk-dah ná.

>> ▶▶ See you.
>> **Láir-o jer gun ná.**

12. Health

antibiotics	yah bpa-dti-chee-wa-ná
antiseptic ointment	yah tah kâh chéu-a
cystitis	gra-pór bpùt-sa-wa ùk-sàyp
dentist	mŏr fun
diarrhoea	tórng sěe-a
doctor	mŏr
hospital	rohng pa-yah-bahn
ill	mâi sa-bai
medicine	yah
painkillers	yah gâir bpòo-ut
pharmacy	ráhn kǎi yah
to prescribe	sùng yah
thrush	ah-gahn ùk-sàyp chéu-a rah

▶ I'm not feeling very well.
Chún róo-sèuk mâi sa-bai kâ.

▶ Can you get a doctor?
Chôo-ay dtahm mŏr dâi mái ká?

▶▶ Where does it hurt?
Jèp têe năi krúp?

▶ It hurts here.
Jèp têe nêe kâ.

▶▶ Is the pain constant?
Jèp dta-lòrt mái krúp?

▶ It's not a constant pain.
Mâi kâ, mâi jèp dta-lòrt.

▶ Can I make an appointment?
Kŏr nút dâi mái ká?

▶ Can you give me something for…?
Hâi yah gâir … dâi mái ká?

▶ Yes, I have insurance.
Kâ, chún mee bpra-gun sòok-ka-pâhp.

13. Hotels

maid	kon tum kwahm sa-àht
manager	pôo jùt-gahn
room service	room ser-wit

▶ Hello, we've booked a double room in the name of Cameron.
Sa-wùt dee kâ, rao jorng hôrng kôo wái, chái chêu Cameron kâ.

▶▶ That was for four nights, wasn't it?
Sŭm-rùp sèe keun châi mái ká?

▶ Yes, we're leaving on Saturday.
Châi kâ, rao jà òrk wun săo kâ.

▶▶ Can I see your passport please?
Kŏr doo núng-sĕu dern tahng kŏrng kOOn nòy kâ?

▶▶ There you are, room 321 on the third floor.
Nêe kâ, hôrng săhm sŏrng nèung, yòo chún săhm kâ.

▶ I can't get this keycard to work.
Chái kee-gáht née mâi dâi kâ.

▶▶ Sorry, I need to reactivate it.
Kŏr-tôht kâ, chún dtôrng tum hâi mun chái ngahn dâi èek krúng kâ.

▶ What time is breakfast?
Bor-ri-gahn ah-hăhn cháo gèe mohng, ká?

▶ There aren't any towels in my room.
Têe hôrng mâi mee pâh chét dtoo-a, kâ.

▶ My flight isn't until this evening, can I keep the room a bit longer?
Kŏr púk nai hôrng nahn nòy dâi mái ká? Têe-o bin kŏrng chún jà òrk dtorn yen.

▶ Can I settle up? Is this card ok?
Kŏr jài kâh têe púk kâ? Rúp bùt née mái ká?

14. Language difficulties

a few words	sŏrng săhm kum
interpreter	lâhm
to translate	bplair

▶▶ Your credit card has been refused.
Bùt kray-dìt kOOn, tòok ra-ngúp chái krúp.

▶ What, I don't understand; do you speak English?
A-rai ná-ká, mâi kâo jai kâ, kOOn pôot pah-săh ung-grìt dâi mái ká?

▶▶ You can't use this credit card any more.
KOOn chái bùt kray-dìt née, mâi dâi láir-o krúp.

▶ Could you say that again?
Chôo-ay pôot èek krúng dâi mái ká?

▶ Slowly.
Cháh cháh.

▶ I understand very little Thai.
Chún kâo jai pah-săh tai dâi nít-nòy kâ.

▶ I speak Thai very badly.
Pôot pah-săh tai dâi mâi dee ler-ee.

▶▶ You can't use this card to pay.
KOon jài ngern dôo-ay bùt née, mâi dâi krúp.

▶▶ Do you understand?
Kâo jai mái krúp?

▶ Sorry, no.
Mâi kâo jai kâ, kŏr-tôht kâ.

▶ Is there someone who speaks English?
Mee krai pôot pah-săh ung-grìt dâi mái ká?

▶ Oh, now I understand.
Ŏr, kâo jai láir-o kâ.

▶ Is that OK now?
Rêe-up róy rěu yung ká?

15. Meeting people

▶ Hello.
Sa-wùt dee krúp.

▶▶ Hello, my name's Ninda.
Sa-wùt dee kâ, chún chêu nin-da kâ.

▶ Graham, from England, Thirsk.
Pŏm chêu graham, mah jàhk thirsk, bpra-tâyt ung-grìt.

▶▶ Don't know that, where is it?
Mâi róo-jùk kâ, meu-ung née yòo têe năi ká?

▶ Not far from York, in the North; and you?
Mâi glai jàhk yórk, tang pâhk něu-a, láir-o kOOn lâ?

▶▶ I'm from Chiangmai; here by yourself?
Chún mah jàhk chee-ang mài, mah kon dee-o rěu ká?

▶ No, I'm with my wife and two kids.
Bplào krúp, mah gùp pun-ra-yah láir lôok sŏrng kon.

▶ What do you do?
Tum ngahn a-rai krúp?

▶▶ I'm in computers.
Dâhn korm-pew-dtêr kâ.

▶ Me too.
Pŏm gôr měu-un gun.

▶ Here's my wife now.
Nêe pun-ra-yah pŏm krúp.

▶▶ Nice to meet you.
Yin dee têe dâi róo-jùk kâ.

16. Nightlife

dancing	gahn dtên rum
electro	don-dtree i-lék-tror
folk	don-dtree péun meu-ung
heavy metal	don-dtree hep-wee may-to
hip-hop	don-dtree híp-hòrp
jazz	don-dtree jáirs
rock	don-dtree rórk

▶ What's a good club for...?
Klùp năi mee chêu sŭm-rùp…?

▶▶ There's going to be a great gig at Thorng Lor
tomorrow night.
**Jà mee gahn sa-dairng don-dtree têe yôrt yêe-am têe
thorng lòr keun prôong née.**

▶ Where can I hear some local music?
Fang don-dtree tórng tìn dâi têe năi ká?

▶ Can you write down the names of the best bars around here?
Chôo-ay kĕe-an chêu bah têe dee têe sòot tăir-o née hâi nòy kâ?

▶▶ That depends what you're looking for.
Kêun yòo wâh koon gum-lung hăh bah bàirp năi.

▶ The place where the locals go.
Têe kon têe nêe chôrp bpai kâ.

▶ A place for a quiet drink.
Têe dèum à-rai ngêe-up ngêe-up dâi kâ.

▶▶ The casino across the river is very good.
Mee ka-si-nôh dtrong kâhm mâir núm jà dee mâhk.

▶ I suppose they have a dress code.
Chán kít wâh káo sài chóot pí-sèt cha-pór.

▶▶ You can wear what you like.
Koon sài chóot à-rai gôr dâi kâ têe koon yàhk sài.

▶ What time does it close?
Jà bpìt gèe mohng ká?

17. Post offices

airmail	air may-o
post card	bprai-sa-nee-ya-bùt
post office	bprai-sa-nee
stamp	sa-dtairm

▶ What time does the post office close?
Bprai-sa-nee bpìt gèe mohng ká?

▶▶ Five o'clock weekdays.
Tóok wun jun tĕung wun sòok dtorn hâh mohng yen krúp.

▶ Is the post office open on Saturdays?
Bprai-sa-nee bpèrt wun săo rĕu bplào ká?

▶▶ Until midday.
Bpèrt tĕung têe-ang krúp.

▶ I'd like to send this registered to England.
Yàhk long ta-bee-an un née láir sòng bpai ung-grìt kâ.

▶▶ Certainly, that will cost 50 baht.
Dâi krúp, túng-mòt hâh-sìp bàht.

▶ And also two stamps for England, please.
Lair kŏr sa-dtairm sŏrng doo-ung sŭm-rùp bpra-tâyt ung-grìt kâ.

▶ Do you have some airmail stickers?
Mee sa-tík-gêr air may-o mái ká?

▶ Do you have any mail for me?
Mee jòt-mǎi sǔm-rùp chún mah mái ká?

ต่างประเทศ	dtàhng bpra-tâyt	international
จดหมาย	jòt-mǎi	letters
ภายในประเทศ	pai nai bpra-tâyt	domestic
บริการไปรษณีย์รอจ่าย	bor-ri-gahn bprai-sa-nee ror jài	poste restante
พัสดุ	pút-sa-doo	parcels

18. Restaurants

bill	bin
menu	may-noo
table	dtó

▶ Can we have a non-smoking table?
Kǒr dtó têe mâi sòop boo-rèe dâi mái krúp?

▶ There are two of us.   ▶ There are four of us.
Sǔm-sùp sǒrng kon krúp.   **Sǔm-rùp sèe kon krúp.**

▶ What's this?
Nêe a-rai krúp?

    ▶▶ It's a type of fish.
    Bplah cha-nít nèung kâ.

    ▶▶ It's a local speciality.
    Bpen ah-hǎhn pi-sàyt pra-jum tórng tìn kâ.

    ▶▶ Come inside and I'll show you.
    Kâo mah kâhng nai si ká, ja hâi doo.

▶ We would like two of these, one of these, and one of those.
Kǒr un née sǒrng têe, un née nèung têe, láir un nóhn nèung têe krúp.

    ▶▶ And to drink?
    Dèum a-rai ká?

▶ Red wine.
Wai dairng.

▶ White wine.
Wai kǎo.

▶ A beer and two orange juices.
Kǒr bee-a nèung gâir-o láir núm sôm sǒrng gâir-o krúp.

▶ Some more bread please.
Kǒr ka-nǒm bpung èek krúp.

▶▶ How was your meal?
Ah-hǎhn a-ròy mái ká?

▶ Excellent, very nice!
A-ròy mâhk krúp!

▶▶ Anything else?
Ja rúp a-rai èek mái ká?

▶ Just the bill thanks.
Chék bin ler-ee, kòrp-kOOn krúp.

19. Self-catering accommodation

air-conditioning	air
apartment	a-páht-mén
cooker	dtao
fridge	dtôo yen
heating	krêu-ung tum kwahm rórn
hot water	náhm rórn
lightbulb	lòrt fai
toilet	hôrng náhm

▶ The toilet's broken, can you get someone to fix it?
Hôrng náhm sǎe-a, chôo-ay sòng kon mah sôrm nòy kâ?

▶ There's no hot water.
Mâi mee náhm rórn.

▶ Can you show me how the air-conditioning works?
Chôo-ay mah sǎh-tít hâi doo nòy, air tum-ngahn yung-ngai?

▶▶ OK, what apartment are you in?
Dâi kâ, púk a-páht-mén nǎi?

▶ We're in number five.
Hôrng ber hâh kâ.

► Can you move us to a quieter apartment?
Chôo-ay yái rao bpai yòo hôrng têe ngêe-up gwàh née nòy dâi mái ká?

► Is there a supermarket nearby?
Mee soo-bper-mah-get glâi glài mái ká?

►► Have you enjoyed your stay?
Yòo têe nêe sa-nòok mái ká?

► Brilliant holiday, thanks!
Bpen gahn púk pòrn têe sa-nòok mâhk kâ, kòrp-kOOn kâ.

20. Shopping

เปิด	bpèrt	open
ปิด	bpìt	closed
โต๊ะจ่ายเงิน	dtó jài ngern	cash desk
ขายลดราคา	kǎi lót rah-kah	sale
แลกเปลี่ยน	lâirk bplèe-un	to exchange

►► Can I help you?
Hâi chôo-ay mái ká?

► Can I just have a look around?
Kǒr doo gòrn krúp?

► Yes, I'm looking for…
Krúp, pǒm gum-lung hǎh…

► How much is this?
Un née tâo-rài krúp?

►► One thousand baht.
Nèung pun bàht kâ.

► OK, I think I'll have to leave it; it's a little too expensive for me.
Rěr krúp, mâi séu ròrk krúp, mun pairng bpai.

►► How about this?
Un née lâ ká?

► Can I pay by credit card?
Jài dôo-ay bùt kray-dìt dâi mái?

► It's too big.
Yài gern bpai krúp.

► It's too small.
Lék gern bpai krúp.

▶ It's for my son – he's about this high.
Dtoo-a née sŭm-rùp lôok chai pŏm – sŏong bpra-mahn née krúp.

▶▶ Will there be anything else?
Rúp a-rai èek mái ká?

▶ That's all thanks.
Króp láir-o, kòrp-kOOn krúp.

▶ Make it six hundred and I'll take it.
Hâi rah-kah hòk róy bàht, láir-o ja séu.

▶ Fine, I'll take it.
Dee, ao krúp.

21. Shopping for clothes

to alter	bplèe-un
bigger	yài gwàh
just right	por dee
smaller	lék gwàh
to try on	lorng sài doo

▶▶ Can I help you?
Hâi chôo-ay mái ká?

▶ No, thanks, I'm just looking.
Mâi bpen rai kâ, kòrp-kOOn, kŏr doo cher-ee cher-ee.

▶▶ Do you want to try that on?
KOOn yàhk lorng sài doo mái ká?

▶ Yes, and I'll try this one too.
Kâ, yàhk lorng sài dtoo-a née doo.

▶ Do you have it in a bigger size?
Mee dtoo-a yài gwàh née mái ká?

▶ Do you have it in a different colour?
Dtoo-a née mee sĕe èun mái ká?

▶▶ That looks good on you.
KOOn sài láir-o doo dee kâ.

▶ Can you shorten this?
Tum hâi sûn long dâi mái ká?

▶▶ Sure, it'll be ready on Friday, after 12.00.
Dâi kâ, jà sèt wun sòok, lŭng têe-ung kâ.

22. Sightseeing

art gallery	hŏr sĭn
bus tour	rót too-a num têe-o
city centre	jai glahng meu-ung
closed	bpìt
guide	múk-koo-tâyt
museum	pí-pít-ta-pun
open	bpèrt

▶ I'm interested in seeing the old town.
A yàhk bpai têe-o meu-ung gào.

▶ Are there guided tours?
Mee too-a têe mee múk-koo-tâyt mái ká?

    ▶▶ I'm sorry, it's fully booked.
    Kŏr-tôht krúp, dtem mòt láir-o.

▶ How much would you charge to drive us around for four hours?
Kùp rót pah têe-o, sùk sèe chôo-a mohng, ja kít ngern tâo-rài ká?

▶ Can we book tickets for the concert here?
Jorng dtŏo-a korn-sèrt têe nêe dâi mái ká?

    ▶▶ Yes, in what name?
    Dâi krúp, chêu a-rai krúp?

▶▶ Which credit card?
Kray-dìt gáht bàirp năi krúp?

▶ Where do we get the tickets?
Rúp dtŏo-a têe nǎi ká?

▶▶ Just pick them up at the entrance.
Rúp têe bpra-dtoo tahng kâo krúp.

▶ Is it open on Sundays?
Wun ah-tít bpèrt mái ká?

▶ How much is it to get in?
Kâh kâo tâo-rài ká?

▶ Are there reductions for groups of six?
Lót rah-kah sǎm-rùp glòom mah dôo-ay gun hòk kon mái ká?

▶ That was really impressive!
Nâh bpra-túp jai jing jing!

23. Taxis

▶ Can you get us a taxi?
Rêe-uk rót táirk-sêe hâi nòy kâ?

▶▶ For now? Where are you going?
Dtorn née rěu ká? Jà bpai nǎi ká?

▶ To the town centre.
Bpai nai meu-ung kâ.

▶ I'd like to book a taxi to the airport for tomorrow.
Dtôrng gahn jorng rót táirk-sêe bpai sa-nǎhm bin prôong née kâ.

▶▶ Sure, at what time? How many people?
Dâi kâ, gèe mohng? Jà bpai gèe kon?

▶ How much is it to Sukhumvit?
Bpai sòo-kŏom-wít tâo-rài ká?

▶ Right here is fine, thanks.
Jòrt dtrong née gôr dâi kâ, kòrp-kOOn kâ.

▶ Can you wait here and take us back?
Ror têe nêe láir pah rao glùp dâi mái ká?

▶▶ How long are you going to be?
Jà hâi ror nahn kâir nǎi ká?

24. Trains

to change trains	dtòr rót fai
platform	chahn chah-lah
return	dtŏo-a bpai glùp
single	dtŏo-a têe-o dee-o
station	sa-tăh-nee rót fai
stop	jòrt
ticket	dtŏo-a

▶ How much is…?
…rah-kah tâo-rài ká?

▶ A single, second class to…
Dtŏo-a têe-o dee-o, chún sŏrng nèung bai bpai…

▶ Two returns, second class to…
Dtŏo-a bpai glùp, chún sŏrng sŏrng bai bpai…

▶ For today.
Sŭm-rùp wun née.

▶ For tomorrow.
Sŭm-rùp wun prôong-née.

▶ For next Tuesday.
Sŭm-rùp wun ung-kahn nâh.

>> There's a supplement for the Sprinter Train.
Dtôrng jài kâh bor-ri-gahn pi-sàyt, sŭm-rùp rót fai
sa-bprín-dtêr krúp.

>> Do you want to make a seat reservation?
Dtôrng-gahn jorng têe nûng mái krúp?

>> You have to change at Don Muang Station.
Koon dtôrng dtòr rót fai têe sa-tăh-nee dorn meu-ung krúp.

▶ What time is the last train to Chiangmai?
Rót fai bpai chee-ung mài, têe-o sòot tái, òrk gèe mohng ká?

▶ Is this seat free?
Têe nêe wâhng mái ká?

▶ Excuse me, which station are we at?
Kŏr-tôht kâ, têe nêe sa-tăh-nee a-rai ká?

▶ Is this where I change for Chiangmai?
Têe nêe, dtòr rót fai bpai chee-ung mài châi mái ká?

ENGLISH
→ THAI

A

a, an (there is no Thai equivalent)

about: about 20 bpra-mahn
yêe-sìp ประมาณยี่สิบ

it's about 5 o'clock
bpra-mahn hâh mohng yen
ประมาณห้าโมงเย็น

a film about Thailand
nǔng rêu-ung meu-ung tai
หนังเรื่องเมืองไทย

above kâhng bon ข้างบน

abroad dtàhng bpra-tâyt
ต่างประเทศ

absolutely (I agree) nâir-norn
แน่นอน

absorbent cotton sǔm-lee สำลี

accelerator kun rêng คันเร่ง

accept rúp รับ

accident OO-bùt-dti-hàyt
อุบัติเหตุ

there's been an accident
mee OO-bùt-dti-hàyt
มีอุบัติเหตุ

accommodation têe púk ที่พัก

accurate tòok-dtôrng ถูกต้อง

ache bpòo-ut ปวด

my back aches bpòo-ut
lǔng ปวดหลัง

across: across the... kâhm...
ข้าม...

adapter (for voltage) krêu-
ung bplairng fai fáh
เครื่องแปลงไฟฟ้า

(plug) bplúk ปลั๊ก

address têe-yòo ที่อยู่

what's your address?
kOOn púk yòo têe-nǎi?
คุณพักอยู่ที่ไหน

address book sa-mÒOt têe-yòo
สมุดที่อยู่

admission charge kâh kâo
ค่าเข้า

adult pôo-yài ผู้ใหญ่

advance: in advance lôo-ung
nâh ล่วงหน้า

aeroplane krêu-ung bin
เครื่องบิน

after lǔng หลัง

after you chern gòrn เชิญก่อน

after lunch lǔng
ah-hǎhn glahng wun
หลังอาหารกลางวัน

afternoon dtorn bài ตอนบ่าย

in the afternoon dtorn bài
ตอนบ่าย

this afternoon bài née บ่ายนี้

aftershave yah tah lǔng gohn
nòo-ut ยาทาหลังโกนหนวด

aftersun cream yah tah lǔng
àhp dàirt ยาทาหลังอาบแดด

afterwards tee lǔng ทีหลัง

again èek อีก

against: I'm against it pŏm (chún) mâi hĕn dôo-ay ผม(ฉัน)ไม่เห็นด้วย

age ah-yóo อายุ

ago: a week ago ah-tít nèung mah láir-o อาทิตย์หนึ่งมาแล้ว

an hour ago chôo-a mohng nèung mah láir-o ชั่วโมงหนึ่งมาแล้ว

agree: I agree pŏm (chún) hĕn dôo-ay ผม(ฉัน)เห็นด้วย

AIDS rôhk áyd โรคเอดส์

air ah-gàht อากาศ

by air tahng ah-gàht ทางอากาศ

air-conditioning krêu-ung air เครื่องแอร์

airmail: by airmail sòng tahng ah-gàht ส่งทางอากาศ

airmail envelope sorng jòt-măi ah-gàht ซองจดหมายอากาศ

airport sa-năhm bin สนามบิน

to the airport, please bpai sa-năhm bin ไปสนามบิน

airport bus rót sa-năhm bin รถสนามบิน

aisle seat têe nûng dtit tahng dern ที่นั่งติดทางเดิน

alarm clock nah-lí-gah bplòok นาฬิกาปลุก

alcohol lâo เหล้า

alcoholic kon kêe lâo mao yah คนขี้เหล้าเมายา

all: all the boys pôo-chai tóok kon ผู้ชายทุกคน

all the girls pôo-yĭng tóok kon ผู้หญิงทุกคน

all of it túng mòt ทั้งหมด

all of them tóok kon ทุกคน

that's all, thanks sèt láir-o kòrp-koon เสร็จแล้วขอบคุณ

allergic: I'm allergic to... pŏm (chún) páir... ผม(ฉัน)แพ้...

allowed: is it allowed? un-nóo-yâht mái? อนุญาตไหม

all right mâi bpen rai ไม่เป็นไร

I'm all right pŏm (chún) sa-bai dee ผม(ฉัน)สบายดี

are you all right? bpen yung-ngai bâhng? เป็นอย่างไรบ้าง

almost gèu-up เกือบ

alone kon dee-o คนเดียว

alphabet dtoo-a uk-sŏrn ตัวอักษร

**already... ** láir-o... แล้ว

also dôo-ay ด้วย

although máir wâh แม้ว่า

altogether túng mòt ทั้งหมด

always sa-mĕr เสมอ

am: I am... pŏm (chún) bpen... ผม(ฉัน)เป็น...

a.m.: at six/seven a.m. hòk/jèt mohng cháo หก/เจ็ดโมงเช้า

amazing (surprising) mâi nâh chêu-a ไม่น่าเชื่อ
(very good) wi-sàyt วิเศษ

ambulance rót pa-yah-bahn รถพยาบาล

call an ambulance! rêe-uk rót pa-yah-bahn! เรียกรถพยาบาล

America a-may-ri-gah อเมริกา

American (adj) a-may-ri-gun อเมริกัน

I'm American pǒm (chún) bpen kon a-may-ri-gun ผม(ฉัน)เป็นคนอเมริกัน

among nai ra-wàhng ในระหว่าง

amount jum-noo-un จำนวน

amp: a 13-amp fuse few sìp sǎhm airm ฟิวส์สิบสามแอมป์

and láir และ

angry gròht โกรธ

animal sùt สัตว์

ankle kôr táo ข้อเท้า

anniversary (wedding) wun cha-lǒrng króp rôrp วันฉลองครบรอบ

annoy: this man's annoying me kon née tum hâi pǒm (chún) rum-kahn คนนี้ทำให้ผม(ฉัน)รำคาญ

annoying nâh rum-kahn น่ารำคาญ

another èek อีก

can we have another room? kǒr bplèe-un hôrng nòy dâi mái? ขอเปลี่ยนห้องหน่อยได้ไหม

another beer, please kǒr bee-a èek kòo-ut nèung ขอเบียร์อีกขวดหนึ่ง

antibiotics yah bpùti-chee-wa-ná ยาปฏิชีวนะ

antihistamines yah airn-dtêe hít-dta-meen ยาแอนตีฮิสตะมีน

antique: is it an antique? bpen kǒrng gào taír táir rěu bplào? เป็นของเก่าแท้ ๆ หรือเปล่า

antique shop ráhn kǎi kǒrng gào ร้านขายของเก่า

antiseptic yah kâh chéu-a ยาฆ่าเชื้อ

any: have you got any bread/ tomatoes? mee ka-nǒm-bpung/ma-kěu-a-tâyt mái? มีขนมปัง/มะเขือเทศไหม

do you have any change? mee sàyt sa-dtahng mái? มีเศษสตางค์ไหม

sorry, I don't have any kǒr-tôht pǒm (chún) mâi mee ขอโทษผม(ฉัน)ไม่มี

anybody krai gôr dâi ใครก็ได้

does anybody speak English? mee krai pôot pah-săh ung-grìt dâi? มีใครพูดภาษาอังกฤษได้

there wasn't anybody there mâi mee krai yòo têe nûn ไม่มีใครอยู่ที่นั่น

anything a-rai gôr dâi อะไรก็ได้

anything else? ao a-rai èek mái?

nothing else, thanks mâi ao krúp (kâ)

would you like anything to drink? dèum a-rai mái?

I don't want anything, thanks mâi krúp (kâ)

apart from nôrk jàhk นอกจาก

apartment a-páht-mén อพาร์ตเม้นท์

apartment block dtèuk a-páht-mén ตึกอพาร์ตเม้นท์

apologize kŏr-tôht ขอโทษ

appendicitis rôhk sâi dtìng โรคไส้ติ่ง

apple air-bpêrn แอปเปิล

appointment nút นัด

good morning, how can I help you? sa-wùt dee krúp mee a-rai ja hâi chôo-ay mái krúp?

I'd like to make an appointment with... yàhk nút póp gùp...

what time would you like? yàhk dâi way-lah tâo-rài?

three o'clock bài săhm mohng

I'm afraid that's not possible, is four o'clock all right? kít wâh kong mâi dâi ao bpen way-lah sèe mohng dâi mái?

yes, that will be fine krúp dtòk-long

the name was? chêu a-rai krúp?

apricot ay-pri-kort เอพริคอท

April may-săh-yon เมษายน

are: we are rao bpen เราเป็น

you are kOOn bpen คุณเป็น

they are káo bpen เขาเป็น

area bor-ri-wayn บริเวณ

area code ra-hùt รหัส

arm kăirn แขน

arrange: will you arrange it for us? chôo-ay jùt gahn hâi nòy dâi mái? ช่วยจัดการให้หน่อยได้ไหม

arrival gahn mah tĕung การมาถึง

arrive mah tĕung มาถึง

when do we arrive? rao ja tĕung mêu-a rài? เราจะถึงเมื่อไร

has my fax arrived yet?
fairks kǒrng pǒm (chún) mah
rěu yung? แฟกซ์ของผม(ฉัน)
มาหรือยัง

we arrived today rao mah
těung wun née เรามาถึงวันนี้

art sǐn-la-bpà ศิลป

art gallery ráhn kǎi pâhp kěe-un
ร้านขายภาพเขียน

artist sǐn-la-bpin ศิลปิน

as: as big as yài tâo gùp
ใหญ่เท่ากับ

as soon as possible yàhng
ray-o têe sòot têe ja ray-o dâi
อย่างเร็วที่สุดที่จะเร็วได้

ashtray têe kèe-a bOO-rèe
ที่เขี่ยบุหรี่

Asia ay-see-a เอเชีย

ask tǎhm ถาม

I didn't ask for this pǒm
(chún) mâi dâi kǒr ao un née
ผม(ฉัน)ไม่ได้ขอเอาอันนี้

could you ask him to...?
chôo-a-y bòrk hâi káo... dâi
mái? ช่วยบอกให้เขา...
ได้ไหม

asleep: she's asleep káo norn
lùp yòo เขานอนหลับอยู่

aspirin airt-pai-rin แอสไพริน

asthma rôhk hèut โรคหืด

astonishing nâh bpra-làht jai
น่าประหลาดใจ

at: at the hotel têe rohng rairm
ที่โรงแรม

at the station têe sa-tǎh-nee
rót fai ที่สถานีรถไฟ

at six o'clock way-lah hòk
mohng เวลาหกโมง

at Noi's têe bâhn kOOn nói
ที่บ้านคุณน้อย

athletics gree-tah กรีฑา

ATM bor-ri-gahn ngern dòo-un
บริการเงินด่วน

at sign, @ àirt แอด

attractive sǒo-ay สวย

aubergine ma-kěu-a มะเขือ

August sǐng-hǎh-kom สิงหาคม

aunt (elder sister of mother/father)
bpâh ป้า

(younger sister of father) ah อา

(younger sister of mother) náh น้า

Australia órt-sa-tray-lee-a
ออสเตรเลีย

Australian (adj) órt-sa-tray-
lee-a ออสเตรเลีย

I'm Australian pǒm (chún)
bpen kon órt-sa-tray-lee-a
ผม(ฉัน)เป็นคนออสเตรเลีย

automatic ùt-dta-noh-mút
อัตโนมัติ

(car) rót ùt-dta-noh-mút
รถอัตโนมัติ

autumn réu-doo bai-mái rôo-
ung ฤดูใบไม้ร่วง

in the autumn dtorn
réu-doo bai-mái rôo-ung
ตอนฤดูใบไม้ร่วง

average tum-ma-dah ธรรมดา

on average doy-ee cha-lèe-a
โดยเฉลี่ย

awake: is he awake? káo
dtèun láir-o rĕu yung?
เขาตื่นแล้วหรือยัง

away: go away! bpài! ไป

is it far away? yòo glai mái?
อยู่ไกลไหม

awful yâir mâhk แย่มาก

axle plao เพลา

B

baby dèk òrn เด็กอ่อน

baby food ah-hăhn dèk
อาหารเด็ก

baby's bottle kòo-ut nom
ขวดนม

baby-sitter pêe lée-ung dèk
พี่เลี้ยงเด็ก

back (of body) lŭng หลัง

(back part) kâhng lŭng ข้างหลัง

at the back kâhng lŭng
ข้างหลัง

**can I have my money
back?** kŏr ngern keun dâi
mái? ขอเงินคืนได้ไหม

to come/go back glùp mah/
glùp bpai กลับมา/กลับไป

backache bpòo-ut lŭng
ปวดหลัง

bacon mŏo bay-korn หมูเบคอน

bad mâi dee ไม่ดี

a bad headache bpòo-ut
hŏo-a mâhk ปวดหัวมาก

badly mâi dee ไม่ดี

bag tŏong ถุง

(handbag) gra-bpăo tĕu
กระเป๋าถือ

(suitcase) gra-bpăo dern tahng
กระเป๋าเดินทาง

baggage gra-bpăo กระเป๋า

baggage check têe fàhk gra-bpǎo ที่ฝากกระเป๋า

baggage claim sǎi pahn lum-lee-ung gra-bpǎo สายพานลำเลียงกระเป๋า

bakery ráhn tum ka-nǒm-bpung ร้านทำขนมปัง

balcony ra-bee-ung ระเบียง

a room with a balcony hôrng mee ra-bee-ung ห้องมีระเบียง

ball lôok born ลูกบอล

ballpoint pen bpàhk-gah lôok lêun ปากกาลูกลื่น

bamboo mái pài ไม้ไผ่

bamboo shoot(s) nòr mái หน่อไม้

banana glôo-ay กล้วย

band (musical) wong don-dtree วงดนตรี

bandage pâh pun plǎir ผ้าพันแผล

Bandaids bplah-sa-dter พลาสเตอร์

Bangkok grOOng-tâyp กรุงเทพฯ

bank (money) ta-nah-kahn ธนาคาร

bank account bun-chee ngern fàhk ta-nah-kahn ปัญชีเงินฝากธนาคาร

Travel tip Travellers soon get so used to the low cost of living in Thailand that they start bargaining at every available opportunity, much as Thai people do. But you shouldn't forget that the few pennies you're making such a fuss over will go a lot further in a Thai person's hands than in your own.

bar bah บาร์

barber's châhng dtùt pǒm ช่างตัดผม

bargaining gahn dtòr rah-kah การต่อราคา

DIALOGUE

how much is this? nêe tâo-rài?

500 baht hâh róy bàht

that's too expensive pairng bpai nòy

how about 400? sèe róy dâi mái?

I'll let you have it for 450 kít sèe róy hâh sìp gôr láir-o gun

can't you reduce it a bit more?/OK, it's a deal lót èek mâi dâi lěu?/oh kay, dtòk long

basket dta-grâh ตะกร้า

bath àhng àhp náhm อ่างอาบน้ำ

can I have a bath?

kǒr àhp náhm dâi mái?
ขออาบน้ำได้ไหม

bathroom hôrng náhm ห้องน้ำ

with a private bathroom
hôrng norn têe mee
hôrng náhm dôo-ay
ห้องนอนที่มีห้องน้ำด้วย

bath towel pâh chét dtoo-a
ผ้าเช็ดตัว

bathtub àhng àhp náhm
อ่างอาบน้ำ

battery bair-dta-rêe
แบตเตอรี

bay ào อ่าว

be bpen เป็น

beach chai hàht ชายหาด

on the beach tee chai haht
ที่ชายหาด

beach mat sèu-a bpoo chai-hàht
เสื่อปูชายหาด

beach umbrella rôm gun dàirt
ร่มกันแดด

beans tòo-a ถั่ว

beansprouts tòo-a ngôrk
ถั่วงอก

beard krao เครา

beautiful sǒo-ay สวย

because prór เพราะ

because of... neû-ung jàhk...
เนื่องจาก...

bed dtee-ung เตียง

I'm going to bed now pǒm
(chún) bpai norn ผม(ฉัน)
ไปนอน

bedroom hôrng norn ห้องนอน

beef néu-a woo-a เนื้อวัว

beer bee-a เบียร์

two beers, please kǒr bee-a
sǒrng kòo-ut ขอเบียร์สองขวด

before gòrn ก่อน

begin rêrm เริ่ม

when does it begin? rêrm
mêu-a rài? เริ่มเมื่อไร

beginner pôo rêrm ree-un
ผู้เริ่มเรียน

beginning: at the beginning
dtorn dtôn ตอนต้น

behind kâhng lǔng ข้างหลัง

behind me kâhng lǔng pǒm
(chún) ข้างหลังผม(ฉัน)

Belgian (adj) bayl-yee-um
เบลเยียม

Belgium bpra-tâyt bayl-yee-
um ประเทศเบลเยียม

below dtâi ใต้

belt kěm kùt เข็มขัด

bend (in road) tahng kóhng
ทางโค้ง

berth (on ship) têe-norn ที่นอน

beside: beside the... kâhng
kâhng... ข้างๆ...

best dee têe sòot ดีที่สุด

better dee gwàh ดีกว่า
  are you feeling better?
  kôy yung chôo-a mái?
  ค่อยยังชั่วไหม

between ra-wàhng ระหว่าง

beyond ler-ee bpai เลยไป

bicycle jùk-gra-yahn จักรยาน

big yài ใหญ่
  too big yài gern bpai
  ใหญ่เกินไป
  it's not big enough yài mâi
  por ใหญ่ไม่พอ

bike jùk-gra-yahn จักรยาน
  (motorbike) jùk-gra-yahn-yon
  จักรยานยนตร์

bikini bi-gi-nee บิกินี

bill bin บิล
  (US) bai báirng ใบแบ๊งค์
  could I have the bill,
  please? chék bin เช็คบิล

bin tǔng ka-yà ถังขยะ

bin liners tǒong ka-yà ถุงขยะ

bird nók นก

birthday wun gèrt วันเกิด
  happy birthday! oo-ay-porn
  wun gèrt! อวยพรวันเกิด

biscuit kóok-gêe คุกกี้

bit: a little bit nít-nòy
  นิดหน่อย
  a big bit chín yài ชิ้นใหญ่

a bit of… …chín nèung
…ชิ้นหนึ่ง
  a bit expensive pairng bpai
  nòy แพงไปหน่อย

bite (by insect, dog) gùt กัด

bitter (taste etc) kǒm ขม

black sěe dum สีดำ

blanket pâh hòm ผ้าห่ม

bleach (for toilet) yah láhng hòrng
  náhm ยาล้างห้องน้ำ

blind dtah bòrt ตาบอด

blinds môo-lêe มู่ลี่

blister plǎir porng แผลพอง

blocked (road, pipe, sink) dtun ตัน

blond (adj) pǒm sěe torng
ผมสีทอง

blood lêu-ut เลือด
  high blood pressure
  kwahm dun loh-hìt sǒong
  ความดันโลหิตสูง

blouse sêu-a pôo-yǐng
เสื้อผู้หญิง

blow-dry bpào pǒm เป่าผม
  I'd like a cut and blow-dry
  yàhk hâi dtùt láir bpào pǒm
  อยากให้ตัดและเป่าผม

blue sěe núm ngern สีน้ำเงิน

boarding pass bùt têe-nûng
บัตรที่นั่ง

boat reu-a เรือ

body râhng-gai ร่างกาย

boiled egg kài dtôm ไข่ต้ม

boiled rice kâo sŏo-ay ข้าวสวย

boiler môr náhm หม้อน้ำ

bone gra-dòok กระดูก

bonnet (of car) gra-bprohng rót กระโปรงรถ

book (*noun*) núng-sĕu หนังสือ

(*verb*) jorng จอง

can I book a seat? kŏr jorng têe-nûng dâi mái? ขอจองที่นั่งได้ไหม

DIALOGUE

I'd like to book a table for two yàhk jorng dtó sŭm-rùp sŏrng kon

what time would you like it booked for? ja jorng way-lah tâo-rài?

half past seven tôOm krêung

that's fine dâi krúp

and your name? chêu a-rai krúp?

bookshop, bookstore ráhn kăi núng-sĕu ร้านขายหนังสือ

boot (footwear) rorng-táo รองเท้า

(of car) gra-bprohng tái rót กระโปรงท้ายรถ

border (of country) chai-dairn ชายแดน

bored: I'm bored pŏm (chún) bèu-a ผม(ฉัน)เบื่อ

boring nâh bèu-a น่าเบื่อ

born: I was born in Manchester pŏm (chún) gèrt têe Manchester ผม(ฉัน)เกิดที่ Manchester

I was born in 1960 pŏm (chún) gèrt bpee nèung pun gâo róy hòk sìp ผม(ฉัน)เกิดปีหนึ่งพันเก้าร้อย หกสิบ

borrow yeum ยืม

may I borrow...? kŏr yeum… dâi mái? ขอยืม… ได้ไหม

both túng sŏrng ทั้งสอง

bother: sorry to bother you kŏr-tôht têe róp-goo-un ขอโทษที่รบกวน

bottle kòo-ut ขวด

bottle-opener têe bpèrt kòo-ut ที่เปิดขวด

bottom (of person) gôn ก้น

at the bottom of the hill cherng kăo เชิงเขา

at the bottom of the street bplai ta-nŏn ปลายถนน

bowl chahm ชาม

box hèep หีบ

box office hôrng kăi dtŏo-a ห้องขายตั๋ว

boy pôo-chai ผู้ชาย

boyfriend fairn แฟน

bra sêu-a yók song เสื้อยกทรง

bracelet gum-lai meu กำไลมือ

brake bràyk เบรค

brandy lâo brùn-dee เหล้าบรั่นดี

bread ka-nŏm-bpung ขนมปัง

break (*verb*) dtàirk แตก

  I've broken the... pŏm
  (chún) tum... dtàirk
  ผม(ฉัน)ทำ... แตก

  I think I've broken my wrist
  pŏm (chún) kít wâh kôr meu
  hùk ผม(ฉัน)คิดว่าข้อมือหัก

break down sĕe-a เสีย

  I've broken down (car) rót
  pŏm (chún) sĕe-a
  รถผม(ฉัน)เสีย

breakdown service bor-ri-
gahn sôrm บริการซ่อม

breakfast ah-hăhn cháo
อาหารเช้า

**break-in: I've had a break-
in** mee ka-moy-ee kâo bâhn
มีขโมยเข้าบ้าน

breast nom นม

breathe hăi jai หายใจ

breeze lom òrn òrn ลมอ่อนๆ

bridge (over river) sa-pahn
สะพาน

brief sûn สั้น

briefcase gra-bpăo กระเป๋า

bright (light etc) sa-wàhng สว่าง

  bright red dairng jùt แดงจัด

brilliant (idea) yêe-um เยี่ยม

bring ao... mah เอา... มา

  I'll bring it back later ja keun
  hâi tee lŭng จะคืนให้ทีหลัง

Britain bpra-tâyt ung-grìt
ประเทศอังกฤษ

British ung-grìt อังกฤษ

brochure rai la-èe-ut
รายละเอียด

broken dtàirk láir-o แตกแล้ว

bronchitis lòrt lom ùk-sàyp
หลอดลมอักเสบ

brooch kĕm glùt sêu-a
เข็มกลัดเสื้อ

broom mái gwàht ไม้กวาด

brother (older) pêe chai พี่ชาย

  (younger) nórng chai น้องชาย

brother-in-law (older) pêe kĕr-ee
พี่เขย

  (younger) nórng kĕr-ee น้องเขย

brown sĕe núm dtahn สีน้ำตาล

bruise fók-chúm ฟกช้ำ

brush (for hair) bprairng pŏm
แปรงผม

  (artist's) bprairng แปรง

  (for cleaning) mái gwàht
ไม้กวาด

bucket tŭng ถัง

Buddha prá-póot-ta-jâo
พระพุทธเจ้า

Buddhism sàh-sa-năh póot
ศาสนาพุทธ

Buddhist (*noun*) chao póot
ชาวพุทธ

buffet car rót sa-bee-ung
รถเสบียง

buggy (for child) rót kĕn dèk
รถเข็นเด็ก

building ah-kahn อาคาร

bulb (light bulb) lòrt fai fáh
หลอดไฟฟ้า

bumper gun chon กันชน

bungalow bung-gah-loh
บังกาโล

bureau de change bor-ri-gahn
lâirk ngern บริการแลกเงิน

burglary ka-moy-ee kâo bâhn
ขโมยเข้าบ้าน

Burma bpra-tâyt pa-mâh
ประเทศพม่า

Burmese pa-mâh พม่า

burn (*noun*) plăir mâi แผลไหม้

burnt: this is burnt un née mâi
อันนี้ไหม้

burst: a burst pipe tôr dtàirk
ท่อแตก

bus rót may รถเมล์

  what number bus is it to...?
rót bpai... ber tâo-rài? รถไป...
เบอร์เท่าไร

  when is the next bus to...?
rót têe-o nâh bpai... òrk gèe

mohng? รถเที่ยวหน้าไป...
ออกกี่โมง

  **what time is the last
bus?** rót têe-o sòot
tái òrk gèe mohng?
รถเที่ยวสุดท้ายออกกี่โมง

does this bus go to...? rót
  kun née bpai... mái?
no, you need a number...
  mâi bpai kOOn dtôrng kêun
  măi-lâyk...

business tóo-rá ธุระ

bus station sa-tăh-nee rót may
สถานีรถเมล์

bus stop bpâi rót may
ป้ายรถเมล์

Travel tip Generally it's best
to travel on the government-
run and licensed long-distance buses that depart from
the main bus terminals, which
have a reputation to main-
tain with their regular Thai
customers, rather than the
temptingly cheap, unlicensed
buses geared towards tourists. The extra comfort, safety
and peace of mind are well
worth the extra baht.

bust nâh òk หน้าอก

busy (restaurant etc) nâirn แน่น

  I'm busy tomorrow prôOng
née mee tóo-rá พรุ่งนี้มีธุระ

but dtàir แต่
butcher's ráhn néu-a ร้านเนื้อ
butter ner-ee sòt เนยสด
button gra-dOOm กระดุม
buy séu ซื้อ

   where can I buy…? pŏm
   (chún) séu… dâi têe
   nǎi? ผม(ฉัน)ซื้อ… ได้ที่ไหน

   by: by bus/car doy-ee rót may/
   rót yon โดยรถเมล์/รถยนต์

   written by… kĕe-un doy-ee…
   เขียนโดย…

   by the window glâi nâh-
   dtàhng ใกล้หน้าต่าง

   by the sea chai ta-lay
   ชายทะเล

   by Monday gòrn wun jun
   ก่อนวันจันทร์

bye lah gòrn ลาก่อน

C

cabbage ga-lùm-bplee กะหล่ำปลี
cake ka-nŏm káyk ขนมเค้ก
call (*verb*) rêe-uk เรียก

   (to phone) toh-ra-sùp, toh
   โทรศัพท์, โทร

   what's it called? rêe-uk wâh
   a-rai? เรียกว่าอะไร

   he/she is called… káo
   chêu… เขาชื่อ…

   please call the doctor
   chôo-ay rêe-uk mŏr hâi nòy
   ช่วยเรียกหมอให้หน่อย

   please give me a call at
   7.30 a.m. chôo-ay toh mah
   way-lah jèt mohng krêung
   ช่วยโทรมาเวลาเจ็ดโมงครึ่ง

please ask him to call me
chôo-ay hâi káo toh mah
ช่วยให้เขาโทรมา

call back: I'll call back
later děe-o ja toh mah mài
เดี๋ยวจะโทรมาใหม่

call round: I'll call round
tomorrow prôOng née ja
wáir mah hǎh
พรุ่งนี้จะแวะมาหา

Cambodia bpra-tâyt gum-poo-
chah ประเทศกัมพูชา

Cambodian (adj) ka-mǎyn เขมร

camcorder glôrng bun-téuk
pâhp กล้องบันทึกภาพ

camera glôrng tài rôop
กล้องถ่ายรูป

camera shop ráhn kǎi glôrng tài
rôop ร้านขายกล้องถ่ายรูป

can gra-bpôrng กระป๋อง

a can of beer bee-a gra-
bpôrng เบียร์กระป๋อง

can: can you...? kOOn... dâi
mái? คุณ... ได้ไหม

can I have...? kǒr... dâi mái?
ขอ ... ได้ไหม

I can't... pǒm (chún)... mâi
dâi ผม(ฉัน) ... ไม่ได้

Canada bpra-tâyt kairn-nah-dah
ประเทศแคนาดา

Canadian (adj) kair-nah-dah
แคนาดา

I'm Canadian pǒm (chún)
bpen kon kair-nah-dah
ผม(ฉัน)เป็นคนแคนาดา

canal klorng คลอง

cancel ngót งด

candies tórp-fêe ท้อฟฟี่

candle tee-un เทียน

can-opener têe bpèrt gra-
bpôrng ที่เปิดกระป๋อง

cap (hat) mòo-uk หมวก

car rót yon รถยนต์

by car doy-ee rót yon
โดยรถยนต์

carburettor kah-ber-ret-dtêr
คาร์บูเรเตอร์

card (business) nahm bùt นามบัตร

here's my card nêe
nahm bùt pǒm (chún)
นี่นามบัตรผม(ฉัน)

cardigan sêu-a nǎo เสื้อหนาว

careful ra-mút ra-wung
ระมัดระวัง

be careful! ra-wung ná!
ระวังนะ

caretaker kon fâo bâhn
คนเฝ้าบ้าน

car ferry pair chái bun-
tóOk rót-yon kâhm fâhk
แพใช้บรรทุกรถยนต์ข้ามฟาก

car hire bor-ri-gahn rót châo
บริการรถเช่า

carnival ngahn งาน

car park têe jòrt rót ที่จอดรถ

carpet prom พรม

car rental bor-ri-gahn rót châo
บริการรถเช่า

carriage (of train) dtôo rót fai
ตู้รถไฟ

carrier bag tŏong hêw ถุงหิ้ว

carrot hŏo-a pùk-gàht dairng
หัวผักกาดแดง

carry (something in the hands)
tĕu ถือ
(something by a handle) hêw หิ้ว
(a heavy load on the back or
shoulder) bàirk แบก
(a child, in one's arms) ôom อุ้ม

carry-cot dta-gráh sài dèk
ตะกร้าใส่เด็ก

carton glòrng กล่อง

carwash bor-ri-gahn láhng rót
บริการล้างรถ

case (suitcase) gra-bpăo dern
tahng กระเป๋าเดินทาง

cash (noun) ngern sòt เงินสด
(verb) kêun ngern ขึ้นเงิน

**will you cash this for
me?** chôo-ay bpai kêun
ngern hâi nòy dâi mái?
ช่วยไปขึ้นเงินให้หน่อยได้ไหม

cash desk dtó jài ngern
โต๊ะจ่ายเงิน

cash dispenser bor-ri-gahn
ngern dòo-un บริการเงินด่วน

cassette móo-un tâyp kah-set
ม้วนเทปคาสเซ็ท

cassette recorder krêu-
ung lên tâyp kah-set
เครื่องเล่นเทปคาสเซ็ท

castle bprah-sàht ปราสาท

casualty department pa-nàirk
oo-bùt-dti-hàyt chòok chěrn
แผนกอุบัติเหตุฉุกเฉิน

cat mair-o แมว

catch (verb) jùp จับ

**where do we catch the bus
to…?** rao kêun rót may bpai…
têe năi? เราขึ้นรถเมล์ไป …
ที่ไหน

Catholic (adj) káirt-oh-lík
แคโทลิค

cauliflower dòrk ga-lùm-bplee
ดอกกะหล่ำปลี

cave tûm ถ้ำ

ceiling pay-dahn เพดาน

cemetery bpàh cháh ป่าช้า

centigrade sen-dti-gràyd
เซ็นติเกรด

centimetre sen-dti-mét
เซ็นติเมตร

central glahng กลาง

centre sŏon glahng
ศูนย์กลาง

how do we get to the
city centre? bpai sŏon
glahng meu-ung yung-ngai?
ไปศูนย์กลางเมืองอย่างไร

certainly nâir-norn แน่นอน

certainly not! mâi ròrk!
ไม่หรอก

chair gâo êe เก้าอี้

champagne chairm-bpayn
แชมเปญ

change (noun: money) sàyt
sa-dtahng เศษสตางค์

(verb: money) bplèe-un
เปลี่ยน

can I change this for...? kŏr
lâirk âi nêe bpen … dâi mái?
ขอแลกไอ้นี่เป็น … ได้ไหม

I don't have any change
pŏm (chún) mâi mee báirnk yôy
yôy ผม(ฉัน)ไม่มีแบงค์ย่อยๆ

can you give me change for
a 100 baht note? kŏr dtàirk
bai la róy nòy, dâi mái?
ขอแตกใบละร้อยหน่อยได้ไหม

DIALOGUE

do we have to change
(trains)? dtôrng bplèe-un
rót fai rěu bplào?

yes, change at Bang
Krathum/no it's a direct
train dtôrng, dtôrng bplèe-
un têe bahng gra-tOOm/
mâi dtôrng, bpen rót dtrong

changed: to get changed
bplèe-un sêu-a เปลี่ยนเสื้อ

charge (noun) kâh ค่า
(verb) kít kâh คิดค่า

cheap tòok ถูก

do you have anything
cheaper? mee a-rai
tòok gwàh rěu bplào?
มีอะไรถูกกว่าหรือเปล่า

check (verb) chék doo เช็คดู

could you check the...,
please? chôo-ay chék doo …
nòy, dâi mái? ช่วยเช็คดู …
หน่อยได้ไหม

check (US: noun) chék เช็ค
(US: bill) bin บิล
see cheque and bill

check book sa-mÒOt chék
สมุดเช็ค

check-in dtròo-ut chûng núm-
nùk ตรวจชั่งน้ำหนัก

check in: where do we have
to check in? rao dtôrng
'check in' têe năi? เราต้อง
'check in' ที่ไหน

cheek (on face) gâirm แก้ม

cheerio! wùt dee hâ! วัสดีฮ่ะ

cheese ner-ee kǎirng เนยแข็ง

chemist's ráhn kǎi yah
ร้านขายยา

cheque chék เช็ค

do you take cheques?
jai bpen chék, dâi mái?
จ่ายเป็นเช็คได้ไหม

cheque book sa-mòot chék
สมุดเช็ค

cheque card bùt chék บัตรเช็ค

cherry cher-rêe เชอร์รี่

chess màhk róok หมากรุก

chest nâh òk หน้าอก

chewing gum màhk fa-rùng
หมากฝรั่ง

Chiangmai chee-ung mài
เชียงใหม่

chicken gài ไก่

chickenpox ee-sòok ee-săi
อีสุกอีใส

child dèk เด็ก

(own) lôok ลูก

child minder kon lée-ung doo
dèk คนเลี้ยงดูเด็ก

children's pool sà wâi náhm dèk
สระว่ายน้ำเด็ก

chilli prík พริก

chin kahng คาง

Chinese (adj) jeen จีน

chips mun fa-rùng tôrt
มันฝรั่งทอด

chocolate chork-goh-lairt
ช็อกโกเลต

choose lêu-uk เลือก

chopsticks dta-gèe-up ตะเกียบ

Christian name chêu ชื่อ

Christmas krít-sa-maht
คริสต์มาส

church bòht โบสถ์

cigar si-gah ซิการ์

cigarette boo-rèe บุหรี่

cigarette lighter fai cháirk
ไฟแช็ค

cinema rohng năng โรงหนัง

circle wong glom วงกลม

city meu-ung เมือง

city centre jai glahng meu-ung
ใจกลางเมือง

clean (adj) sa-àht สะอาด

**can you clean these for
me?** tum kwahm sa-àht nêe
hâi nòy dâi mái? ทำความสะ
อาดนี่ให้หน่อยได้ไหม

cleaning solution (for contact
lenses) núm yah tum kwahm
sa-àht น้ำยาทำความสะอาด

cleansing lotion núm
yah tum kwahm sa-àht
น้ำยาทำความสะอาด

clear chút ชัด

(obvious) hěn dâi chút เห็นได้ชัด

clever cha-làht ฉลาด

cliff nâh pǎh หน้าผา

clinic klee-ník คลีนิค

cloakroom têe fàhk kǒrng
ที่ฝากของ

clock nah-li-gah นาฬิกา

close (*verb*) bpìt ปิด

what time do you close?
kOOn bpìt gèe mohng?

we close at 8 p.m. on weekdays and 6 p.m. on Saturdays rao bpìt way-lah sŏrng tôOm ra-wàhng wun jun wun sÒOk láir hòk mohng wun sǎo

do you close for lunch?
bpìt way-lah ra-hǎhn glahng wun rěu bplào?

yes, between 1 and 3.30 p.m. krúp ra-wàhng way-lah bài mohng těung sǎhm mohng krêung

closed bpìt ปิด

cloth (fabric) pâh ผ้า

(for cleaning etc) pâh kêe réw ผ้าขี้ริ้ว

clothes sêu-a pâh เสื้อผ้า

clothes line rao dtàhk pâh ราวตากผ้า

clothes peg mái nèep pâh ไม้หนีบผ้า

cloud mâyk เมฆ

cloudy mâyk kréum เมฆครึ้ม

clutch klút คลัทช์

coach (bus) rót too-a รถทัวร์

(on train) dtôo rót fai ตู้รถไฟ

coach station sa-tǎhn-nee rót may สถานีรถเมล์

coach trip rót num têe-o รถนำเที่ยว

coast chai ta-lay ชายทะเล

on the coast chai ta-lay ชายทะเล

coat (long coat) sêu-a klOOm เสื้อคลุม

(jacket) sêu-a nôrk เสื้อนอก

coathanger mái kwǎirn sêu-a ไม้แขวนเสื้อ

cockroach ma-lairng sàhp แมลงสาบ

cocoa goh-gôh โกโก้

coconut ma-práo มะพร้าว

coconut milk núm ma-práo น้ำมะพร้าว

code (for phoning) ra-hùt รหัส

what's the (dialling) code for Chiangmai? ra-hùt chee-ung mài ber a-rai? รหัสเชียงใหม่เบอร์อะไร

coffee gah-fair กาแฟ

two coffees, please kǒr gah-fair sŏrng tôo-ay ขอกาแฟสองถ้วย

coffee shop kòrp-fèe chórp คอฟฟี่ช็อบ

coin ngern rěe-un เงินเหรียญ

Coke koh-láh โคล่า

cold (*adj*) nǎo หนาว

I'm cold pŏm (chún) nǎo
ผม(ฉัน)หนาว

I have a cold pŏm (chún)
bpen wùt ผม(ฉัน)เป็นหวัด

collapse: he's collapsed káo
mòt sa-dtì เขาหมดสติ

collar kor bpòk sêu-a
คอปกเสื้อ

collect gèp เก็บ

I've come to collect… pŏm
(chún) mah gèp… ผม(ฉัน)
มาเก็บ…

collect call toh-ra-sùp
gèp ngern bplai tahng
โทรศัพท์เก็บเงินปลายทาง

college wít-ta-yah-lai วิทยาลัย

colour sěe สี

**do you have this in other
colours?** mee sěe èun mái?
มีสีอื่นไหม

colour film feem sěe ฟิล์มสี

comb (*noun*) wěe หวี

come mah มา

where do you come from?
kOOn mah jàhk nǎi krúp
(ká?)

I come from Edinburgh
pŏm (chún) mah jàhk
Edinburgh

come back glùp mah กลับมา

I'll come back tomorrow
prôOng née glùp mah mài
พรุ่งนี้กลับมาใหม่

come in chern kâo mah
เชิญเข้ามา

comfortable sa-dòo-uk สะดวก

compact disc pàirn see dee
แผ่นซีดี

company (business) bor-ri-sùt
บริษัท

compartment (on train) hôrng
pôo doy-ee sǎhn ห้องผู้โดยสาร

compass kěm-tít เข็มทิศ

complain bòn บ่น

complaint rêu-ung rórng ree-un
เรื่องร้องเรียน

I have a complaint pŏm
(chún) mee rêu-ung rórng ree-
un ผม(ฉัน)มีเรื่องร้องเรียน

completely túng mòt ทั้งหมด

computer korm-pew-dter
คอมพิวเตอร์

concert gahn sa-dairng don-
dtree การแสดงดนตรี

concussion sa-mǒrng
tòok gra-tóp gra-teu-un
สมองถูกกระทบกระเทือน

conditioner (for hair) kreem nôo-
ut pŏm ครีมนวดผม

condom tǒong yahng ถุงยาง

conference gahn bpra-chOOm
การประชุม

confirm rúp-rorng รับรอง

congratulations! kŏr sa-dairng kwahm yin dee! ขอแสดงความยินดี

connecting flight têe-o bin dtòr เที่ยวบินต่อ

connection dtòr ต่อ

conscious mee sa-dtì มีสติ

constipation tórng pòok ท้องผูก

consulate sa-tăhn gong-sŏOn สถานกงสุล

contact (verb) dtìt dtòr ติดต่อ

contact lenses korn-táirk layn คอนแทคเล็นซ์

contraceptive krêu-ung kOOm gum-nèrt เครื่องคุมกำเนิด

convenient sa-dòo-uk สะดวก

that's not convenient nûn mâi kóy sa-dòo-uk นั่นไม่ค่อยสะดวก

cook (verb) tum ah-hăhn ทำอาหาร

not cooked dìp dìp ดิบๆ

cooker dtao เตา

cookie kóok-gêe คุกกี้

cooking utensils krêu-ung chái nai kroo-a เครื่องใช้ในครัว

cool yen เย็น

cork jòok kòo-ut จุกขวด

corkscrew têe bpèrt kòo-ut ที่เปิดขวด

corner: on the corner têe mOOm ที่มุม

in the corner yòo dtrong hŏo-a mum อยู่ตรงหัวมุม

correct (right) tòok ถูก

corridor tahng dern ทางเดิน

cosmetics krêu-ung sŭm-ahng เครื่องสำอาง

cost (noun) rah-kah ราคา

how much does it cost? rah-kah tâo-rài? ราคาเท่าไร

cot bplay เปล

cotton fâi ฝ้าย

cotton wool sŭm-lee สำลี

couch (sofa) têe nûng rúp kàirk ที่นั่งรับแขก

cough ai ไอ

cough medicine yah gâir ai ยาแก้ไอ

could: could you...? kOOn... dâi mái? คุณ ... ได้ไหม

could I have...? kŏr ... dâi mái? ขอ ... ได้ไหม

I couldn't... pŏm (chún) ... mâi dâi ผม(ฉัน) ... ไม่ได้

country (nation) bpra-tâyt ประเทศ

countryside chon-na-bòt ชนบท

couple (two people) kôo คู่

a couple of... sŏrng săhm... สองสาม ...

courier múk-kOO-tâyt มัคคุเทศก์

course (main course etc) chóot ah-hǎhn ชุดอาหาร

of course nâir-norn แน่นอน

of course not mâi ròrk ไม่หรอก

cousin lôok pêe lôok nórng ลูกพี่ลูกน้อง

cow woo-a วัว

crab bpoo ปู

crash (noun) rót chon รถชน

I've had a crash pǒm (chún) gèrt rót chon ผม(ฉัน)เกิดรถชน

crazy bâh บ้า

cream kreem ครีม

credit card bùt kray-dìt บัตรเครดิต

can I pay by credit card? jài doy-ee bùt kray-dìt dâi mái? จ่ายโดยบัตรเครดิตได้ไหม

DIALOGUE

can I pay by credit card? jài doy-ee bùt kray-dìt dâi mái?

which card do you want to use? ja chái bùt a-rai krúp?

American Express/Visa yes, sir dâi krúp

what's the number? ber a-rai krúp?

and the expiry date? láir-o bùt mòt ah-yóo mêu-raí?

credit crunch bpan-hǎh sǐn-chêu ปัญหาสินเชื่อ

crisps mun fa-rùng tôrt มันฝรั่งทอด

crockery tôo-ay chahm ถ้วยชาม

crossing (by sea) kâhm ta-lay ข้ามทะเล

crossroads sèe yâirk สี่แยก

crowd fǒong kon ฝูงคน

crowded kon nâirn คนแน่น

crown (on tooth) lèe-um fun เหลี่ยมฟัน

cruise lôrng reu-a ล่องเรือ

crutches mái yun rúk ráir ไม้ยันรักแร้

cry (verb) rórng hâi ร้องไห้

cucumber dtairng gwah แตงกวา

cup tôo-ay ถ้วย

a cup of..., please kǒr ... tôo-ay nèung ขอ ... ถ้วยหนึ่ง

cupboard dtôo ตู้

cure (verb) gâir แก้

curly pǒm yìk ผมหยิก

current (electrical) gra-sǎir fai fáh กระแสไฟฟ้า

(in water) gra-sǎir náhm กระแสน้ำ

curtains mâhn ม่าน

cushion mǒrn หมอน

custom bpra-pay-nee ประเพณี

Customs sŏOn-la-gah-gorn
ศุลกากร

cut (*noun*) dtùt ตัด

(*verb*) roy bàht รอยบาด

I've cut myself pŏm (chún)
mee roy bàht ผม(ฉัน)
มีรอยบาด

cutlery chórn sòrm ช้อนส้อม

cycling gahn tèep jùk-ra-yahn
การถีบจักรยาน

cyclist kon tèep jùk-ra-yahn
คนถีบจักรยาน

D

dad pôr พ่อ

daily bpra-jum wun ประจำวัน

damage (*verb*) kwahm sěe-a hǎi
ความเสียหาย

damaged sěe-a láir-o เสียแล้ว

**I'm sorry, I've damaged
this** kŏr-tôht pŏm
(chún) tum hâi sěe-a
ขอโทษผม(ฉัน)ทำให้เสีย

damn! chìp-hǎi! ฉิบหาย

damp (*adj*) chéun ชื้น

dance (*noun*) ra-bum ระบำ

(*verb*) dtên rum เต้นรำ

would you like to dance?
yàhk dtên rum mái?
อยากเต้นรำไหม

dangerous un-dta-rai อันตราย

Danish den-mahk เดนมาร์ก

dark (*adj*: colour) gàir แก่

(hair) dum ดำ

it's getting dark mêut láir-o
มืดแล้ว

date: what's the date today?
wun née wun têe tâo-rài?
วันนี้วันที่เท่าไร

**let's make a date for next
Monday** nút póp gun wun jun
nâh นัดพบกันวันจันทร์หน้า

dates (fruit) in-ta-pa-lǔm
อินทผลัม

daughter lôok sǎo ลูกสาว

daughter-in-law lôok sa-pái
ลูกสะใภ้

dawn (*noun*) rôong รุ่ง

  at dawn rôong cháo รุ่งเช้า

day wun วัน

  the day after tomorrow wun
ma-reun née วันมะรืนนี้

  the day before wun gòrn
วันก่อน

  the day before yesterday
mêu-a wun seun née
เมื่อวานซืนนี้

  every day tóok wun ทุกวัน

  all day túng wun ทั้งวัน

  in two days' time èek sŏrng
wun อีกสองวัน

day trip bpai glùp wun dee-o
ไปกลับวันเดียว

dead dtai ตาย

deaf hŏo nòo-uk หูหนวก

deal (business) tóo-ra-gìt ธุรกิจ

  it's a deal dtòk long láir-o
ตกลงแล้ว

death gahn dtai การตาย

decaffeinated coffee gah-
fair mâi mee kah-fay-in
กาแฟไม่มีคาเฟอีน

December tun-wah-kom
ธันวาคม

decide dtùt sĭn jai ตัดสินใจ

  we haven't decided yet

rao yung mâi dâi dtùt sĭn jai
เรายังไม่ได้ตัดสินใจ

decision gahn dtùt sĭn jai
การตัดสินใจ

deck (on ship) dàht fáh ดาดฟ้า

deckchair gâo êe pâh bai
เก้าอี้ผ้าใบ

deep léuk ลึก

definitely nâir-norn แน่นอน

  definitely not! mâi ròrk!
ไม่หรอก

degree (qualification) bpa-rin-yah
ปริญญา

delay (*noun*) kwahm chúk cháh
ความชักช้า

deliberately doy-ee ay-dta-nah
โดยเจตนา

delicatessen ráhn kǎi
ah-hǎhn sǔm-rèt rôop
ร้านขายอาหารสำเร็จรูป

delicious a-ròy อร่อย

deliver sòng ส่ง

delivery (of mail) gahn sòng jòt-
mǎi การส่งจดหมาย

Denmark bpra-tâyt den-mahk
ประเทศเดนมาร์ก

dentist mŏr fun หมอฟัน

DIALOGUE

it's this one here un nêe ná
this one? un née, châi mái?
no that one mâi châi, un nún
here? un nêe, châi mái?
yes châi

dentures chóot fun tee-um
ชุดฟันเทียม

deodorant yah dùp glìn dtoo-a
ยาดับกลิ่นตัว

department pa-nàirk แผนก

department store hâhng ห้าง

departure kǎh òrk ขาออก

departure lounge hôrng
pôo doy-ee sǎhn kǎh òrk
ห้องผู้โดยสารขาออก

depend: it depends láir-o dtàir
แล้วแต่

  it depends on… láir-o dtàir…
  แล้วแต่…

deposit (as security) ngern fàhk
เงินฝาก

  (as part payment) kâh mút-jum
  ค่ามัดจำ

description kum ùt-ti-bai
คำอธิบาย

dessert kǒrng wǎhn ของหวาน

destination jòot-mǎi bplai
tahng จุดหมายปลายทาง

diabetic (noun) bpen rôhk bao
wǎhn เป็นโรคเบาหวาน

dial (verb) mǒon หมุนe

dialling code ra-hùt toh-ra-sùp
รหัสโทรศัพท์

diamond pét เพชร

diaper pâh ôrm ผ้าอ้อม

diarrhoea tórng sěe-a
ท้องเสีย

**do you have something
for diarrhoea?** mee
yah gâir tórng sěe-a mái?
มียาแก้ท้องเสียไหม

diary sa-mòot bun-téuk bpra-
jum wun สมุดบันทึกประจำวัน

dictionary pót-ja-nah-nóo-
grom พจนานุกรม

didn't mâi dâi… ไม่ได้…
see **not**

die dtai ตาย

diesel núm mun rót dee-sen
น้ำมันรถดีเซล

diet ah-hǎhn pi-sàyt
อาหารพิเศษ

  I'm on a diet pǒm (chún)
  gum-lung lót núm nùk
  ผม(ฉัน)กำลังลดน้ำหนัก

  **I have to follow a special
  diet** pǒm (chún) dtôrng tahn
  ah-hǎhn pi-sàyt ผม(ฉัน)
  ต้องทานอาหารพิเศษ

difference kwahm dtàirk dtàhng
ความแตกต่าง

  what's the difference?
  dtàirk dtàhng gun yung-ngai?
  แตกต่างกันอย่างไร

different dtàhng ต่าง

  this one is different un née
  dtàhng gun อันนี้ต่างกัน

  a different table/room èek
  dtó/hôrng nèung อีกโต๊ะ/
  ห้องหนึ่ง

difficult yâhk ยาก

difficulty bpun-hǎh ปัญหา

dinghy reu-a bòt เรือบด

dining room hôrng rúp-
bpra-tahn ah-hǎhn
ห้องรับประทานอาหาร

dinner (evening meal) ah-hǎhn
yen อาหารเย็น

  to have dinner tahn ah-hǎhn
yen ทานอาหารเย็น

direct (*adj*) dtrong ตรง

  is there a direct train?
mee rót fai dtrong bpai mái?
มีรถไฟตรงไปไหม

direction tahng ทาง

  which direction is it? yòo
tahng nǎi? อยู่ทางไหน

  is it in this direction?
bpai tahng née, châi mái?
ไปทางนี้ใช่ไหม

directory enquiries bor-ri-gahn
sòrp tǎhm ber toh-ra-sùp
บริการสอบถามเบอร์โทรศัพท์

dirt kêe fòon ขี้ฝุ่น

dirty sòk-ga-bpròk สกปรก

disabled pí-gahn พิการ

disappear hǎi bpai หายไป

  it's disappeared mun
hǎi bpai nǎi gôr mâi róo
มันหายไปไหนก็ไม่รู้

disappointed pìt wǔng ผิดหวัง

disappointing mâi dee tâo têe
kít wái ไม่ดีเท่าที่คิดไว้

disaster hǎi-ya-ná หายนะ

disco dit-sa-gôh ดิสโก้

discount lót rah-kah ลดราคา

  is there a discount?
lót rah-kah nòy dâi mái?
ลดราคาหน่อยได้ไหม

disease rôhk โรค

disgusting nâh glèe-ut
น่าเกลียด

dish (meal) gùp kâo กับข้าว

  (bowl) chahm ชาม

dishcloth pâh chét jahn
ผ้าเช็ดจาน

disinfectant yah kâh chéu-a
rôhk ยาฆ่าเชื้อโรค

disk (for computer) jahn bun-téuk
จานบันทึก

**disposable diapers/
nappies** pâh ôrm sǔm-rèt
rôop chái krúng dee-o
ผ้าอ้อมสำเร็จรูปใช้ครั้งเดียว

distance ra-yá tahng ระยะทาง

  in the distance yòo nai ra-yá
glai อยู่ในระยะไกล

district kàyt เขต

disturb róp-goo-un รบกวน

diversion (detour) bplèe-un sên
tahng dern เปลี่ยนเส้นทางเดิน

diving board têe gra-dòht náhm
ที่กระโดดน้ำ

divorced yàh gun láir-o
หย่ากันแล้ว

dizzy: I feel dizzy pǒm (chún)
wee-un hǒo-a ผม(ฉัน)เวียนหัว

do (*verb*) tum ทำ

what shall we do? rao ja tum
yung-ngai? เราจะทำอย่างไร

how do you do it? tum yung-
ngai? ทำอย่างไร

will you do it for me?
chôo-ay tum hâi nòy, dâi mái?
ช่วยทำให้หน่อยได้ไหม

how do you do? sa-wùt dee
krúp (kà)

nice to meet you yin dee
têe dâi róo-jùk gun

what do you do? (work) koon
tum ngahn a-rai krúp (ká)?

I'm a teacher, and you?
bpen kroo, láir-o kOOn lâ?

I'm a student bpen núk
sèuk-sǎh

**what are you doing this
evening?** yen née bpai
nǎi?

**we're going out for a
drink, do you want to
join us?** rao bpai gin lào,
bpai dôo-ay gun mái?

do you want fish sauce?
sài núm bplah mái?

I do, but she doesn't mâi
sài dtàir káo gôr sài

doctor mǒr หมอ

we need a doctor rao
dtôrng gahn hǎh mǒr
เราต้องการหาหมอ

please call a doctor chôo-ay
rêe-uk mǒr ช่วยเรียกหมอ

where does it hurt? jèp
dtrong nǎi?

right here dtrong née

does that hurt now? yung
jèp yòo rěu bplào?

yes jèp

take this to the pharmacy
ao nêe bpai ráhn kǎi yah

document àyk-ga-sǎhn เอกสาร

dog mǎh หมา

doll dtóok-ga-dtah ตุ๊กตา

domestic flight têe-o bin pai nai
เที่ยวบินภายใน

don't! yàh! อย่า

don't do that! yàh tum yàhng
nún! อย่าทำอย่างนั้น

door bpra-dtoo ประตู

doorman kon fâo bpra-dtoo
คนเฝ้าประตู

double kôo คู่

double bed dtee-ung yày
เตียงใหญ่

double room hôrng kôo ห้องคู่

doughnut doh-nút โดนัท

down: down here yòo têe nêe
อยู่ที่นี่

put it down over there wahng
bpai têe nôhn วางไปที่โน่น

it's down there on the right
ler-ee bpai kâhng nâh tahng
dâhn kwǎh meu เลยไปข้างหน้
าทางด้านขวามือ

it's further down the road
bpai dtahm ta-nǒn kâhng nâh
ไปตามถนนข้างหน้า

download dahw-lòht
ดาวน์โหลด

downmarket (restaurant etc) rah-
kah tòok ราคาถูก

downstairs kâhng lâhng
ข้างล่าง

dozen lǒh โหล

half a dozen krêung lǒh
ครึ่งโหล

drain (in sink, in street) tôr ra-bai
ท่อระบาย

draughty: it's draughty mee
lom yen kâo มีลมเย็นเข้า

draw wâht วาด

drawer lín-chúk ลิ้นชัก

drawing rôop wâht รูปวาด

dreadful yâir แย่

dream (noun) kwahm fǔn
ความฝัน

dress (noun) sêu-a chóot เสื้อชุด

dressed: to get dressed
dtàirng dtoo-a แต่งตัว

dressing (for cut) pâh pun plǎir
ผ้าพันแผล

salad dressing núm (râht)
sa-lùt น้ำ(ราด)สลัด

dressing gown sêu-a kloOm
chóot norn เสื้อคลุมชุดนอน

drink (noun) krêu-ung dèum
เครื่องดื่ม

(verb) dèum ดื่ม

a cold drink krêu-ung dèum
yen yen เครื่องดื่มเย็นๆ

can I get you a drink?
kOOn ja dèum a-rai mái?
คุณจะดื่มอะไรไหม

**what would you like (to
drink)?** kOOn ja dèum a-rai?
คุณจะดื่มอะไร

no thanks, I don't drink mâi
krúp (kâ) pǒm (chún) mâi
dèum ไม่ครับ(ค่ะ)ผม(ฉัน)
ไม่ดื่ม

**I'll just have a drink of
water** kǒr náhm bplào tâo-
nún ขอน้ำเปล่าเท่านั้น

drinking water náhm dèum
น้ำดื่ม

is this drinking water?
náhm née gin dâi mái?
น้ำนี้กินได้ไหม

drive (verb) kùp ขับ

we drove here rao kùp rót mah เราขับรถมา

I'll drive you home pŏm (chún) kùp rót bpai sòng ผม(ฉัน)ขับรถไปส่ง

driver kon kùp คนขับ

driving licence bai kùp kèe ใบขับขี่

drop: just a drop, please (of drink) nít dee-o tâo-nún นิดเดียวเท่านั้น

drug yah ยา

drugs (narcotics) yah-sàyp-dtìt ยาเสพติด

Travel tip Thai police actively look for tourists taking drugs, reportedly searching people regularly and randomly on Thanon Khao San, for example. They have the power to order a urine test if they have reasonable grounds for suspicion, and a positive result for marijuana consumption could lead to a year's imprisonment.

drunk (adj) mao เมา

drunken driving kùp rót ka-nà mao ขับรถขณะเมา

dry (adj) hâirng แห้ง

dry-cleaner ráhn súk hâirng ร้านซักแห้ง

duck bpèt เป็ด

due: he was due to arrive

yesterday káo koo-un ja mah mêu-a wahn née เขาควรจะมาเมื่อวานนี้

when is the train due? rót fai mah gèe mohng? รถไฟมากี่โมง

dull (pain) mâi rOOn rairng ไม่รุนแรง

(weather) mêut moo-a มืดมัว

dummy (baby's) hŏo-a nom lòrk หัวนมหลอก

during nai ra-wàhng ในระหว่าง

dust fÒOn ฝุ่น

dustbin tŭng ka-yà ถังขยะ

dusty mee fÒOn yér มีฝุ่นเยอะ

Dutch horl-lairn ฮอลแลนด์

duty-free (goods) mâi dtôrng sĕe-a pah-sĕe ไม่ต้องเสียภาษี

duty-free shop ráhn káh sĭn-káh bplòrt pah-sĕe ah-gorn ร้านค้าสินค้าปลอดภาษีอากร

DVD dee wee dee ดีวีดี

E

each (every) tÓOk ทุก

how much are they each? un la tâo-rài? อันละเท่าไร

ear hŏo หู

earache: I have earache pŏm (chún) bpòo-ut hŏo ผม(ฉัน)ปวดหู

early ray-o เร็ว

  early in the morning cháo dtròo เช้าตรู่

  I called by earlier pŏm (chún) mah hăh mêu-a gòrn née ผม(ฉัน)มาหาเมื่อก่อนนี้

earrings dtôOm hŏo ตุ้มหู

east dta-wun òrk ตะวันออก

  in the east tahng dta-wun òrk ทางตะวันออก

Easter ee-sa-dtêr อีสเตอร์

easy ngâi ง่าย

eat gin kâo กินข้าว

  we've already eaten, thanks rao gin kâo láir-o เรากินข้าวแล้ว

eau de toilette núm òp น้ำอบ

egg kài ไข่

egg noodles ba-mèe บะหมี่

either: either... or... ... rĕu ... ... หรือ ...

  either of them un năi gôr dâi อันไหนก็ได้

elastic (*noun*) săi yahng yêut สายยางยืด

elastic band yahng rút ยางรัด

elbow kôr sòrk ข้อศอก

electric fai fáh ไฟฟ้า

electrical appliances krêu-ung fai fáh เครื่องไฟฟ้า

electrician châhng fai fáh ช่างไฟฟ้า

electricity fai fáh ไฟฟ้า

elephant cháhng ช้าง

elevator líf ลิฟท์

else: something else a-rai èek อะไรอีก

  somewhere else têe èun ที่อื่น

would you like anything else? ao a-rai èek mái?

no, nothing else, thanks mâi krúp (kâ), kòrp-kOOn

email ee-mayl อีเมล์

embassy sa-tǎhn tôot สถานทูต

emergency chÒOk chěrn ฉุกเฉิน

this is an emergency! bpen pah-wá chÒOk chěrn! เป็นภาวะฉุกเฉิน

emergency exit tahng òrk chÒOk chěrn ทางออกฉุกเฉิน

empty wâhng ว่าง

end (*noun*) jòp จบ

(*verb*) sîn sÒOt, jòp สิ้นสุด, จบ

at the end of the soi sÒOt soy สุดซอย

when does it end? jòp mêu-rài? จบเมื่อไร

engaged (toilet, telephone) mâi wâhng ไม่ว่าง

(to be married) mûn หมั้น

engine (car) krêu-ung yon เครื่องยนต์

England bpra-tâyt ung-grìt ประเทศอังกฤษ

English (*adj*) ung-grìt อังกฤษ

(language) pah-sǎh ung-grìt ภาษาอังกฤษ

I'm English pǒm (chún) bpen kon ung-grìt ผม(ฉัน) เป็นคนอังกฤษ

do you speak English? kOOn pôot pah-sǎh ung-grìt bpen mái? คุณพูดภาษาอังกฤษเป็นไหม

enjoy: to enjoy oneself sa-nÒOk สนุก

how did you like the film? nǔng sa-nÒOk mái?

I enjoyed it very much, did you enjoy it? sa-nÒOk mâhk, kOOn kít wâh sa-nÒOk mái?

enjoyable sa-nÒOk dee สนุกดี

enlargement (of photo) pâhp ka-yǎi ภาพขยาย

enormous yài bêr-rêr ใหญ่เบ้อเร่อ

enough por พอ

there's not enough mâi por ไม่พอ

it's not big enough yài mâi por ใหญ่ไม่พอ

that's enough por láir-o พอแล้ว

entrance (*noun*) tahng kâo ทางเข้า

envelope sorng jòt-mǎi ซองจดหมาย

epileptic bpen rôhk lom bâh mǒo เป็นโรคลมบ้าหมู

equipment òop-bpa-gorn อุปกรณ์

error têe pìt ที่ผิด

especially doy-ee cha-pòr โดยเฉพาะ

essential jum-bpen จำเป็น

it is essential that... jum-bpen têe... จำเป็นที่ ...

Europe yOO-rohp ยุโรป

European (adj) yOO-rohp ยุโรป

even máir dtàir แม้แต่

even if... máir wâh... แม้ว่า ...

evening (early evening) dtorn yen ตอนเย็น

(late evening) dtorn glahng keun ตอนกลางคืน

this evening (early evening) yen née เย็นนี้

(late evening) keun née คืนนี้

in the evening (early evening) dtorn yen ตอนเย็น

(late evening) dtorn glahng keun ตอนกลางคืน

evening meal ah-hǎhn yen อาหารเย็น

eventually nai têe sòot ในที่สุด

ever ker-ee เคย

DIALOGUE

have you ever been to Phuket? kOOn ker-ee bpai poo-gèt mái?

yes, I was there two years ago ker-ee, ker-ee bpai mêu-a sǒrng bpee gòrn

every tóok ทุก

every day tóok wun ทุกวัน

everyone tóok kon ทุกคน

everything tóok yàhng ทุกอย่าง

everywhere tôo-a bpai ทั่วไป

exactly! châi láir-o! ใช่แล้ว

exam gahn sòrp การสอบ

example dtoo-a yàhng ตัวอย่าง

for example chên... เช่น...

excellent yêe-um เยี่ยม

excellent! yêe-um ler-ee! เยี่ยมเลย

except yók wáyn ยกเว้น

excess baggage núm nùk gern น้ำหนักเกิน

exchange rate ùt-dtrah lâirk bplèe-un อัตราแลกเปลี่ยน

exciting nâh dtèun dtên น่าตื่นเต้น

excuse me (to get past, to say sorry) kǒr-tôht ขอโทษ

(to get attention) koon krúp (kâ) คุณครับ (คะ)

(to say pardon?) a-rai ná? อะไรนะ

exhaust (pipe) tôr ai sěe-a
ท่อไอเสีย

exhausted (tired) nèu-ay เหนื่อย

exhibition ní-tá-sa-gahn
นิทรรศการ

exit tahng òrk ทางออก

**where's the nearest
exit?** tahng òrk glâi
têe sÒOt yòo têe năi?
ทางออกใกล้ที่สุดอยู่ที่ไหน

expect kâht คาด

expensive pairng แพง

experienced mee bpra-sòp-ba-
gahn มีประสบการณ์

explain ùt-ti-bai อธิบาย

can you explain that?
chôo-ay ùt-ti-bai
hâi nòy, dâi mái?
ช่วยอธิบายให้หน่อยได้ไหม

express (mail) bprai-sa-nee dòo-
un ไปรษณีย์ด่วน
(train) rót fai dòo-un
รถไฟด่วน

extension (telephone) dtòr ต่อ

extension 341, please kǒr
dtòr ber săhm sèe nèung
ขอต่อเบอร์สามสี่หนึ่ง

extension lead săi pôo-ung
สายพ่วง

**extra: can we have an extra
one?** kǒr èek un nèung
ขออีกอันหนึ่ง

**do you charge extra for
that?** kít dtàhng hàhk rěu
bplào? คิดต่างหากหรือเปล่า

extraordinary bplàirk mâhk
แปลกมาก

extremely mâhk lěu-a gern
มากเหลือเกิน

eye dtah ตา

**will you keep an eye on my
suitcase for me?** chôo-ay
fâo gra-bpǎo hâi nòy, dâi mái?
ช่วยเฝ้ากระเป๋าให้หน่อยได้
ไหม

eyebrow pencil din-sǒr kěe-un
kéw ดินสอเขียนคิ้ว

eye drops yah yòrt dtah
ยาหยอดตา

eyeglasses (US) wâirn dtah
แว่นตา

eyeliner têe kěe-un kòrp dtah
ที่เขียนขอบตา

eye make-up remover núm
yah láhng têe kěe-un kòrp dtah
น้ำยาล้างที่เขียนขอบตา

eye shadow kreem tah nǔng
dtah ครีมทาหนังตา

F

face nâh หน้า

factory rohng ngahn โรงงาน

Fahrenheit fah-ren-háit
ฟาเรนไฮท์

faint (*verb*) bpen lom เป็นลม

   she's fainted káo bpen lom เขาเป็นลม

   I feel faint pŏm (chún) róo-sèuk bpen lom ผม(ฉัน) รู้สึกเป็นลม

fair (funfair) ngahn òrk ráhn งานออกร้าน

   (trade) ngahn sa-dairng sĭn-káh งานแสดงสินค้า

   (*adj*) yóot-dti-tum ยุติธรรม

fairly kôrn-kâhng ค่อนข้าง

fake kŏrng bplorm ของปลอม

fall (US) réu-doo bai-mái rôo-ung ฤดูใบไม้ร่วง

   in the fall dtorn réu-doo bai-mái rôo-ung ตอนฤดูใบไม้ร่วง

fall (*verb*) hòk lóm หกล้ม

   she's had a fall káo hòk lóm เขาหกล้ม

false mâi jing ไม่จริง

family krôrp-kroo-a ครอบครัว

famous mee chêu sĕe-ung มีชื่อเสียง

fan (electrical) pút lom พัดลม

   (handheld) pút พัด

   (sports) kon chôrp doo gee-lah คนชอบดูกีฬา

fan belt săi pahn สายพาน

fantastic yêe-um yôrt เยี่ยมยอด

far glai ไกล

DIALOGUE

   is it far from here? yòo glai mái?

   no, not very far mâi glai

   well, how far? gèe gi-loh-met?

   it's about 20 kilometres bpra-mahn yêe-sìp gi-loh-met

fare kâh doy-ee săhn ค่าโดยสาร

farm fahm ฟาร์ม

fashionable tun sa-măi ทันสมัย

fast ray-o เร็ว

fat (person) ôo-un อ้วน

   (on meat) mun มัน

father pôr พ่อ

father-in-law (of a man) pôr dtah พ่อตา

   (of a woman) pôr pŏo-a พ่อผัว

faucet górk náhm ก๊อกน้ำ

fault kwahm pìt ความผิด

   sorry, it was my fault kŏr-tôht kwahm pìt kŏrng pŏm (chún) ขอโทษ ความผิดของผม(ฉัน)

   it's not my fault mâi châi kwahm pìt kŏrng pŏm (chún) ไม่ใช่ความผิดของผม(ฉัน)

faulty pìt ผิด

favourite bpròht โปรด

fax (machine) krêu-ung toh-ra-săhn เครื่องโทรสาร

(verb: person) sòng toh-ra-sǎhn bpai hâi **ส่งโทรสารไปให้**
(document) bun-téuk toh-ra-sǎhn, fáirks **บันทึกโทรสาร, แฟกซ์**

February gOOm-pah-pun **กุมภาพันธ์**

feel róo-sèuk **รู้สึก**

I feel hot pǒm (chún) róo-sèuk rórn **ผม(ฉัน)รู้สึกร้อน**

I feel unwell pǒm (chún) róo-sèuk mâi sa-bai **ผม(ฉัน)รู้สึกไม่สบาย**

I feel like going for a walk pǒm (chún) yàhk ja bpai dern lên **ผม(ฉัน)อยากจะไปเดินเล่น**

how are you feeling? kOOn róo-sèuk bpen yung-ngai bâhng? **คุณรู้สึกเป็นอย่างไรบ้าง**

I'm feeling better pǒm (chún) róo-sèuk kôy yung chôo-a **ผม(ฉัน)รู้สึกค่อยยังชั่ว**

felt-tip (pen) bpàhk-gah may-jik **ปากกาเมจิก**

fence róo-a **รั้ว**

fender gun chon **กันชน**

ferry reu-a kâhm fàhk **เรือข้ามฟาก**

festival ngahn **งาน**

fetch rúp **รับ**

I'll fetch him pǒm (chún) ja bpai rúp káo **ผม(ฉัน)จะไปรับเขา**

will you come and fetch me later? mah rúp pǒm (chún) tee lǔng dâi mái? **มารับผม(ฉัน)ทีหลังได้ไหม**

feverish bpen kâi **เป็นไข้**

few: a few sǒrng sǎhm **สองสาม**

a few days sǒrng sǎhm wun **สองสามวัน**

fiancé(e) kôo mûn **คู่หมั้น**

field sa-nǎhm **สนาม**

fight (noun) gahn chók dtòy **การชกต่อย**

file fah-ee **ไฟล์**

fill dterm **เติม**

fill in gròrk **กรอก**

do I have to fill this in? dtôrng gròrk un née rěu bplào? **ต้องกรอกอันนี้หรือเปล่า**

fill up tum hâi dtem **ทำให้เต็ม**

fill it up, please dterm núm mun hâi dtem **เติมน้ำมันให้เต็ม**

filling (in tooth) ò̀ot fun **อุดฟัน**

film (movie) nǔng **หนัง**

film processing láhng feem **ล้างฟิล์ม**

filthy sòk-ga-bpròk **สกปรก**

find (verb) jer **เจอ**

I can't find it pŏm (chún) hăh mâi jer ผม(ฉัน)หาไม่เจอ

I've found it pŏm (chún) jer láir-o ผม(ฉัน)เจอแล้ว

find out hăh rai la-êe-ut หารายละเอียด

  could you find out for me? chôo-ay hăh rai la-êe-ut hâi nòy dâi mái? ช่วยหารายละเอียดให้หน่อยได้ไหม

fine (weather) dee ดี

  (punishment) kâh bprùp ค่าปรับ

finger néw meu นิ้วมือ

finish (verb) jòp จบ

  I haven't finished yet pŏm (chún) yung mâi sèt ผม(ฉัน)ยังไม่เสร็จ

  when does it finish? jòp gèe mohng? จบกี่โมง

fire: fire! fai mâi! ไฟไหม้

  can we light a fire here? gòr fai dtrong née dâi mái? ก่อไฟตรงนี้ได้ไหม

fire alarm săn-yahn fay mâi สัญญาณไฟไหม้

fire brigade gorng dtum-ròo-ut dùp plerng กองตำรวจดับเพลิง

fire escape bun-dai sŭm-rùp née fai บรรไดสำหรับหนีไฟ

fire extinguisher krêu-ung dùp plerng เครื่องดับเพลิง

first râirk แรก

  I was first pŏm (chún) bpen kon râirk ผม(ฉัน)เป็นคนแรก

  at first tee râirk ทีแรก

  the first time krúng râirk ครั้งแรก

  first on the left lée-o sái têe tahng yâirk kâhng nâh เลี้ยวซ้ายที่ทางแยกข้างหน้า

first aid gahn bpa-tŏm pa-yah-bahn การปฐมพยาบาล

first-aid kit chóot bpa-thŏm pa-yah-bahn ชุดปฐมพยาบาล

first class (travel etc) chún nèung ชั้นหนึ่ง

first floor chún sŏrng ชั้นสอง
  (US) chún nèung ชั้นหนึ่ง

first name chêu ชื่อ

fish (noun) bplah ปลา

fisherman kon jùp bplah คนจับปลา

fishing gahn jùp bplah การจับปลา

fishing boat reu-a bpra-mong
เรือประมง

fishing village mòo bâhn bpra-
mong หมู่บ้านประมง

fishmonger's ráhn kǎi bplah
ร้านขายปลา

fit (attack) ah-gahn bpen lom
อาการเป็นลม

fit: it doesn't fit me sài mâi dâi
ใส่ไม่ได้

fitting room hôrng lorng sêu-a
pâh ห้องลองเสื้อผ้า

fix (*verb:* arrange) jùt จัด

  can you fix this? (repair)
  un née gâir dâi mái?
  อันนี้แก้ได้ไหม

fizzy sâh ซ่า

flag tong ธง

flannel (facecloth) pâh chét nâh
ผ้าเช็ดหน้า

flash (for camera) fláirt แฟลช

flat (*noun:* apartment) fláirt แฟลต
  (*adj*) bairn แบน

  I've got a flat tyre yahng
  bairn ยางแบน

flavour rót รส

flea mùt หมัด

flight têe-o bin เที่ยวบิน

flight number têe-o bin mǎi-
lâyk เที่ยวบินหมายเลข

flippers rorng táo ma-nóOt gòp
รองเท้ามนุษย์กบ

floating market dta-làht náhm
ตลาดน้ำ

flood núm tôo-um น้ำท่วม

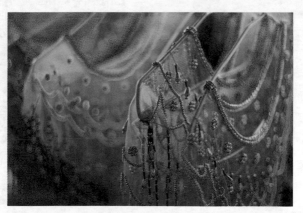

floor (of room) péun พื้น

(storey) chún ชั้น

on the floor yòo bon péun
อยู่บนพื้น

florist ráhn kăi dòrk-mái
ร้านขายดอกไม้

flour bpâirng săh-lee แป้งสาลี

flower dòrk-mái ดอกไม้

flu kâi wùt ไข้หวัด

**fluent: John speaks
fluent Thai** John pôot
pah-săh tai dâi khlôrng
จอห์นพูดภาษาไทยได้คล่อง

fly (*noun*) ma-lairng wun แมลงวัน

(*verb*) bin บิน

can we fly there? bpai
krêu-ung bin dâi mái?
ไปเครื่องบินได้ไหม

fly in bin kâo mah บินเข้ามา

fly out bin òrk bpai บินออกไป

fog mòrk long หมอกลง

foggy: it's foggy mòrk long
หมอกลง

folk dancing gahn fórn
rum péun meu-ung
การฟ้อนรำพื้นเมือง

folk music don-dtree péun meu-
ung ดนตรีพื้นเมือง

follow dtahm ตาม

follow me dtahm pŏm (chún)
mah ตามผม(ฉัน)มา

food ah-hăhn อาหาร

food poisoning ah-hăhn bpen
pít อาหารเป็นพิษ

food shop/store ráhn kăi kŏrng
chum ร้านขายของชำ

foot (of person) táo เท้า

on foot dern bpai เดินไป

football (game) fóot-born
ฟุตบอล

(ball) lôok fóot-born ลูกฟุตบอล

football match gahn kàirng kŭn
fóot-born การแข่งขันฟุตบอล

**for: do you have something
for…?** (headache/diarrhoea
etc) mee a-rai gâir… mái?
มีอะไรแก้ … ไหม

I've been here for two days, how about you? yòo sŏrng wun, láir-o kOOn lâ?

I've been here for a week pŏm (chún) yòo têe nêe ah-tít nèung láir-o

forehead nâh pàhk หน้าผาก

foreign dtàhng bpra-tâyt ต่างประเทศ

foreigner chao dtàhng bpra-tâyt ชาวต่างประเทศ

forest bpàh ป่า

forget leum ลืม

I forget, I've forgotten pŏm (chún) leum láir-o ผม(ฉัน) ลืมแล้ว

fork sôrm ส้อม

(in road) tahng yâirk ทางแยก

form (document) bàirp form แบบฟอร์ม

formal (dress) bpen tahng gahn เป็นทางการ

fortnight sŏrng ah-tít สองอาทิตย์

fortunately chôhk dee โชคดี

forward: could you forward my mail? chôo-ay sòng jòt-măi dtòr bpai hâi dôo-ay ช่วยส่งจดหมายต่อไปให้ด้วย

forwarding address têe yòo sŭm-rùp sòng jòt-măi bpai hâi ที่อยู่สำหรับส่งจดหมายไปให้

foundation cream kreem rorng péun ครีมรองพื้น

fountain núm póo น้ำพุ

foyer (of hotel) hôrng tôhng glahng sŭm-rùp rúp kàirk ห้องโถงกลางสำหรับรับแขก

(of theatre) bor-ri-wayn nûng púk ror บริเวณนั่งพักรอ

fracture (noun) gra-dòok hùk กระดูกหัก

France bpra-tâyt fa-rùng-sàyt ประเทศฝรั่งเศส

free ì-sa-rá อิสระ

(no charge) free ฟรี

is it free (of charge)? free rĕu bplào? ฟรีหรือเปล่า

freeway tahng dòo-un ทางด่วน

freezer dtôo châir kăirng ตู้แช่แข็ง

French (adj) fa-rùng-sàyt ฝรั่งเศส

(language) pah-săh fa-rùng-sàyt ภาษาฝรั่งเศส

French fries mun fa-rùng tôrt มันฝรั่งทอด

frequent bòy bòy บ่อย ๆ

how frequent is the bus to Pattaya? mee rót bpai pút-ta-yah bòy kâir năi? มีรถไปพัทยาบ่อยแค่ไหน

fresh (weather, breeze) sòt chêun สดชื่น

(fruit etc) sòt สด

fresh orange núm sôm kún
น้ำส้มคั้น

Friday wun sòok วันศุกร์

fridge dtôo yen ตู้เย็น

fried pùt ผัด

fried egg kài dao ไข่ดาว

fried noodles (Thai-style) pùt tai
ผัดไทย

(Chinese-style) pùt see éw
ผัดซีอิ๊ว

fried rice kâo pùt ข้าวผัด

friend pêu-un เพื่อน

friendly bpen pêu-un เป็นเพื่อน

frog gòp กบ

from jàhk จาก

**when does the next train
from Ubon arrive?** rót
fai jàhk OO-bon têe-o náh
mah tĕung gèe mohng?
รถไฟจากอุบลเที่ยวหน้ามา
ถึงกี่โมง **from Monday
to Friday** dtûng dtàir wun
jun jon tĕung wun sòok
ตั้งแต่วันจันทร์จนถึงวันศุกร์
from next Thursday
dtûng dtàir wun pa-réu-hùt
ตั้งแต่วันพฤหัส

where are you from? kOOn
mah jàhk năi?
I'm from Slough pŏm
(chún) mah jàhk Slough

front nâh หน้า

in front kâhng nâh ข้างหน้า

in front of the hotel
kâhng nâh rohng rairm
ข้างหน้าโรงแรม

at the front kâhng nâh
ข้างหน้า

frozen châir kăirng แช่แข็ง

frozen food ah-hăhn châir
kăirng อาหารแช่แข็ง

fruit pŏn-la-mái ผลไม้

fruit juice núm pŏn-la-mái
น้ำผลไม้

fry (deep-fry) tôrt ทอด

(stir-fry) pùt ผัด

frying pan ga-tá กะทะ

full dtem เต็ม

it's full of... dtem bpai dôo-
ay... เต็มไปด้วย...

I'm full pŏm (chún) ìm láir-o
ผม(ฉัน)อิ่มแล้ว

full board gin yòo prórm
กินอยู่พร้อม

fun: it was fun sa-nòok dee
สนุกดี

funeral ngahn sòp งานศพ

funny (strange) bplàirk แปลก

(amusing) dta-lòk ตลก

furniture krêu-ung reu-un
เครื่องเรือน

further ler-ee bpai เลยไป

it's further down the road
bpai dtahm ta-nŏn kâhng nâh
ไปตามถนนข้างหน้า

DIALOGUE

**how much further is it to
Hua Hin?** bpai hŏo-a hĭn
èek glai mái?
about 5 kilometres bpra-
mahn hâh gi-loh-met

fuse few ฟิวส์

the lights have fused few
kàht ฟิวส์ขาด

fuse box glòrng few กล่องฟิวส์

fuse wire săi few สายฟิวส์

future a-nah-kót อนาคต

in future nai a-nah-kót
ในอนาคต

G

game (cards etc) gaym เกม

(match) gahn lên การเล่น

(meat) néu-a sùt bpàh
เนื้อสัตว์ป่า

garage (for fuel) bpúm núm mun
ปั๊มน้ำมัน

(for repairs) òo sôrm rót
อู่ซ่อมรถ

(for parking) rohng rót โรงรถ

garbage (waste) ka-yà ขยะ

garden sŏo-un สวน

garlic gra-tee-um กระเทียม

gas gáirt แก๊ส

(US) núm mun น้ำมัน

see **petrol**

gas cylinder (camping gas) tŭng
gáirt ถังแก๊ส

gasoline núm mun น้ำมัน

gas station bpúm núm mun
ปั๊มน้ำมัน

gate bpra-dtoo ประตู

(at airport) chôrng kâo ช่องเข้า

gay gay เกย์

gay bar bah gay บาร์เกย์

gearbox glòrng gee-a
กล่องเกียร์

gear lever kun gee-a คันเกียร์

gears gee-a เกียร์

general (adj) tôo-a bpai ทั่วไป

gents (toilet) boo-ròot บุรุษ

genuine (antique etc) táir แท้

German (adj) yer-ra-mun
เยอรมัน

(language) pah-săh yer-ra-mun
ภาษาเยอรมัน

German measles rôhk hùt yer-
ra-mun โรคหัดเยอรมัน

Germany bpra-tâyt yer-ra-mun
ประเทศเยอรมัน

get (fetch) dâi ได้

will you get me another one, please? kŏr ao èek un nèung dâi mái? ขอเอาอีกอันหนึ่งได้ไหม

how do I get to...? bpai ... yung-ngai? ไป ... อย่างไร

do you know where I can get them? sâhp mái wâh ja séu dâi têe nǎi? ทราบไหมว่าจะซื้อได้ที่ไหน

get back (return) glùp กลับ

get in (arrive) těung ถึง

get off long ลง

where do I get off? pǒm (chún) long têe nǎi? ผม(ฉัน) ลงที่ไหน

get on (to train etc) kêun ขึ้น

get out (of car etc) long ลง

get up (in the morning) dtèun ตื่น

gift kŏrng kwǔn ของขวัญ

gin lâo yin เหล้ายิน

a gin and tonic, please kŏr yin toh-nik ขอยินโทนิค

girl pôo-yǐng ผู้หญิง

girlfriend fairn แฟน

give hâi ให้

can you give me some change? kŏr lâirk sàyt sa-dtahng dâi mái? ขอแลกเศษสตางค์ได้ไหม

I gave it to him pǒm (chún) hâi káo bpai láir-o ผม(ฉัน) ให้เขาไปแล้ว

will you give this to...? chôo-ay ao née bpai hâi ... nòy, dâi mái? ช่วยเอานี้ไปให้ ... หน่อยได้ไหม

give back keun คืน

glad yin dee ยินดี

glass gâir-o แก้ว

glasses (spectacles) wâirn dtah แว่นตา

gloves tǒong meu ถุงมือ

glue (*noun*) gao กาว

go bpai ไป

we'd like to go to the waterfalls rao yàhk ja bpai têe-o núm dtòk เราอยากจะไปเที่ยวน้ำตก

where are you going? kOOn bpai nǎi? คุณไปไหน

where does this bus go? rót may sǎi née bpai nǎi? รถเมล์สายนี้ไปไหน

let's go! bpai tèr! ไปเถอะ

she's gone (left) káo bpai láir-o เขาไปแล้ว

where has he gone? káo bpai nǎi? เขาไปไหน

I went there last week pǒm (chún) bpai têe nûn mêu-a ah-tít têe láir-o ผม(ฉัน) ไปที่นั่นเมื่ออาทิตย์ที่แล้ว

go away bpai ไป

go away! bpai hâi pón! ไปให้พ้น

go back (return) glùp กลับ

go down (the stairs etc) long bpai ลงไป

go in (enter) kâo bpai เข้าไป

go out (in the evening) têe-o bpai ไปเที่ยว

do you want to go out tonight? keun née yàhk bpai têe-o mái? คืนนี้อยากไปเที่ยวไหม

go through pàhn bpai ผ่านไป

go up (the stairs etc) kêun bpai ขึ้นไป

goat páir แพะ

God pra-jâo พระเจ้า

goggles wâirn dtah dum náhm แว่นตาดำน้ำ

gold torng ทอง

Golden Triangle sǎhm lèe-um torng kum สามเหลี่ยมทองคำ

goldsmith châhng torng ช่างทอง

golf górp กอล์ฟ

golf course sa-nǎhm górp สนามกอล์ฟ

good dee ดี

good! dee láir-o! ดีแล้ว

goodbye lah gòrn ná ลาก่อนนะ

good evening sa-wùt dee krúp (kâ) สวัสดีครับ(ค่ะ)

good morning sa-wùt dee krúp (kâ) สวัสดีครับ(ค่ะ)

good night sa-wùt dee krúp (kâ) สวัสดีครับ(ค่ะ)

goose hàhn ห่าน

got: we've got to leave rao dtôrng bpai เราต้องไป

have you got any...? mee ... mái? มี ... ไหม

government rút-ta-bahn รัฐบาล

gradually tee la nòy ทีละหน่อย

grammar wai-yah-gorn ไวยากรณ์

gram(me) grum กรัม

granddaughter lǎhn sǎo หลานสาว

grandfather (maternal) dtah ตา (paternal) bpòo ปู่

grandmother (maternal) yai ยาย (paternal) yâh ย่า

grandson lǎhn chai หลานชาย

grapefruit sôm oh ส้มโอ

grapes a-ngòOn องุ่น

grass yâh หญ้า

grateful róo-sèuk kòrp-kOOn
รู้สึกขอบคุณ

great (excellent) yôrt ยอด

   that's great! yôrt! ยอด

Great Britain bpra-tâyt ung-grìt
ประเทศอังกฤษ

Greece bpra-tâyt greet
ประเทศกรีซ

greedy dta-glà ตะกละ

green sěe kěe-o สีเขียว

greengrocer's ráhn kǎi pùk
ร้านขายผัก

grey sěe tao สีเทา

grill (noun) dtao bping เตาปิ้ง

grilled yâhng ย่าง

grocer's ráhn kǎi kǒrng chum
ร้านขายของชำ

ground péun din พื้นดิน

   on the ground bon péun din
บนพื้นดิน

ground floor chún nèung
ชั้นหนึ่ง

group glòOm กลุ่ม

guarantee (noun) bai rúp-rorng
ใบรับรอง

   is it guaranteed? mee
bai rúp bpra-gun mái?
มีใบรับประกันไหม

guest kàirk แขก

guesthouse gáyt háot เกสต์เฮาส์

guide (noun: person) múk-kOO-
tâyt มัคคุเทศก์

guidebook kôo meu num têe-o คู่มือนำเที่ยว

guided tour rai-gahn num têe-o รายการนำเที่ยว

guitar gee-dtah กีตาร์

Gulf of Thailand ào tai อ่าวไทย

gum (in mouth) ngèu-uk เหงือก

gun (pistol) bpeun pók ปืนพก

(rifle) bpeun yao ปืนยาว

gym rohng yim โรงยิม

H

hair pŏm ผม

hairbrush bprairng pŏm แปรงผม

haircut dtùt pŏm ตัดผม

hairdresser's (men's) ráhn dtàirng pŏm chai ร้านแต่งผมชาย

(women's) ráhn tum pŏm sa-dtree ร้านทำผมสตรี

hairdryer krêu-ung bpào pŏm เครื่องเป่าผม

hair gel kreem sài pŏm ครีมใส่ผม

hairgrips gíp nèep pŏm กิ๊บหนีบผม

hair spray sa-bpray chèet pŏm สเปรย์ฉีดผม

half krêung ครึ่ง

half an hour krêung chôo-a mohng ครึ่งชั่วโมง

half a litre krêung lít ครึ่งลิตร

about half that bpra-mahn krêung nèung ประมาณครึ่งหนึ่ง

half-price krêung rah-kah ครึ่งราคา

ham mŏo hairm หมูแฮม

hamburger hairm-ber-gêr แฮมเบอร์เกอร์

hammer (noun) kórn ฆ้อน

hand meu มือ

handbag gra-bpǎo tĕu กระเป๋าถือ

handbrake brayk meu เบรคมือ

handkerchief pâh chét nâh ผ้าเช็ดหน้า

handle (on door, suitcase) dâhm ด้าม

hand luggage gra-bpǎo tĕu กระเป๋าถือ

hang-gliding gahn hŏhn rôrn การโหนร่อน

hangover bpòo-ut hŏo-a ปวดหัว

I've got a hangover pŏm (chún) bpòo-ut hŏo-a

happen gèrt kêun เกิดขึ้น

what's happening? gèrt a-rai kêun? เกิดอะไรขึ้น

what has happened?
mee a-rai gèrt kêun?
มีอะไรเกิดขึ้น

happy dee jai ดีใจ

I'm not happy about this
rêu-ung née pǒm (chún)
mâi sa-bai jai เรื่องนี้ผม(ฉัน)
ไม่สบายใจ

harbour tâh reu-a ท่าเรือ

hard kǎirng แข็ง

(difficult) yâhk ยาก

hard-boiled egg kài dtôm
kǎirng ไข่ต้มแข็ง

hardly mâi kôy… ไม่ค่อย…

hardly ever mâi kôy…
ไม่ค่อย…

hardware shop ráhn kǎi krêu-
ung lèk ร้านขายเครื่องเหล็ก

hat mòo-uk หมวก

hate (verb) glèe-ut เกลียด

have mee มี

can I have a…? kǒr … nòy
ขอ … หน่อย

do you have…? mee … mái?
มี … ไหม

what'll you have? (drink)
kOOn ja dèum a-rai?
คุณจะดื่มอะไร

I have to leave now pǒm
(chún) dtông bpai děe-o née
ผม(ฉัน)ต้องไปเดี๋ยวนี้

do I have to…? pǒm (chún)
dtông … rěu bplào? ผม(ฉัน)
ต้อง … หรือเปล่า

can we have some…?
kǒr … nòy dâi mái? ขอ …
หน่อยได้ไหม

hayfever rôhk hèut โรคหืด

he kǎo เขา

head hǒo-a หัว

headache bpòo-ut hǒo-a
ปวดหัว

headlights fai nâh rót ไฟหน้ารถ

headphones hǒo fung หูฟัง

healthy (person) mee sòOk-ka-
pâhp dee มีสุขภาพดี

(food) bpen bpra-
yòht gàir râhng-gai
เป็นประโยชน์แก่ร่างกาย

hear dâi yin ได้ยิน

DIALOGUE

can you hear me? dâi yin
mái?

**I can't hear you, could you
repeat that?** pǒm (chún)
mâi dâi yin, pôot èek tee
dâi mái?

hearing aid krêu-ung chôo-ay
fung เครื่องช่วยฟัง

heart hǒo-a jai หัวใจ

heart attack hǒo-a jai wai
หัวใจวาย

heat kwahm rórn ความร้อน

heating krêu-ung tum kwahm rórn เครื่องทำความร้อน

heavy nùk หนัก

heel (of foot) sôn táo ส้นเท้า

(of shoe) sôn rorng táo ส้นรองเท้า

could you heel these? bplèe-un sôn mài hâi nòy, dâi mái? เปลี่ยนส้นใหม่ให้หน่อยได้ไหม

height kwahm sŏong ความสูง

helicopter hay-li-korp-dter เฮลิคอปเตอร์

hello sa-wùt dee สวัสดี

(answer on phone) hun-loh ฮัลโหล

helmet (for motorbike) mòo-uk gun chon หมวกกันชน

help (noun) kwahm chôo-ay lěu-a ความช่วยเหลือ

(verb) chôo-ay ช่วย

help! chôo-ay dôo-ay! ช่วยด้วย

can you help me? chôo-ay pŏm (chún) nòy, dâi mái? ช่วยผม(ฉัน)หน่อยได้ไหม

thank you very much for your help kòrp-kOOn têe dâi chôo-ay lěu-a ขอบคุณที่ได้ช่วยเหลือ

helpful bpen bpra-yòht mâhk เป็นประโยชน์มาก

hepatitis dtùp ùk-sàyp ตับอักเสบ

her: I haven't seen her pŏm (chún) mâi dâi hĕn káo ผม(ฉัน)ไม่ได้เห็นเขา

to her gàir káo แก่เขา

with her gùp káo กับเขา

for her sŭm-rùp káo สำหรับเขา

that's her nûn káo นั่นเขา

that's her towel bpen pâh chét dtoo-a kŏrng káo เป็นผ้าเช็ดตัวของเขา

herbs (for cooking) krêu-ung tâyt เครื่องเทศ

(medicinal) sa-mŎOn prai สมุนไพร

here têe-nêe ที่นี่

here is/are… nêe… นี่…

here you are (offering) nêe ngai นี่ไง

hers kŏrng káo ของเขา

that's hers nûn kŏrng káo นั่นของเขา

hey! háy! เฮ้

hi! (hello) bpai năi? ไปไหน

hide (verb) sôrn ซ่อน

high sŏong สูง

highchair gâo êe sŏong เก้าอี้สูง

highway tahng dòo-un ทางด่วน

hill kăo เขา

him: I haven't seen him
pŏm (chún) mâi dâi hĕn káo
ผม(ฉัน)ไม่ได้เห็นเขา

to him gàir káo แก่เขา

with him gùp káo กับเขา

for him sŭm-rùp káo
สำหรับเขา

that's him nûn káo นั่นเขา

hip sa-pôhk สะโพก

hire châo เช่า

for hire hâi châo ให้เช่า

where can I hire a bike?
(bicycle) châo jùk-ra-yahn dâi
têe nǎi? เช่าจักรยานได้ที่ไหน

his: it's his car bpen rót kŏrng
káo เป็นรถของเขา

that's his nûn kŏrng káo
นั่นของเขา

hit (verb) dtee ตี

hitch-hike bòhk rót โบกรถ

hobby ngahn a-di-ràyk
งานอดิเรก

hold (verb) tĕu ถือ

hole roo รู

holiday wun yòot วันหยุด

on holiday yòot púk pòrn
หยุดพักผ่อน

Holland bpra-tâyt hor-lairn
ประเทศฮอลแลนด์

home bâhn บ้าน

at home (in my house etc) têe
bâhn ที่บ้าน

(in my country) nai bpra-tâyt pŏm
(chún) ในประเทศผม(ฉัน)

we go home tomorrow (to
country) rao glùp bâhn prôOng
née เรากลับบ้านพรุ่งนี้

honest sêu dtrong ซื่อตรง

honey núm pêung น้ำผึ้ง

honeymoon hun-nee-moon
ฮันนีมูน

hood (US: car) gra-bprohng rót
กระโปรงรถ

hope wǔng หวัง

I hope so wǔng wâh yung
ngún หวังว่าอย่างนั้น

I hope not wǔng wâh kong
mâi หวังว่าคงไม่

hopefully wǔng wâh… หวังว่า…

horn (of car) dtrair แตร

horrible nâh glèe-ut น่าเกลียด

horse máh ม้า

horse riding kèe máh ขี่ม้า

hospital rohng pa-yah-bahn
โรงพยาบาล

hospitality gahn dtôrn rúp kùp
sôo การต้อนรับขับสู่

**thank you for your
hospitality** kòrp-kOOn
têe dtôrn rúp kùp sôo
ขอบคุณที่ต้อนรับขับสู่

hostess (in bar) pôo-yǐng bah
ผู้หญิงบาร์

hot rórn ร้อน

(spicy) pèt เผ็ด

I'm hot pǒm (chún) rórn ผม(ฉัน)ร้อน

it's hot today wun née ah-gàht rórn jung ler-ee วันนี้อากาศร้อนจังเลย

hotel rohng rairm โรงแรม

hotel room hôrng nai rohng rairm ห้องในโรงแรม

hour chôo-a mohng ชั่วโมง

house bâhn บ้าน

how? yung-ngai? อย่างไร

how many? gèe? กี่

how do you do? sa-wùt dee krúp (kâ) สวัสดีครับ(ค่ะ)

how are you? bpen yung-ngai bâhng?

fine, thanks, and you? sa-bai dee krúp (kâ) láir-o kOOn lâ?

how much is it? tâo-rài?

50 baht hâh sìp baht

I'll take it ao

humid chéun ชื้น

hungry hěw kâo หิวข้าว

are you hungry? hěw kâo mái? หิวข้าวไหม

hurry (verb) rêep รีบ

I'm in a hurry pǒm (chún) dtôrng rêep ผม(ฉัน)ต้องรีบ

there's no hurry mâi dtôrng rêep ไม่ต้องรีบ

hurry up! ray-o ray-o kâo! เร็ว ๆ เข้า

hurt (verb) jèp เจ็บ

it really hurts jèp jing jing เจ็บจริง ๆ

husband sǎh-mee สามี

I (male) pǒm ผม

(female) chún; dee-chún ฉัน; ดิฉัน

ice núm kǎirng น้ำแข็ง

with ice sài núm kǎirng ใส่น้ำแข็ง

no ice, thanks mâi sài núm kǎirng ไม่ใส่น้ำแข็ง

ice cream ait-greem ไอศกรีม

ice-cream cone groo-ay sài ait-greem กรวยใส่ไอศกรีม

iced coffee gah-fair yen กาแฟเย็น

ice lolly ait-greem tâirng ไอศครีมแท่ง

idea kwahm kít ความคิด

idiot kon bâh คนบ้า

if tâh ถ้า

ignition fai krêu-ung yon ไฟเครื่องยนต์

ill mâi sa-bai ไม่สบาย

   I feel ill pǒm (chún) mâi sa-bai ผม(ฉัน)ไม่สบาย

illness kwahm jèp bpòo-ay ความเจ็บป่วย

imitation (leather etc) tee-um เทียม

immediately tun-tee ทันที

important sǔm-kun สำคัญ

   it's very important sǔm-kun mâhk สำคัญมาก

   it's not important mâi sǔm-kun ไม่สำคัญ

impossible bpen bpai mâi dâi เป็นไปไม่ได้

impressive nâh têung น่าทึ่ง

improve dee kêun ดีขึ้น

   I want to improve my Thai pǒm (chún) yàhk ja pôot pah-sǎh tai hâi dee kêun อยากจะพูดภาษาไทยให้ดีขึ้น

in: it's in the centre nai jai glahng meu-ung ในใจกลางเมือง

   in my car nai rót pǒm (chún) ในรถผม(ฉัน)

   in Chiangmai têe chee-ung-mài ที่เชียงใหม่

   in two days from now èek sǒrng wun dtòr jàhk née อีกสองวันต่อจากนี้

in five minutes èek hâh nah-tee อีกห้านาที

in May deu-un préut-sa-pah-kom เดือนพฤษภาคม

in English bpen pah-sǎh ung-grit เป็นภาษาอังกฤษ

in Thai bpen pah-sǎh tai เป็นภาษาไทย

is he in? káo yòo mái? เขาอยู่ไหม

inch néw นิ้ว

include roo-um รวม

   does that include meals? roo-um ah-hǎhn dôo-ay rěu bplào? รวมอาหารด้วยหรือเปล่า?

   is that included? roo-um yòo dôo-ay rěu bplào? รวมอยู่ด้วยหรือเปล่า

inconvenient mâi sa-dòo-uk ไม่สะดวก

incredible mâi nâh chêu-a ไม่น่าเชื่อ

India bpra-tâyt in-dee-a ประเทศอินเดีย

Indian (adj) kàirk แขก

indicator (on car) fai lée-o ไฟเลี้ยว

indigestion ah-hǎhn mâi yôy อาหารไม่ย่อย

Indonesia bpra-tâyt in-doh-nee-see-a ประเทศอินโดนีเซีย

indoors kâhng nai ข้างใน

inexpensive mâi pairng, tòok ไม่แพง, ถูก

infection ah-gahn ùk-sàyp อาการอักเสบ

infectious rôhk dtìt dtòr โรคติดต่อ

inflammation ah-gahn bpòo-ut boo-um อาการปวดบวม

informal bpen gun ayng เป็นกันเอง

information kào-sǎhn ข่าวสาร

  do you have any information about...? mee rai la-èe-ut gèe-o gùp … mái? มีรายละเอียดเกี่ยวกับ … ไหม

information desk têe sòrp tǎhm ที่สอบถาม

injection chèet yah ฉีดยา

injured bàht jèp บาดเจ็บ

  she's been injured kǎo bàht jèp เขาบาดเจ็บ

inner tube (for tyre) yahng nai ยางใน

innocent bor-ri-sòOt บริสุทธิ์

insect ma-lairng แมลง

insect bite ma-lairng gùt แมลงกัด

  do you have anything for insect bites? mee yah

tah gâir ma-lairng gùt mái? มียาทาแก้แมลงกัดไหม

insect repellent yah gun ma-lairng ยากันแมลง

inside kâhng nai ข้างใน

  inside the hotel kâhng nai rohng rairm ข้างในโรงแรม

  let's sit inside bpai nûng kâhng nai tèr ไปนั่งข้างในเถอะ

insist ka-yún ka-yor คะยั้นคะยอ

  I insist pǒm (chún) ka-yún ka-yor ผม(ฉัน)คะยั้นคะยอ

insomnia norn mâi lùp นอนไม่หลับ

instant coffee gah-fair pǒng กาแฟผง

instead tairn แทน

  give me that one instead ao un nún tairn เอาอันนั้นแทน

  instead of... tairn têe ja... แทนที่จะ...

insulin in-soo-lin อินซูลิน

insurance gahn bpra-gun pai การประกันภัย

intelligent cha-làht ฉลาด

interested: I'm interested in... pǒm (chún) sǒn jai... ผม(ฉัน) สนใจ...

interesting nâh sǒn jai น่าสนใจ

  that's very interesting nâh sǒn jai mâhk น่าสนใจมาก

international săh-gon สากล

internet in-dter-nèt
อินเทอร์เน็ต

interpret bplair แปล

interpreter lâhm ล่าม

intersection sèe yâirk สี่แยก

interval (at theatre) púk krêung
พักครึ่ง

into nai ใน

I'm not into... pŏm (chún)
mâi chôrp...
ผม(ฉัน)ไม่ชอบ...

introduce náir-num แนะนำ

may I introduce...?
pŏm (chún) kŏr náir-
num hâi róo-jùk gùp...
ผม(ฉัน)ขอแนะนำให้รู้จักกับ...

invitation kum chern คำเชิญ

invite chern choo-un เชิญชวน

Ireland ai-lairn ไอร์แลนด์

iron (for ironing) dtao rêet เตารีด

can you iron these for me?
chôo-ay rêet hâi này dâi mái?
ช่วยรีดให้หน่อยได้ไหม

is bpen เป็น

island gòr เกาะ

it mun มัน

it is... bpen... เป็น...

is it...? ... châi mái? ...
ใช่ไหม

where is it? yòo têe năi?
อยู่ที่ไหน

it's him kăo nûn làir
เขานั่นแหละ

it was... bpen... เป็น...

Italy bpra-tâyt ì-dtah-lee
ประเทศอิตาลี

itch: it itches kun คัน

J

jack (for car) mâir rairng แม่แรง

jacket sêu-a nórk เสื้อนอก

jam yairm แยม

jammed: it's jammed mun dtìt
nâirn มันติดแน่น

January mók-ga-rah-kom
มกราคม

Japan yêe-bpòon ญี่ปุ่น

Japanese yêe-bpòon ญี่ปุ่น

jar (*noun*) hăi ไห

jaw kăh-gun-grai ขากรรไกร

jazz jáirt แจ๊ส

jealous hěung หึง

jeans yeen ยีนส์

jellyfish mairng ga-prOOn
แมงกะพรุน

jersey sêu-a sa-wét-dtêr
เสื้อสเวตเตอร์

jetty tâh reu-a ท่าเรือ

jeweller's ráhn kǎi
krêu-ung pét ploy
ร้านขายเครื่องเพชรพลอย

jewellery pét ploy **เพชรพลอย**

Jewish yew **ยิว**

job ngahn **งาน**

jogging jórk-gîng **จ็อกกิ้ง**

   to go jogging bpai jórk-gîng
   ไปจ็อกกิ้ง

joke dta-lòk **ตลก**

journey gahn dern tahng
การเดินทาง

   have a good journey!
   dern tahng dôo-ay dee ná!
   เดินทางด้วยดีนะ

jug yèu-uk **เหยือก**

   a jug of water yèu-uk náhm
   เหยือกน้ำ

juice náhm pǒn-la-mái
น้ำผลไม้

July ga-rúk-ga-dah-kom
กรกฎาคม

jump (verb) gra-dòht **กระโดด**

jumper sêu-a sa-wét-dtêr
เสื้อสเวตเตอร์

junction tahng yâirk **ทางแยก**

June mí-tOO-nah-yon **มิถุนายน**

jungle bpàh **ป่า**

just (only) tâo-nún **เท่านั้น**

   just two sǒrng un tâo-nún
   สองอันเท่านั้น

   just for me sǔm-rùp
   pǒm (chún) kon dee-o
   สำหรับผม(ฉัน)คนเดียว

   just here dtrong née **ตรงนี้**

   not just now mâi ao děe-o
   née ไม่เอาเดี๋ยวนี้

   we've just arrived rao pêrng
   mah mêu-a gêe née ayng
   เราเพิ่งมาเมื่อกี้นี้เอง

K

keep gèp เก็บ

keep the change mâi dtôrng
torn ไม่ต้องทอน

can I keep it? pŏm (chún)
gèp wái dâi mái? ผม(ฉัน)
เก็บไว้ได้ไหม

please keep it ao wái ler-ee
เอาไว้เลย

ketchup sórt ma-kěu-a tâyt
ซอสมะเขือเทศ

kettle gah náhm กาน้ำ

key gOOn-jair กุญแจ

**the key for room 201,
please** kŏr gOOn-jair
hôrng sŏrng sŏon sèe
ขอกุญแจห้องสองศูนย์สี่

keyring hòo-ung gOOn-jair
ห่วงกุญแจ

kidneys (in body) dtai ไต

(food) krêu-ung nai เครื่องใน

kill kâh ฆ่า

kilo gi-loh กิโล

kilometre gi-loh-mét กิโลเมตร

**how many kilometres is it
to...?** bpai ... gèe gi-loh? ไป
... กี่กิโล

kind (generous) jai dee ใจดี

that's very kind kOOn jai dee
mâhk คุณใจดีมาก

which kind do you want?
ao bàirp nǎi?
I want this/that kind ao
bàirp née/nún
DIALOGUE

king nai lŏo-ung ในหลวง

kiosk dtôo ตู้

kiss jòop จูบ

kitchen hôrng kroo-a ห้องครัว

knee hǒo-a kào หัวเข่า

knickers gahng gayng nai
sa-dtree กางเกงในสตรี

knife mêet มีด

knock (verb) kór เคาะ

knock down (road accident) rót
chon รถชน

**he's been knocked
down** kao tòok rót chon
เขาถูกรถชน

knock over (object, pedestrian)
chon lóm ชนล้ม

know (somebody) róo-jùk รู้จัก

(something) róo; (formal) sâhp รู้;
ทราบ

(a place) róo-jùk รู้จัก

I don't know pŏm (chún) mâi
róo/sâhp ผม(ฉัน)ไม่รู้/ทราบ

I didn't know that pŏm
(chún) mâi róo/sâhp mah
gòrn ผม(ฉัน)
ไม่รู้/ทราบมาก่อน

do you know where I can find...? sàhp mái wâh ja hǎh ... dâi têe nǎi? ทราบไหมว่าจะหา ... ได้ที่ไหน

L

label bpâi ป้าย

ladies' (room) sa-dtree สตรี

ladies' wear krêu-ung dtàirng gai sa-dtree เครื่องแต่งกายสตรี

lady pôo-yǐng ผู้หญิง

lager lah-ger ลาเกอร์

lake ta-lay sàhp ทะเลสาบ

lamb (meat) néu-a gàir เนื้อแกะ

lamp kohm fai fáh โคมไฟฟ้า

lane (motorway) chôrng ช่อง

(small road) soy ซอย

language pah-sǎh ภาษา

language course bàirp ree-un pah-sǎh แบบเรียนภาษา

Laos bpra-tâyt lao ประเทศลาว

laptop láirp-tòrp แล็ปท็อป

large yài ใหญ่

last sòrt tái สุดท้าย

last week mêu-a ah-tít gòrn เมื่ออาทิตย์ก่อน

last Friday mêu-a wun sòok gòrn เมื่อวันศุกร์ก่อน

last night mêu-a keun née เมื่อคืนนี้

what time is the last train to Ubon? rót fai bpai OO-bon têe-o sòrt tái òrk gèe mohng? รถไฟไปอุบลเที่ยวสุดท้าย ออกกี่โมง

late cháh ช้า

sorry I'm late kǒr-tôht têe mah cháh ขอโทษที่มาช้า

the train was late rót fai mah tǔeng cháh รถไฟมาถึงช้า

we must go – we'll be late rao dtôrng bpai dǐe-o ja mâi tun เราต้องไป เดี๋ยวจะไม่ทัน

it's getting late dèuk láir-o ดึกแล้ว

later tee lǔng ทีหลัง

I'll come back later dǐe-o ja glùp mah เดี๋ยวจะกลับมา

see you later dǐe-o jer gun èek เดี๋ยวเจอกันอีก

later on tee lǔng ทีหลัง

latest yàhng cháh têe sòrt อย่างช้าที่สุด

by Wednesday at the latest wun póot yàhng cháh têe sòrt วันพุธอย่างช้าที่สุด

laugh (verb) hǒo-a rór หัวเราะ

laundry (clothes) sêu-a pâh เสื้อผ้า

(place) ráhn súk pâh ร้านซักผ้า

lavatory hôrng náhm ห้องน้ำ

law gòt-măi กฎหมาย

lawn sa-năhm yâh สนามหญ้า

lawyer ta-nai kwahm
ทนายความ

laxative yah tài ยาถ่าย

lazy kêe gèe-ut ขี้เกียจ

lead (electrical) săi fai fáh
สายไฟฟ้า

   (verb) num นำ

   where does this lead to?
   nêe bpai těung năi? นี่ไปถึงไหน

leaf bai mái ใบไม้

leaflet bai bplew ใบปลิว

leak rôo-a รั่ว

   the roof leaks lŭng-kah rôo-a
   หลังคารั่ว

learn ree-un เรียน

least: not in the least mâi ler-
ee ไม่เลย

   at least yàhng nóy têe sòot
   อย่างน้อยที่สุด

leather nŭng หนัง

leave (verb: behind) tíng wái ทิ้งไว้

   (go away) jàhk bpai จากไป

   I am leaving tomorrow
   pŏm (chún) bpai prôOng née
   ผม(ฉัน)ไปพรุ่งนี้

   he left yesterday káo
   bpai mêu-a wahn née
   เขาไปเมื่อวานนี้

may I leave this here? kŏr
fàhk wái têe nêe dâi mái?
ขอฝากไว้ที่นี่ได้ไหม

I left my coat in the bar
pŏm (chún) tíng sêu-a wái têe
bah ผม(ฉัน)ทิ้งเสื้อไว้ที่บาร์

**when does the bus for
Bangsaen leave?** rót bpai
bahng-săirn òrk gèe mohng?
รถไปบางแสนออกกี่โมง

left sái ซ้าย

   on the left tahng sái ทางซ้าย

   to the left tahng sái ทางซ้าย

   turn left lée-o sái เลี้ยวซ้าย

   there's none left mâi mee
   lěu-a yòo ไม่มีเหลืออยู่

left-handed ta-nùt meu sái
ถนัดมือซ้าย

left luggage (office) têe fàhk gra-
bpăo ที่ฝากกระเป๋า

leg kăh ขา

lemon ma-nao มะนาว

lemonade núm ma-nao
น้ำมะนาว

lemon tea núm chah sài ma-nao
น้ำชาใส่มะนาว

lend: will you lend me your...?
kŏr yeum … nòy, dâi mái?
ขอยืม … หน่อยได้ไหม

lens (of camera) layn เลนส์

lesbian 'lesbian' เล็สเบียน

less nóy gwàh น้อยกว่า

less than... nóy gwàh ...
น้อยกว่า...

less expensive tòok gwàh
ถูกกว่า

lesson bòt ree-un บทเรียน

let (allow) hâi ให้

will you let me know? chôo-ay bòrk hâi pǒm (chún) sâhp dôo-ay
ช่วยบอกให้ผม(ฉัน)ทราบด้วย

I'll let you know pǒm (chún) ja bòrk hâi sâhp
ผม(ฉัน)จะบอกให้ทราบ

let's go for something to eat bpai tahn kâo mái?
ไปทานข้าวไหม

let off: will you let me off at...? kǒr long têe ... dâi mái?
ขอลงที่ ... ได้ไหม

letter jòt-mǎi จดหมาย

do you have any letters for me? mee jòt-mǎi mah těung pǒm (chún) mái?
มีจดหมายมาถึงผม(ฉัน)ไหม

letterbox dtôo jòt-mǎi
ตู้จดหมาย

lettuce pùk-gàht ผักกาด

lever (noun) kun yók คันยก

library hǒr sa-mòot หอสมุด

licence bai un-nóO-yâht
ใบอนุญาต

lid fǎh ฝา

lie (verb: tell untruth) goh-hòk
โกหก

lie down norn นอน

life chee-wít ชีวิต

lifebelt choo chêep ชูชีพ

life jacket sêu-a choo chêep
เสื้อชูชีพ

lift (in building) líf ลิฟท์

could you give me a lift? chôo-ay bpai sòng nòy, dâi mái? ช่วยไปส่งหน่อยได้ไหม

would you like a lift? bpai sòng hâi ao mái?
ไปส่งให้เอาไหม

light (noun) fai ไฟ

(not heavy) bao เบา

do you have a light? (for cigarette) mee fai mái? มีไฟไหม

light green sěe kěe-o òrn
สีเขียวอ่อน

light bulb lòrt fai fáh
หลอดไฟฟ้า

I need a new light bulb pǒm (chún) dtôrng-gahn lòrt fai fáh
ผม(ฉัน)ต้องการหลอดไฟฟ้า

lighter (cigarette) fai cháirk
ไฟแช็ก

lightning fáh lâirp ฟ้าแลบ

like (verb) chôrp ชอบ

I like it pǒm (chún) chôrp
ผม(ฉัน)ชอบ

I like going for walks pǒm (chún) chôrp bpai dern lên ผม(ฉัน)ชอบไปเดินเล่น

I like you pǒm (chún) chôrp kOOn ผม(ฉัน)ชอบคุณ

I don't like it pǒm (chún) mâi chôrp ผม(ฉัน)ไม่ชอบ

do you like...? kOOn chôrp … mái? คุณชอบ ...ไหม

I'd like a beer pǒm (chún) ao bee-a kòo-ut nèung ผม(ฉัน) เอาเบียร์ขวดหนึ่ง

I'd like to go swimming pǒm (chún) yàhk bpai wâi náhm ผม(ฉัน)อยากไปว่ายน้ำ

would you like a drink? kOOn dèum a-rai mái? คุณดื่มอะไรไหม

would you like to go for a walk? kOOn yàhk bpai dern lên mái? คุณอยากไปเดินเล่นไหม

what's it like? bpen yung ngai? เป็นอย่างไร

I want one like this ao bàirp née เอาแบบนี้

lime ma-nao มะนาว

line (on paper) sên เส้น

(phone) sǎi สาย

could you give me an outside line? chôo-ay dtòr sǎi kâhng nôrk hâi nòy, dâi mái? ช่วยต่อสายข้างนอกให้หน่อย ได้ไหม

lips rim fěe bpàhk ริมฝีปาก

lip salve kêe pêung tah rim fěe bpàhk ขี้ผึ้งทาริมฝีปาก

lipstick líp sa-dtík ลิปสติก

listen fung ฟัง

litre lít ลิตร

little lék เล็ก

just a little, thanks nít dee-o nít dee-o tâo-nún นิดเดียวเท่านั้น

a little milk nom nít nòy นมนิดหน่อย

a little bit more èek nít nèung อีกนิดหนึ่ง

live (verb) mee chee-wít yòo มีชีวิตอยู่

we live together rao yòo dôo-ay gun เราอยู่ด้วยกัน

DIALOGUE

where do you live? kOOn yòo têe nǎi?

I live in London pǒm (chún) yòo têe lorn-dorn

lively (person, town) mee chee-wít chee-wah มีชีวิตชีวา

liver (in body, food) dtùp ตับ

loaf bporn ปอนด์

lobby (in hotel) pa-nàirk dtôrn rúp แผนกต้อนรับ

lobster gÔOng yài กุ้งใหญ่

local tăir-o née แถวนี้

can you recommend a local restaurant? chôo-ay náir-num ráhn ah-hǎhn tǎir-o née hâi nòy dâi mái? ช่วยแนะนำร้านอาหารแถวนี้ให้หน่อยได้ไหม

lock (*noun*) gOOn-jair กุญแจ
(*verb*) sài gOOn-jair ใส่กุญแจ

it's locked sài gOOn-jair láir-o ใส่กุญแจแล้ว

lock out: I've locked myself out bpìt gOOn-jair láir-o kâo hôrng mâi dâi ปิดกุญแจแล้วเข้าห้องไม่ได้

locker (for luggage etc) dtôo ตู้

lollipop om-yím อมยิ้ม

London lorn-dorn ลอนดอน

long yao ยาว

how long will it take to fix it? chái way-lah sôrm nahn tâo-rài? ใช้เวลาซ่อมนานเท่าไร

how long does it take? chái way-lah nahn tâo-rài? ใช้เวลานานเท่าไร

a long time nahn นาน

one day/two days longer èek wun sŏrng wun อีกวันสองวัน

long-distance call toh tahng glai โทรทางไกล

long-tailed boat reu-a hǎhng yao เรือหางยาว

look: I'm just looking, thanks pŏm (chún) chom doo tâo-nún ผม(ฉัน)ชมดูเท่านั้น

you don't look well kOOn tâh tahng mâi sa-bai คุณท่าทางไม่สบาย

look out! ra-wung ná! ระวังนะ

can I have a look? kŏr doo nòy, dâi mái? ขอดูหน่อยได้ไหม

look after doo lair ดูแล

look at doo ดู

look for hǎh หา

I'm looking for... pŏm (chún) gum-lung hǎh... ผม(ฉัน)กำลังหา...

loose (handle etc) lòot หลุด

lorry rót bun-tóok รถบรรทุก

lose hǎi หาย

I've lost my way pŏm (chún) lŏng tahng ผม(ฉัน)หลงทาง

I'm lost, I want to get to... pŏm (chún) lŏng tahng, dtôrng-gahn bpai... ผม(ฉัน)หลงทาง ต้องการไป...

I've lost my bag gra-bpǎo pŏm (chún) hǎi กระเป๋าผม(ฉัน)หาย

lost property (office) têe jâirng kŏrng hăi ที่แจ้งของหาย

lot: a lot, lots mâhk มาก

not a lot mâi mâhk ไม่มาก

a lot of people kon mâhk คนมาก

a lot bigger yài mâhk gwàh ใหญ่มากกว่า

I like it a lot pŏm (chún) chôrp mâhk ผม(ฉัน)ชอบมาก

lotion yah tah ยาทา

loud dung ดัง

lounge (in house, hotel) hôrng nûng lên ห้องนั่งเล่น
(in airport) hôrng púk pôo doy-ee săhn ห้องพักผู้โดยสาร

love (*noun*) kwahm rúk ความรัก
(*verb*) rúk รัก

I love Thailand pŏm (chún) rúk meu-ung tai ผม(ฉัน)รักเมืองไทย

lovely sŏo-ay สวย

low (prices, bridge) dtùm ต่ำ

luck chôhk โชค

good luck! chôhk dee! โชคดี

luggage gra-bpăo กระเป๋า

luggage trolley rót kĕn รถเข็น

lump (on body) néu-a ngôrk เนื้องอก

lunch ah-hăhn glahng wun อาหารกลางวัน

lungs bpòrt ปอด

luxurious (hotel, furnishings) rŏo-răh หรูหรา

luxury kŏrng fôOm feu-ay ของฟุ่มเฟือย

M

machine krêu-ung เครื่อง

mad (insane) bâh บ้า
(angry) gròht โกรธ

magazine nít-ta-ya-săhn นิตยสาร

maid (in hotel) kon tum kwahm sa-àht คนทำความสะอาด

maiden name nahm sa-gOOn derm นามสกุลเดิม

mail (*noun*) jòt-măi จดหมาย
(*verb*) sòng jòt-măi ส่งจดหมาย

is there any mail for me? mee jòt-măi sŭm-rùp pŏm (chún) mái? มีจดหมายสำหรับผม(ฉัน)ไหม

mailbox dtôo jòt-măi ตู้จดหมาย

main sŭm-kun สำคัญ

main post office bprai-sa-nee glahng ไปรษณีย์กลาง

main road ta-nŏn yài ถนนใหญ่

mains switch (for electricity) sa-wít săi fai yài

สวิชสายไฟใหญ่

make (brand name) yêe hôr ยี่ห้อ
(*verb*) tum ทำ

I make it 500 baht pŏm
(chún) kít wâh hâh róy bàht
ผม(ฉัน)คิดว่าห้าร้อยบาท

what is it made of? tum
dôo-ay a-rai? ทำด้วยอะไร

make-up krêu-ung sŭm-ahng
เครื่องสำอาง

malaria kâi jùp sùn, mah-lay-
ree-a ไข้จับสั่น, มาเลเรีย

malaria tablets yah gâir mah-
lay-ree-a ยาแก้มาเลเรีย

Malay (*adj*) ma-lah-yoo มลายู

Malaysia bpra-tàyt mah-lay-
see-a ประเทศมาเลเซีย

man pôo-chai ผู้ชาย

manager pôo-jùt-gahn ผู้จัดการ

can I see the manager?
kŏr póp pôo-jùt-gahn nòy
ขอพบผู้จัดการหน่อย

mango ma-môo-ung มะม่วง

many mâhk มาก

not many mâi mâhk ไม่มาก

map păirn-têe แผนที่

March mee-nah-kom มีนาคม

margarine ner-ee tee-um
เนยเทียม

market dta-làht ตลาด

marmalade yairm แยม

married: I'm married pŏm
(chún) dtàirng ngahn láir-o
ผม(ฉัน)แต่งงานแล้ว

are you married? koOn
dtàirng ngahn láir-o rĕu yung?
คุณแต่งงานแล้วหรือยัง

mascara mair-sa-kah-rah
แมสคารา

massage nôo-ut นวด

match (football etc) gahn kàirng
kŭn การแข่งขัน

matches mái kèet ไม้ขีด

material (fabric) pâh ผ้า

matter: it doesn't matter mâi
bpen rai ไม่เป็นไร

what's the matter? bpen
a-rai? เป็นอะไร

mattress têe norn ที่นอน

May préut-sa-pah-kom
พฤษภาคม

**may: may I have another
one?** kŏr èek un nèung dâi

mái? ขออีกอันหนึ่งได้ไหม

may I come in? kâo mah dâi mái? เข้ามาได้ไหม

may I see it? kŏr doo nòy dâi mái? ขอดูหน่อยได้ไหม

may I sit here? nûng têe nêe dâi mái? นั่งที่นี่ได้ไหม

maybe bahng tee บางที

mayonnaise núm sa-lùt น้ำสลัด

me (*male*) pŏm ผม

(*female*) dee-chún, chún ดิฉัน, ฉัน

that's for me nûn sǔm-rùp pŏm (chún) นั่นสำหรับผม(ฉัน)

send it to me sòng mah hâi pŏm (chún) ส่งมาให้ผม(ฉัน)

me too pŏm (chún) gôr měu-un gun ผม(ฉัน)ก็เหมือนกัน

meal ah-hǎhn อาหาร

did you enjoy your meal? ah-hǎhn a-ròy mái?

it was excellent, thank you a-ròy mâhk

mean (*verb*) mǎi kwahm หมายความ

what do you mean? koOn mǎi kwahm wâh a-rai? คุณหมายความว่าอะไร

what does this word mean? kum née bplàir wâh a-rai?

it means… in English pah-sǎh ung-grìt bplair wâh…

measles rôhk hùt โรคหัด

meat néu-a เนื้อ

mechanic châhng krêu-ung
ช่างเครื่อง

medicine yah ยา

medium (*adj*: size) glahng กลาง

medium-rare (steak) sòok sòok
dìp dìp สุกๆดิบๆ

medium-sized ka-nàht glahng
ขนาดกลาง

meet (*verb*) póp พบ

nice to meet you yin
dee têe dâi róo-jùk gun
ยินดีที่ได้รู้จักกัน

where shall I meet you? póp
gun têe nǎi? พบกันที่ไหน

meeting bpra-choom ประชุม

meeting place têe nút póp
ที่นัดพบ

melon dtairng tai แตงไทย

memory stick mem-moh-rêe
sa-dtík เม็มโมรี่ สติ๊ก

men pôo-chai ผู้ชาย

mend sôrm ซ่อม

could you mend this for
me? koon sôrm hâi dâi mái?
คุณซ่อมให้ได้ไหม

men's room boo-ròot บุรุษ

menswear krêu-ung dtàirng gai
boo-ròot เครื่องแต่งกายบุรุษ

mention (*verb*) glào tǔeng
กล่าวถึง

don't mention it mâi bpen rai
ไม่เป็นไร

menu may-noo เมนู

may I see the menu,
please? kǒr doo may-
noo nòy krúp (kâ)
ขอดูเมนูหน่อยครับ(ค่ะ)

see **Menu Reader** page 235

message kào kàao ข่าว

are there any messages
for me? mee krai sùng
a-rai wái rěu bplào?
มีใครสั่งอะไรไว้หรือเปล่า

I want to leave a message
for... pǒm (chún) yàhk ja
fàhk bòrk a-rai hâi... ผม(ฉัน)
อยากจะฝากบอกอะไรให้...

metal (*noun*) loh-hà โลหะ

metre mét เมตร

midday têe-ung wun เที่ยงวัน

at midday têe-ung wun
เที่ยงวัน

middle: in the middle yòo
dtrong glahng อยู่ตรงกลาง

in the middle of the
night dtorn glahng keun
ตอนกลางคืน

the middle one un glahng
อันกลาง

midnight têe-ung keun เที่ยงคืน

at midnight têe-ung keun
เที่ยงคืน

might: I might... bahng tee pǒm

(chún) àht ja... บางทีผม(ฉัน)
อาจจะ...

I might not... bahng tee
pŏm (chún) àht ja mâi...
บางทีผม(ฉัน)อาจจะไม่...

**I might want to stay another
day** bahng tee pŏm (chún)
àht ja yòo èek wun nèung
บางทีผม(ฉัน)อาจจะอยู่อีกวัน
หนึ่ง

migraine bpòo-ut hŏo-a kâhng
dee-o ปวดหัวข้างเดียว

mild (taste) mâi pèt ไม่เผ็ด

mile mai ไมล์

milk nom นม

millimetre min-li-mét มิลลิเมตร

minced meat néu-a sùp เนื้อสับ

mind: never mind mâi bpen rai
ไม่เป็นไร

I've changed my mind pŏm
(chún) bplèe-un jai láir-o
ผม(ฉัน)เปลี่ยนใจแล้ว

**do you mind if I open the
window?** kŏr bpèrt nâh-
dtàhng nòy, dâi mái?
no, I don't mind dâi

mine: it's mine kŏrng pŏm
(chún) ของผม(ฉัน)

mineral water núm râir น้ำแร่

minute nah-tee นาที

in a minute èek bpra-dĕe-o
อีกประเดี๋ยว

just a minute dĕe-o, dĕe-o
เดี๋ยว ๆ

mirror gra-jòk ngao กระจกเงา

Miss nahng-sǎo นางสาว

miss: I missed the bus pŏm
(chún) dtòk rót may ผม(ฉัน)
ตกรถเมล์

missing hǎi bpai หายไป

one of my... is missing
kŏng pŏm (chún) hǎi bpai...
ของผม(ฉัน)หายไป...

there's a suitcase missing
mee gra-bpǎo hǎi bpai
มีกระเป๋าหายไป

mist mòrk หมอก

mistake (noun) kwahm pìt
ความผิด

**I think there's a
mistake** pŏm (chún) kít
wâh mee kôr pìt lék nóy
ผม(ฉัน)คิดว่ามีข้อผิดเล็กน้อย

sorry, I've made a mistake
kŏr-tôht, pŏm (chún) tum pìt
ขอโทษผม(ฉัน)ทำผิด

misunderstanding kwahm kâo
jai pìt ความเข้าใจผิด

**mix-up: sorry, there's been
a mix-up** kŏr-tôht, mee
kwahm kâo jai pìt ขอโทษ
มีความเข้าใจผิด

mobile phone toh-ra-sùp rái săi
โทรศัพท์ไร้สาย

modern tun sa-măi ทันสมัย

moisturizer kreem bum-rOOng pěw ครีมบำรุงผิว

moment: I won't be a moment ror děe-o รอเดี๋ยว

monastery wút วัด

> **Travel tip** Theoretically, monks are forbidden from having any close contact with women, which means women mustn't sit or stand next to a monk, or even brush against his robes; if it's essential to pass him something, put the object down so that he can then pick it up – never hand it over directly.

Monday wun jun วันจันทร์

money ngern เงิน

monk prá พระ

monsoon mor-ra-sŎOm มรสุม

month deu-un เดือน

monument a-nÓO-săh-wa-ree อนุสาวรีย์

moon prá-jun พระจันทร์

moped rót mor-dter-sai รถมอร์เตอร์ไซค์

more èek อีก

can I have some more water, please? kŏr

náhm èek nòy krúp (kâ)
ขอน้ำอีกหน่อยครับ(ค่ะ)

more expensive /interesting pairng /nâh sŏn jai gwàh
แพง/น่าสนใจกว่า

more than 50 hâh sìp gwàh
ห้าสิบกว่า

more than that mâhk gwàh nún มากกว่านั้น

a lot more èek mâhk
อีกมาก

would you like some more? ao èek mái?

no, no more for me, thanks por láir-o, kòrp-kOOn krúp (kâ)

how about you? láir-o kOOn lâ?

I don't want any more, thanks por láir-o krúp (kâ)

morning dtorn cháo ตอนเช้า

this morning cháo née เช้านี้

in the morning dtorn cháo
ตอนเช้า

mosquito yOOng ยุง

mosquito net mÓOng มุ้ง

mosquito repellent yah gun yOOng ยากันยุง

most: I like this one most of all pŏm (chún) chôrp un

née mâhk têe sòot ผม(ฉัน)
ชอบอันนี้มากที่สุด

most of the time sòo-un
mâhk ส่วนมาก

most tourists núk
tôrng têe-o sòo-un mâhk
นักท่องเที่ยวส่วนมาก

mostly sòo-un mâhk ส่วนมาก

mother mâir แม่

mother-in-law (of a man) mâir
yai แม่ยาย
(of a woman) mâir pǒo-a แม่ผัว

motorbike rót mor-dter-sai
รถมอร์เตอร์ไซค์

motorboat reu-a yon
เรือยนตร์

motorway tahng dòo-un
ทางด่วน

mountain poo-kǎo ภูเขา

in the mountains nai poo-
kǎo ในภูเขา

mouse nǒo หนู

moustache nòo-ut หนวด

mouth bpàhk ปาก

mouth ulcer plǎir nai bpàhk
แผลในปาก

**move: he's moved to
another room** káo yái
bpai yòo èek hôrng nèung
เขาย้ายไปอยู่อีกห้องหนึ่ง

could you move your

car? chôo-ay lêu-un rót
kǒrng kOOn, dâi mái?
ช่วยเลื่อนรถของคุณได้ไหม

**could you move up a
little?** chít nai nòy dâi mái?
ชิดในหน่อยได้ไหม

where has it moved to?
(shop, restaurant etc) yái bpai yòo
têe nǎi? ย้ายไปอยู่ที่ไหน

movie nǔng หนัง

movie theater rohng nǔng
โรงหนัง

MP3 format for-mairt em pee
sǎhm ฟอร์แมต เอ็มพี สาม

Mr nai นาย

Mrs nahng นาง

much mâhk มาก

much better/worse dee/yâir
mâhk gwàh ดี/แย่มากกว่า

much hotter rórn mâhk gwàh
ร้อนมากกว่า

not much mâi mâhk ไม่มาก

not very much mâi kôy mâhk
ไม่ค่อยมาก

I don't want very much pǒm
(chún) mâi ao mâhk ผม(ฉัน)
ไม่เอามาก

mud klohn โคลน

mug: I've been mugged pǒm
(chún) tòok jêe ผม(ฉัน)ถูกจี้

mum mâir แม่

mumps kahng toom คางทูม

museum pí-pít-ta-pun
พิพิธภัณฑ์

mushrooms hèt เห็ด

music don-dtree ดนตรี

musician núk don-dtree
นักดนตรี

Muslim (adj) ì-sa-lahm อิสลาม

mussels hǒy mairng pôo
หอยแมงภู่

must: I must pǒm (chún)
dtôrng ผม(ฉัน)ต้อง

I mustn't drink alcohol pǒm
(chún) dtôrng mâi gin lâo
ผม(ฉัน)ต้องไม่กินเหล้า

mustard núm jîm mut-sa-dtàht
น้ำจิ้มมัสตาด

my kǒrng pǒm (chún)
ของผม(ฉัน)

myself: I'll do it myself
pǒm (chún) ja tum ayng
ผม(ฉัน)จะทำเอง

by myself dôo-ay dton ayng
ด้วยตนเอง

N

nail (finger) lép meu เล็บมือ
(metal) dta-bpoo ตะปู

nailbrush bprairng kùt lép
แปรงขัดเล็บ

nail varnish yah tah lép
ยาทาเล็บ

name chêu ชื่อ

my name's... pǒm chêu...
ผมชื่อจอห์น...

what's your name? kOOn
chêu a-rai? คุณชื่ออะไร

**what is the name of this
street?** nêe ta-nǒn a-rai?
นี่ถนนอะไร

napkin pâh chét bpàhk
ผ้าเช็ดปาก

nappy pâh ôrm ผ้าอ้อม

narrow (street) kâirp แคบ

nasty nâh tOO-râyt น่าทุเรศ

national hàirng châht แห่งชาติ

nationality sǔn-châht สัญชาติ

natural tum-ma-châht
ธรรมชาติ

nausea ah-gahn klêun hěe-un
อาการคลื่นเหียน

navy (blue) sěe fáh gàir สีฟ้าแก่

near glâi ใกล้

is it near the city centre?
yòo glâi meu-ung mái?
อยู่ใกล้เมืองไหม

**do you go near the
museum?** kOOn pàhn
bpai glâi glâi pí-pít-ta-pun
mái? คุณผ่านไปใกล้ๆ
พิพิธภัณฑ์ไหม

where is the nearest...?
...glâi têe sòOt yòo têe nǎi?
...ใกล้ที่สุดอยู่ที่ไหน

nearby yòo glâi อยู่ใกล้

nearly gèu-up เกือบ

necessary jum-bpen จำเป็น

neck kor คอ

necklace sôy kor สร้อยคอ

necktie nék-tai เน็คไท

need: I need... pǒm (chún)
dtôrng-gahn... ผม(ฉัน)
ต้องการ...

do I need to pay?
dtôrng jài rěu bplào?
ต้องจ่ายหรือเปล่า

needle kěm เข็ม

negative (film) feem nay-gah-
dteef ฟิล์มเนกาตีฟ

nephew lǎhn chai หลานชาย

net (in sport) dtah-kài ตาข่าย

never mâi ker-ee ไม่เคย

new mài ใหม่

news (radio, TV etc) kào ข่าว

newsagent's ráhn kǎi núng-sěu

pim ร้านขายหนังสือพิมพ์

newspaper núng-sěu pim
หนังสือพิมพ์

newspaper kiosk dtôo núng-
sěu pim ตู้หนังสือพิมพ์

New Year bpee mài ปีใหม่

Happy New Year! sa-wùt dee
bpee mài! สวัสดีปีใหม่

New Year's Eve wun sîn bpee
วันสิ้นปี

New Zealand bpra-tâyt new see-
láirn ประเทศนิวซีแลนด์

**New Zealander: I'm a New
Zealander** pǒm (chún) bpen
kon new see-láirn ผม(ฉัน)
เป็นคนนิวซีแลนด์

next nâh หน้า

**the next turning on
the left** lée-o sái têe
tahng yâirk kâhng nâh
เลี้ยวซ้ายที่ทางแยกข้างหน้า

at the next stop bpâi nâh
ป้ายหน้า

next week ah-tít nâh
อาทิตย์หน้า

next to dtìt gùp ติดกับ

nice (food) a-ròy อร่อย

(looks, view etc) sǒo-ay สวย

(person) dee ดี

niece lǎhn sǎo หลานสาว

night glahng keun กลางคืน

at night dtorn glahng keun
ตอนกลางคืน

good night sa-wàt dee สวัสดี

DIALOGUE

do you have a single room for one night? mee hôrng sǔm-rùp keun dee-o mái?

yes, madam mee krúp

how much is it per night? keun la tâo-rài?

it's 1,000 baht for one night keun la pun bàht

thank you, I'll take it kòrp-kOOn ao hôrng née

nightclub náit klùp ไนทคลับ

nightdress chóot norn ชุดนอน

no mâi ไม่

I've no change mâi mee sàyt sa-dtahng ไม่มีเศษสตางค์

there's no… left mâi mee … lěu-a yòo ไม่มี … เหลืออยู่

no way! mâi mee tahng! ไม่มีทาง

oh no! (upset) dtai jing! ตายจริง

nobody mâi mee krai ไม่มีใคร

there's nobody there mâi mee krai yòo ไม่มีใครอยู่

noise sěe-ung เสียง

noisy: it's too noisy nòo-uk hǒo หนวกหู

non-alcoholic mâi mee un-gor-horl ไม่มีอัลกอฮอล

nonsmoking hâhm sòop bOO-rèe ห้ามสูบบุหรี่

> **Travel tip** Most inexpensive Thai restaurants specialize in one general food type or preparation method. A "noodle shop", for example, will offer fried noodles and/or noodle soups, plus maybe a basic fried rice, but they won't have curries or meat or fish dishes, while in "curry shops" your options are limited to the vats of curries stewing away in the hot cabinet.

noodles gǒo-ay dtěe-o ก๋วยเตี๋ยว

noodle shop ráhn gǒo-ay dtěe-o ร้านก๋วยเตี๋ยว

noon têe-ung wun เที่ยงวัน

at noon têe-ung wun เที่ยงวัน

no-one mâi mee krai ไม่มีใคร

nor: nor do I pǒm (chún) gôr mâi měu-un gun ผม(ฉัน)ก็ไม่เหมือนกัน

normal tum-ma-dah ธรรมดา

north něu-a เหนือ

in the north nai pâhk něu-a ในภาคเหนือ

to the north tahng něu-a ทางเหนือ

north of Bangkok tahng něu-a kǒrng grOOng-tâyp

ทางเหนือของกรุงเทพฯ

northeast dta-wun òrk chěe-ung
něu-a ตะวันออกเฉียงเหนือ

Northern Ireland ai-lairn něu-a
ไอร์แลนด์เหนือ

northwest dta-wun dtòk chěe-
ung něu-a ตะวันตกเฉียงเหนือ

Norway bpra-tâyt nor-way
ประเทศนอรเว

nose ja-mòok จมูก

nosebleed lêu-ut gum-dao òrk
เลือดกำเดาออก

not mâi ไม่

  no thanks, I'm not hungry
  mâi krúp (kâ) pǒm (chún)
  mâi hěw
  ไม่ครับ(ค่ะ)ผม(ฉัน)ไม่หิว

  **I don't want any, thank
  you** pǒm (chún) mâi ao kòrp-
  kOOn ผม(ฉัน)ไม่เอาขอบคุณ

  it's not necessary mâi jum-
  bpen ไม่จำเป็น

  I didn't know that pǒm
  (chún) mâi sâhp rêu-ung nún
  ผม(ฉัน)ไม่ทราบเรื่องนั้น

  not that one – this one
  mâi châi un nún – un nêe
  ไม่ใช่อันนั้นอันนี้

note (banknote) bai báirng
ใบแบ๊งค์

notebook sa-mòot สมุด

notepaper (for letters) gra-

dàht kěe-un jòt-mǎi
กระดาษเขียนจดหมาย

nothing mâi mee a-rai ไม่มีอะไร

  nothing for me, thanks mâi
  ao a-rai krúp (kâ) kòrp-kOOn
  ไม่เอาอะไรครับ(ค่ะ)ขอบคุณ

  nothing else mâi mee a-rai
  èek ไม่มีอะไรอีก

novel na-wa-ni-yai นวนิยาย

November préut-sa-ji-gah-yon
พฤศจิกายน

now děe-o née เดี๋ยวนี้

number mǎi-lâyk หมายเลข

  I've got the wrong number
  toh pìt ber โทรผิดเบอร์

  **what is your phone
  number?** ber toh-ra-sùp
  kǒrng kOOn lâyk a-rai?เบอร์โ
  ทรศัพท์ของคุณเลขอะไร

number plate bpâi ta-bee-un rót
ป้ายทะเบียนรถ

nurse (female) nahng pa-yah-
bahn นางพยาบาล

nut (for bolt) glee-o เกลียว

nuts tòo-a ถั่ว

O

occupied (line etc) mâi wâhng
ไม่ว่าง

o'clock mohng โมง

October dtOO-lah-kom ตุลาคม

odd (strange) bplàirk แปลก

of kŏrng ของ

off (lights) bpìt ปิด

it's just off Sukhumwit Road
yòo tăir-o ta-nŏn sOO-kŏOm-wít อยู่แถวถนนสุขุมวิท

we're off tomorrow
(leaving) rao bpai prôong née
เราไปพรุ่งนี้

offensive nâh rung-gèe-ut
น่ารังเกียจ

office (place of work) sŭm-núk
ngahn สำนักงาน

officer (said to policeman) nai
dtum-ròo-ut นายตำรวจ

often bòy bòy บ่อย ๆ

not often mâi bòy ไม่บ่อย

how often are the buses?
rót mah bòy kâir nǎi?
รถมาบ่อยแค่ไหน

oil núm mun น้ำมัน

(motor) núm mun krêu-ung
น้ำมันเครื่อง

ointment yah tah ยาทา

OK oh-kay โอเค

are you OK? kOOn oh-kay
mái? คุณโอเคไหม

is that OK with you? kOOn
oh-kay mái? คุณโอเคไหม

is it OK to...? ...dâi mái?
...ได้ไหม

that's OK thanks (it doesn't
matter) mâi bpen rai ไม่เป็นไร

I'm OK (nothing for me, I've got enough) pǒm (chún) por láir-o ผม(ฉัน)พอแล้ว

(I feel OK) pǒm (chún) oh kay ผม(ฉัน)โอเค

is this train OK for...? rót fai née bpai ... châi mái? รถไฟนี้ไป ... ใช่ไหม

old (person) gàir แก่

(thing) gào เก่า

> **how old are you?** kOOn ah-yÓO tâo-rài?
> **I'm 25** pǒm (chún) ah-yÓO yêe-sìp hâh bpee
> **and you?** láir-o kOOn lâ?

old-fashioned láh sa-mǎi ล้าสมัย

old town (old part of town) meu-ung gào เมืองเก่า

olive oil núm mun ma-gòrk น้ำมันมะกอก

olives ma-gòrk มะกอก

omelette kài jee-o ไข่เจียว

on bon บน

on the beach têe chai hàht ที่ชายหาด

on the street bon ta-nǒn บนถนน

is it on this road? yòo ta-nǒn née rěu bplào?

on the plane bon krêu-ung bin บนเครื่องบิน

on Saturday wun sǎo วันเสาร์

on television nai tee wee ในทีวี

I haven't got it on me pǒm (chún) mâi dâi ao mah dôo-ay ผม(ฉัน)ไม่ได้เอามาด้วย

this one's on me (drink) pǒm (chún) lée-ung ผม(ฉัน)เลี้ยง

the light wasn't on fai mâi bpèrt yòo ไฟไม่เปิดอยู่

what's on tonight? keun née mee a-rai? คืนนี้มีอะไร

once (one time) krúng nèung ครั้งหนึ่ง

at once (immediately) tun-tee ทันที

one nèung หนึ่ง

the white one un sěe kǎo อันสีขาว

one-way ticket dtǒo-a bpai ตั๋วไป

onion hǒo-a hǒrm หัวหอม

online orn-lai ออนไลน์

only tâo-nún เท่านั้น

only one un dee-o tâo-nún อันเดียวเท่านั้น

it's only 6 o'clock pee-

ung hòk mohng tâo-nún
เพียงหกโมงเท่านั้น

I've only just got here
pŏm (chún) pêung mah
dĕe-o née ayng **ผม(ฉัน)**
เพิ่งมาเดี๋ยวนี้เอง

on/off switch sa-wít bpèrt/bpìt
สวิชเปิด/ปิด

open (adj, verb) bpèrt **เปิด**

when do you open? bpèrt
gèe mohng? **เปิดกี่โมง**

I can't get it open bpèrt mâi
dâi **เปิดไม่ได้**

in the open air glahng jâirng
กลางแจ้ง

opening times way-lah bpìt-
bpèrt **เวลาปิดเปิด**

open ticket dtŏo-a mâi jum-gùt
way-lah **ตั๋วไม่จำกัดเวลา**

operation (medical) gahn pàh
dtùt **การผ่าตัด**

operator (telephone)
pa-núk ngahn toh-ra-sùp
พนักงานโทรศัพท์

opposite: the opposite
direction tahng dtrong kâhm
ทางตรงข้าม

the bar opposite bah dtrong
kâhm **บาร์ตรงข้าม**

opposite my hotel
dtrong kâhm rohng rairm
ตรงข้ามโรงแรม

optician jùk-sÒO pâirt
จักษุแพทย์

or rĕu **หรือ**

orange (fruit) sôm **ส้ม**

(colour) sĕe sôm **สีส้ม**

orange juice núm sôm **น้ำส้ม**

orchestra wong don-dtree
วงดนตรี

order: can we order now? (in
restaurant) kŏr sùng dĕe-o née
dâi mái? **ขอสั่งเดี๋ยวนี้ได้ไหม**

I've already ordered,
thanks pŏm (chún) sùng
láir-o **ผม(ฉัน)สั่งแล้ว**

I didn't order this pŏm (chún)
mâi dâi sùng **ผม(ฉัน)ไม่ได้สั่ง**

out of order sĕe-a **เสีย**

ordinary tum-ma-dah **ธรรมดา**

other èun **อื่น**

the other one (person) èek kon
nèung **อีกคนหนึ่ง**

(thing) èek un nèung **อีกอันหนึ่ง**

the other day (recently) mêu-a
mâi gèe wun **เมื่อไม่กี่วัน**

I'm waiting for the others
(other people) pŏm (chún) ror
kon èun **ผม(ฉัน)รอคนอื่น**

do you have any others?
mee yàhng èun mái?
มีอย่างอื่นไหม

otherwise mí-cha-nún **มิฉะนั้น**

our kǒrng rao ของเรา

ours kǒrng rao ของเรา

out: he's out (not at home) káo mâi yòo เขาไม่อยู่

three kilometres out of town nôrk meu-ung bpai sǎhm gi-loh นอกเมืองไปสามกิโล

outdoors glahng jàirng กลางแจ้ง

outside kâhng nôrk ข้างนอก

can we sit outside? nûng kâhng nôrk dâi mái? นั่งข้างนอกได้ไหม

oven dtao เตา

over: over here têe nêe ที่นี่

over there têe nôhn ที่โน่น

over 500 hâh róy gwàh ห้าร้อยกว่า

it's over (finished) jòp láir-o จบแล้ว

overcharge: you've overcharged me kOOn kít ngern mâhk bpai คุณคิดเงินมากไป

overcoat sêu-a nôrk เสื้อนอก

overnight (travel) dern tahng glahng keun เดินทางกลางคืน

overtake sairng แซง

owe: how much do I owe you? pǒm (chún) bpen nêe kOOn tâo-rài? ผม(ฉัน) เป็นหนี้คุณเท่าไร

own: my own... kǒrng pǒm (chún) ayng... ของผม(ฉัน) เอง ...

are you on your own? kOOn mah kon dee-o rěu bplào? คุณมาคนเดียวหรือเปล่า

I'm on my own pǒm (chún) mah kon dee-o ผม(ฉัน) มาคนเดียว

owner jâo-kǒrng เจ้าของ

oyster hǒy nahng rom หอยนางรม

P

pack (verb) jùt gra-bpǎo จัดกระเป๋า

a pack of... hòr... ห่อ...

package (parcel) hòr ห่อ

packed lunch ah-hǎhn glahng wun glòrng อาหารกลางวันกลอง

packet: a packet of cigarettes sorng bOO-rèe ซองบุหรี่

paddy field nah นา

page (of book) nâh หน้า

could you page Mr...? chôo-ay hǎh ber toh-ra-sùp kOOn ... hâi dôo-ay ช่วยหาเบอร์โทรศัพท์คุณ ... ให้ด้วย

pagoda jay-dee เจดีย์

pain kwahm jèp bpòo-ut
ความเจ็บปวด

  I have a pain here jèp dtrong
née เจ็บตรงนี้

painful jèp bpòo-ut เจ็บปวด

painkillers yah ra-ngúp bpòo-ut
ยาระงับปวด

paint (*noun*) sěe สี

painting (picture) pâhp kěe-un
ภาพเขียน

pair: a pair of... ...kôo nèung
... คู่หนึ่ง

Pakistani (*adj*) kon bpah-gee-sa-
tǎhn คนปากีสถาน

palace wung วัง

pale sěe òrn สีอ่อน

  pale blue sěe fáh òrn สีฟ้าอ่อน

pan (frying pan) gra-tá กระทะ

panties gahng gayng nai sa-dtree
กางเกงในสตรี

pants (underwear: men's) gahng
gayng nai กางเกงใน

  (women's) gahng gayng nai
sa-dtree กางเกงในสตรี

  (US: trousers) gahng-gayng
กางเกง

pantyhose tǒong yai boo-a
ถุงใยบัว

paper gra-dàht กระดาษ

  (newspaper) núng-sěu-pim

หนังสือพิมพ์

a piece of paper gra-dàht
pàirn nèung กระดาษแผ่นหนึ่ง

paper handkerchiefs gra-dàht
chét náh กระดาษเช็ดหน้า

parcel hòr ห่อ

pardon (me)? (didn't understand,
hear) a-rai ná krúp (ká)?
อะไรนะครับ(คะ)

parents pôr mâir พ่อแม่

parents-in-law (wife's
parents) pôr dtah mâir yai
พ่อตาแม่ยาย

  (husband's parents) pôr pǒo-a
mâir pǒo-a พ่อผัวแม่ผัว

park (*noun*) sǒo-un sǎh-tah-ra-ná
สวนสาธารณะ

  (*verb*) jòrt จอด

  can I park here? jòrt têe nêe
dâi mái? จอดที่นี่ได้ไหม

parking lot têe jòrt rót ที่จอดรถ

part (*noun*) sòo-un ส่วน

partner (boyfriend, girlfriend etc)
fairn แฟน

party (group) glòom kon กลุ่มคน

  (celebration) ngahn lée-ung
งานเลี้ยง

pass (in mountains) chôrng kǎo
ช่องเขา

passenger pôo doy-ee sǎhn
ผู้โดยสาร

passport núng-sĕu dern tahng หนังสือเดินทาง

password ra-hùt pàhn รหัสผ่าน

past: in the past mêu-a gòrn เมื่อก่อน

just past the post office ler-ee bprai-sa-nee bpai èek nít nèung เลยไปรษณีย์ไปอีกนิดหนึ่ง

path tahng ทาง

pattern bàirp แบบ

pavement bàht wít-tĕe บาทวิถี

on the pavement bon bàht wít-tĕe บนบาทวิถี

pay (verb) jài จ่าย

can I pay, please? kŏr bin nòy ขอบิลหน่อย

it's already paid for jài láir-o จ่ายแล้ว

pay phone toh-ra-sùp săh-tah-ra-ná โทรศัพท์สาธารณะ

peaceful (quiet) ngêe-up เงียบ

peach lôok pêech ลูกพีช

peanuts tòo-a ถั่ว

pear lôok pair ลูกแพร์

peculiar (taste, custom) bplàirk แปลก

pedestrian crossing tahng máh-lai ทางม้าลาย

pedestrian precinct têe hâhm rót kâo ที่ห้ามรถเข้า

peg (for washing) mái nèep pâh ไม้หนีบผ้า

pen bpàhk-gah ปากกา

pencil din-sŏr ดินสอ

penfriend pêu-un tahng jòt-măi เพื่อนทางจดหมาย

penicillin yah pen-ni-seen-lin ยาเพนนิซีลลิน

penknife mêet púp มีดพับ

people kon คน

the other people in the hotel kon èun nai rohng rairm คนอื่นในโรงแรม

too many people kon mâhk bpai คนมากไป

pepper (spice) prík tai พริกไทย

(vegetable) prík yòo-uk พริกหยวก

per: per night keun la… คืนละ…

how much per day? wun la tâo-rài? วันละเท่าไร

per cent bper-sen เปอร์เซ็นต์

perfect yôrt yêe-um ยอดเยี่ยม

perfume núm hŏrm น้ำหอม

perhaps bahng tee บางที

perhaps not bahng tee mâi
บางทีไม่

period (of time) chôo-a rá-yá
ชั่วระยะ

(menstruation) bpra-jum deu-un
ประจำเดือน

perm dùt pŏm ดัดผม

permit (noun) bai un-nóo-yâht
ใบอนุญาต

person kon คน

personal stereo work-mairn
วอล์กแมน

petrol núm mun น้ำมัน

petrol can gra-bpŏrng núm
mun กระป๋องน้ำมัน

petrol station bpúm núm mun
ปั๊มน้ำมัน

pharmacy hâhng kăi yah
ห้างขายยา

phone toh-ra-sùp โทรศัพท์

phone book sa-mòot
măi-lâyk toh-ra-sùp
สมุดหมายเลขโทรศัพท์

phone box dtôo toh-ra-sùp
ตู้โทรศัพท์

phonecard bùt toh-ra-sùp
บัตรโทรศัพท์

phone charger krêu-ung
cháht toh-ra-sùp เครื่องชาร์จ
โทรศัพท์

phone number ber toh-ra-sùp
เบอร์โทรศัพท์

photo rôop tài รูปถ่าย

excuse me, could you take
a photo of us? kŏr-tôht krúp
(kâ), chôo-ay tài rôop rao hâi
nòy dâi mái? ขอโทษครับ(ค่ะ)
ช่วยถ่ายรูปเราให้หน่อย
ได้ไหม

phrasebook kôo meu sŏn-ta-
nah คู่มือสนทนา

Phuket poo-gèt ภูเก็ต

piano bpee-a-noh เปียโน

pickpocket ka-moy-ee lóo-ung
gra-bpăo ขโมยล้วงกระเป๋า

pick up: will you be there to
pick me up? ja bpai rúp pŏm
(chún) mái? จะไปรับผม(ฉัน)
ไหม

picnic (noun) bpìk-ník ปิคนิค

picture (painting, photo) rôop รูป

pie pai ไพ

piece chín ชิ้น

a piece of... ...chín nèung
...ชิ้นหนึ่ง

pill (contraceptive pill) yah koom
gum-nèrt ยาคุมกำเนิด

I'm on the pill chún chái
yah koom gum-nèrt
ฉันใช้ยาคุมกำเนิด

pillow mŏrn หมอน

pillow case bplòrk mŏrn ปลอกหมอน

pin (*noun*) kĕm mòot เข็มหมุด

pineapple sùp-bpa-rót สับปะรด

pineapple juice núm sùp-bpa-rót น้ำสับปะรด

pink sĕe chom-poo สีชมพู

pipe (for smoking) glôrng yah sên กล้องยาเส้น
(for water) tôr ท่อ

pipe cleaners mái tum kwahm sà-aht glôrng yah sên ไม้ทำความสะอาดกล้องยาเส้น

pity: it's a pity nâh sŏng-sǎhn น่าสงสาร

pizza pee-sâh พีซซ่า

place (*noun*) sa-tǎhn-têe สถานที่
at your place têe bâhn kOOn ที่บ้านคุณ
at his place têe bâhn káo ที่บ้านเขา

plain (not patterned) mâi mee lôo-ut lai ไม่มีลวดลาย

plane krêu-ung bin เครื่องบิน
by plane doy-ee krêu-ung bin โดยเครื่องบิน

plant dtôn mái ต้นไม้

plaster cast fèu-uk เฝือก

plasters bplah-sa-dter พลาสเตอร์

plastic bplah-sa-dtik ปลาสติค
(credit cards) bùt kray-dìt บัตรเครดิต

plastic bag tǒong bplah-sa-dtik ถุงปลาสติค

plate jahn จาน

platform chahn chah-lah ชานชาลา
which platform is it for Chiangmai? bpai chee-ung-mài chahn chah-lah a-rai? ไปเชียงใหม่ชานชาลาอะไร

play (*verb*) lên เล่น
(*noun*: in theatre) la-korn ละคร

playground (for children) sa-nǎhm dèk lên สนามเด็กเล่น

pleasant sa-nòok สนุก

please (requesting something) kŏr... ขอ...
(offering) chern krúp (kâ) เชิญครับ(ค่ะ)
yes please ao krúp (kâ) เอาครับ(ค่ะ)
could you please...? chôo-ay ... nòy dâi mái? ช่วยหน่อย ... ได้ไหม
please don't yàh ler-ee krúp (kâ) อย่าเลยครับ(ค่ะ)

pleased: pleased to meet you yin dee têe dâi róo-jùk gun ยินดีที่ได้รู้จักกัน

pleasure: my pleasure (response to thanks) mâi bpen rai ไม่เป็นไร

plenty: plenty of... ...mâhk ...มาก

  there's plenty of time mee way-lah mâhk มีเวลามาก

  that's plenty, thanks por láir-o kòrp-kOOn พอแล้วขอบคุณ

pliers keem bpàhk kêep คีมปากคีบ

plug (electrical) bplúk ปลั๊ก

  (for car) hŏo-a tee-un หัวเทียน

  (in sink) jòok òot จุกอุด

plumber châhng bpra-bpah ช่างประปา

p.m. (see pages 10–11)

pocket gra-bpǎo กระเป๋า

point: two point five sŏrng jòot hâh สองจุดห้า

  there's no point mâi mee bpra-yòht ไม่มีประโยชน์

points (in car) torng kǎo ทองขาว

poisonous bpen pít เป็นพิษ

police dtum-ròo-ut ตำรวจ

  call the police! rêe-uk dtum-ròo-ut mah! เรียกตำรวจมา

policeman dtum-ròo-ut ตำรวจ

police station sa-tǎh-nee dtum-ròo-ut สถานีตำรวจ

policewoman dtum-ròo-ut yǐng ตำรวจหญิง

polish (noun) yah kùt ยาขัด

polite sOO-pâhp สุภาพ

polluted bpen pít เป็นพิษ

pony máh glàirp ม้าแกลบ

pool (for swimming) sà wâi náhm สระว่ายน้ำ

poor (not rich) jon จน

  (quality) mâi ao nǎi ไม่เอาไหน

pop music don-dtree pórp ดนตรีป๊อพ

pop singer núk rórng นักร้อง

popular bpen têe nee-yom เป็นที่นิยม

population bpra-chah-gorn ประชากร

pork néu-a mǒo เนื้อหมู

port (for boats) tâh reu-a ท่าเรือ

porter (in hotel) kon fâo bpra-dtoo คนเฝ้าประตู

portrait pâhp kěe-un dtoo-a jing ภาพเขียนตัวจริง

posh (restaurant, people) rŏo-rǎh หรูหรา

possible bpen bpai dâi เป็นไปได้

  is it possible to...? ...bpen bpai dâi mái? ...เป็นไปได้ไหม

  as... as possible yàhng ... têe sòOt têe ja ... dâi อย่าง ... ที่สุดที่จะ ... ได้

post (noun: mail) jòt-mǎi จดหมาย

  (verb) sòng jòt-mǎi ส่งจดหมาย

  could you post this for

me? chôo-ay sòng jòt-mǎi née hâi nòy dâi mái? ช่วยส่งจดหมายนี้ให้หน่อยได้ไหม

postbox dtôo bprai-sa-nee ตู้ไปรษณีย์

postcard bpóht-gáht โปสการ์ด

postcode ra-hùt bprai-sa-nee รหัสไปรษณีย์

poster bpoh-sa-dter โปสเตอร์

poste restante 'poste restante'

post office bprai-sa-nee ไปรษณีย์

potato mun fa-rùng มันฝรั่ง

potato chips (US) mun fa-rùng tôrt มันฝรั่งทอด

pots and pans môr kâo môr gairng หม้อข้าวหม้อแกง

pottery krêu-ung bpûn din pǎo เครื่องปั้นดินเผา

pound (money) bporn ปอนด์

power cut dtùt fai ตัดไฟ

power point bplúk fai ปลั๊กไฟ

practise: I want to practise my Thai pǒm (chún) yàhk ja fèuk pôot pah-sǎh tai ผม(ฉัน)อยากจะฝึกพูดภาษาไทย

prawns gôOng กุ้ง

prefer: I prefer... pǒm (chún) chôrp ... mâhk gwàh ผม(ฉัน)ชอบ ... มากกวา

pregnant mee tórng มีท้อง

prescription (for medicine) bai sùng yah ใบสั่งยา

present (gift) kŏrng kwŭn ของขวัญ

president (of country) bpra-tah-nah-tí-bor-dee ประธานาธิบดี

pretty sŏo-ay สวย

　it's pretty expensive pairng měu-un gun ná แพงเหมือนกันนะ

price rah-kah ราคา

priest prá พระ

prime minister nah-yók rút-ta-mon-dtree นายกรัฐมนตรี

printed matter sìng dtee pim สิ่งตีพิมพ์

priority (in driving) sìt pàhn bpai gòrn สิทธผ่านไปก่อน

prison kóok คุก

private sòo-un dtoo-a ส่วนตัว

private bathroom hôrng náhm sòo-un dtoo-a ห้องน้ำส่วนตัว

probably kong-ja คงจะ

problem bpun-hǎh ปัญหา

　no problem! mâi mee bpun-hǎh! ไม่มีปัญหา

program(me) (noun) bproh-grairm โปรแกรม

promise: I promise pŏm (chún) sŭn-yah ผม(ฉัน)สัญญา

pronounce: how is this pronounced? nêe òrk sĕe-ung

yung-ngai? นี่ออกเสียงอย่างไร

properly (repaired, locked etc) tòok dtôrng ถูกต้อง

Protestant krít คริสต์

public convenience sôo-um sǎh-tah-ra-ná ส้วมสาธารณะ

public holiday wun yòot râht-cha-gahn วันหยุดราชการ

pudding (dessert) kŏrng wǎhn ของหวาน

pull deung ดึง

pullover sêu-a sa-wét-dtêr เสื้อสเวตเตอร์

puncture (noun) yahng dtàirk ยางแตก

purple sĕe môo-ung สีม่วง

purse (for money) gra-bpǎo sa-dtahng กระเป๋าสตางค์
　(US) gra-bpǎo tĕu กระเป๋าถือ

push plùk ผลัก

pushchair rót kĕn รถเข็น

put sài ใส่

　where can I put...? ... sài dâi têe nǎi? ... ใส่ได้ที่ไหน

　could you put us up for the night? kŏr káhng keun têe nêe nòy dâi mái? ขอค้างคืนที่นี่หน่อยได้ไหม

pyjamas sêu-a gahng-gayng norn เสื้อกางเกงนอน

Q

quality kOOn-na-pâhp คุณภาพ

quarantine (place) dâhn gùk
rôhk ด่านกักโรค

    (period) ra-yá way-lah têe gùk
rôhk wái ระยะเวลาที่กักโรคไว้

quarter nèung nai sèe หนึ่งในสี่

quayside: on the quayside têe
tâh reu-a ที่ท่าเรือ

question kum tǎhm คำถาม

queue (*noun*) kew คิว

quick ray-o เร็ว

    that was quick ray-o jing
เร็วจริง

    **what's the quickest way
there?** bpai tahng nǎi ray-o têe
sòot? ไปทางไหนเร็วที่สุด

    fancy a quick drink?
yàhk bpai dèum a-rai mái?
อยากไปดื่มอะไรไหม

quickly ray-o เร็ว

quiet (place, hotel) ngêe-up เงียบ

    quiet! ngêe-up ngêe-up nòy!
เงียบ ๆ หน่อย

quite (fairly) por sǒm-koo-un
พอสมควร

    (very) tee dee-o ทีเดียว

    that's quite right tòok láir-o
ถูกแล้ว

    quite a lot mâhk por sǒm-

koo-un มากพอสมควร

R

rabbit (meat) gra-dtài กระต่าย

race (for runners, cars) gahn kàirng
kǔn การแข่งขัน

racket (tennis, squash) mái dtee
ไม้ตี

radiator môr náhm หม้อน้ำ

radio wít-ta-yóo วิทยุ

    on the radio tahng wít-ta-
yóo ทางวิทยุ

rail: by rail doy-ee rót fai
โดยรถไฟ

railway tahng rót fai ทางรถไฟ

rain (*noun*) fǒn ฝน

    in the rain dtàhk fǒn ตากฝน

    it's raining fǒn dtòk ฝนตก

raincoat sêu-a fǒn เสื้อฝน

rape (*noun*) kòm kěun ข่มขืน

rare (uncommon) hǎh yâhk หายาก

    (steak) sòok sòok dìp dìp สุก
ๆ ดิบ ๆ

rash (on skin) pèun ผื่น

rat nǒo หนู

rate (for changing money) ùt-dtrah
อัตรา

rather: it's rather good kôrn
kâhng dee ค่อนข้างดี

I'd rather... pŏm (chún) yàhk ja … dee gwàh ผม(ฉัน) อยากจะ ... ดีกว่า

razor (dry, electric) mêet gohn มีดโกน

razor blades bai mêet gohn ใบมีดโกน

read àhn อ่าน

ready prórm, sèt พร้อม , เสร็จ

are you ready? sèt láir-o rĕu yung? เสร็จแล้วหรือยัง

I'm not ready yet pŏm (chún) yung mâi sèt ผม(ฉัน) ยังไม่เสร็จ

when will it be ready? sèt mêu-a rài?

it should be ready in a couple of days èek sŏrng săhm wun koo-un ja sèt

real jing จริง

really jing jing จริง ๆ

I'm really sorry pŏm (chún) sĕe-a jai jing jing ผม(ฉัน) เสียใจจริง ๆ

that's really great dee jung ler-ee ดีจังเลย

really? (doubt) jing lĕr? จริงหรือ

(polite interest) lĕr? หรือ

rear lights fai lŭng rót ไฟหลังรถ

rearview mirror gra-jòk lŭng กระจกหลัง

reasonable (price) rah-kah yao ราคาเยา

receipt bai sèt rúp ngern ใบเสร็จรับเงิน

recently mêu-a ray-o ray-o née เมื่อเร็ว ๆ นี้

reception (in hotel) pa-nàirk dtôrn rúp แผนกต้อนรับ

(for guests) ngahn lée-ung dtôrn rúp งานเลี้ยงต้อนรับ

at reception têe pa-nàirk dtôrn rúp ที่แผนกต้อนรับ

reception desk pa-nàirk dtôrn rúp แผนกต้อนรับ

receptionist pa-núk ngahn dtôrn rúp พนักงานต้อนรับ

recognize jum dâi จำได้

recommend: could you recommend...? kOOn náir-num … dâi mái? คุณแนะนำ ... ได้ไหม

record (music) pàirn sĕe-ung แผ่นเสียง

red sĕe dairng สีแดง

red wine lâo wai dairng เหล้าไวน์แดง

refund (noun) keun ngern คืนเงิน

can I have a refund? keun ngern hâi dâi mái?

คืนเงินให้ได้ไหม

region pâhk ภาค

registered: by registered mail jòt-mǎi long ta-bee-un จดหมายลงทะเบียน

registration number ta-bee-un rót ทะเบียนรถ

relative (*noun*) yâht ญาติ

religion sàh-sa-nǎh ศาสนา

remember: I don't remember pǒm (chún) jum mâi dâi ผม(ฉัน)จำไม่ได้

I remember pǒm (chún) jum dâi ผม(ฉัน)จำได้

do you remember? jum dâi mái? จำได้ไหม

rent (*noun*: for apartment etc) kâh châo ค่าเช่า

(*verb*: car etc) châo เช่า

rented car rót châo รถเช่า

repair (*verb*) sôrm ซ่อม

can you repair it? sôrm dâi mái? ซ่อมได้ไหม

repeat pôot èek tee พูดอีกที

could you repeat that? pôot èek tee dâi mái? พูดอีกทีได้ไหม

reservation jorng จอง

I'd like to make a reservation kŏr jorng ขอจอง

I have a reservation pǒm (chún) dâi jorng wái láir-o

yes sir, what name please? krúp kOOn chêu a-rai?

reserve (*verb*) jorng จอง

can I reserve a table for tonight? chún kŏr jorng dtór sǔm-rùp keun née dâi mái?

yes madam, for how many people? dâi krúp mee gèe kon?

for two sŏrng kon

and for what time? láir-o gèe mohng?

for eight o'clock sŏrng tôOm

and could I have your name, please? láir-o kOOn chêu a-rai krúp?

rest: I need a rest pǒm (chún) dtôrng púk pòrn ผม(ฉัน)ต้องพักผ่อน

the rest of the group pôo-uk kon èun พวกคนอื่น

restaurant ráhn ah-hǎhn ร้านอาหาร

restaurant car rót sa-bee-ung รถเสบียง

rest room hôrng náhm ห้องน้ำ

retired: I'm retired pǒm (chún)

ga-see-un ผม(ฉัน)เกษียน

return: a return to... dtŏo-a
bpai glùp... ตั๋วไปกลับ...

return ticket dtŏo-a bpai glùp
ตั๋วไปกลับ

reverse charge call toh-ra-
sùp gèp ngern bplai tahng
โทรศัพท์เก็บเงินปลายทาง

reverse gear gee-a tŏy lǔng
เกียร์ถอยหลัง

revolting nâh rung-gèe-ut
น่ารังเกียจ

rib sêe krohng ซี่โครง

rice kâo ข้าว

rich (person) roo-ay รวย

(food) mun มัน

ridiculous nâh hŏo-a rór
น่าหัวเราะ

right (correct) tòok ถูก

(not left) kwǎh ขวา

you were right kOOn tòok
láir-o คุณถูกแล้ว

that's right tòok láir-o ถูกแล้ว

this can't be right mâi tòok
nâir nâir ไม่ถูกแน่ๆ

right! ao lá! เอาละ

is this the right road for...?
bpai ... tahng ta-nŏn née tòok
mái? ไป ... ทางถนนนี้ถูกไหม

on the right tahng kwǎh
ทางขวา

turn right lée-o kwǎh
เลี้ยวขวา

right-hand drive poo-ung
ma-lai kwǎh พวงมาลัยขวา

ring (on finger) wǎirn แหวน

I'll ring you pŏm
(chún) ja toh bpai tĕung
ผม(ฉัน)จะโทรไปถึง

ring back toh glùp mah
โทรกลับมา

ripe (fruit) sòok สุก

rip-off: it's a rip-off lòrk dtôm
หลอกต้ม

rip-off prices rah-kah lòrk
dtôm ราคาหลอกต้ม

risky sèe-ung เสี่ยง

river mâir náhm แม่น้ำ

road (in town, country) ta-nŏn
ถนน

is this the road for...? nêe
ta-nŏn bpai ... châi mái?
นี่ถนนไป ... ใช่ไหม

down the road yòo glâi glâi
kâir née อยู่ใกล้ๆแค่นี้

road accident rót chon gun
รถชนกัน

road map pǎirn-têe ta-nŏn
แผนที่ถนน

roadsign krêu-ung mǎi ja-rah
jorn เครื่องหมายจราจร

rob: I've been robbed pŏm
(chún) tòok ka-moy-ee

ผม(ฉัน)ถูกขโมย

rock hǐn หิน

(music) rórk ร็อค

on the rocks (with ice) sài núm kǎirng ใส่น้ำแข็ง

roll (bread) ka-nǒm-bpung ขนมปัง

roof lǔng-kah หลังคา

roof rack gròrp dtìt lǔng-kah rót กรอบติดหลังคารถ

room hôrng ห้อง

in my room nai hôrng pǒm (chún) ในห้องผม(ฉัน)

room service bor-ri-gahn rúp chái nai hôrng púk บริการรับใช้ในห้องพัก

rope chêu-uk เชือก

roughly (approximately) bpra-mahn ประมาณ

round: it's my round bpen tee kǒrng pǒm เป็นที่ของผม

roundabout (for traffic) wong wee-un วงเวียน

round trip ticket dtǒo-a bpai glùp ตั๋วไปกลับ

route tahng ทาง

what's the best route? bpai tahng nǎi dee têe sòot? ไปทางไหนดีที่สุด

rubber (material) yahng ยาง

(eraser) yahng lóp ยางลบ

rubber band yahng rút ยางรัด

rubbish (waste) ka-yà ขยะ

(poor quality goods) mâi ao nǎi ไม่เอาไหน

rubbish! (nonsense) mâi bpen rêu-ung! ไม่เป็นเรื่อง

rucksack bpây lǔng เป้หลัง

rude mâi sOO-pâhp ไม่สุภาพ

ruins sâhk sa-lùk hùk pung ซากสลักหักพัง

rum lâo rum เหล้ารัม

rum and Coke rum airn kóhk รัมแอนด์โค้ก

run (verb: person) wîng วิ่ง

how often do the buses run? rót may wîng têe mái? รถเมล์วิ่งถี่ไหม

I've run out of money pǒm (chún) mót ngern ผม(ฉัน)หมดเงิน

S

sad sâo เศร้า

saddle (for bike) ahn jùk-gra-yahn อานจักรยาน

(for horse) ahn máh อานม้า

safe (not in danger) bplòrt-pai ปลอดภัย

(not dangerous) mâi un-dta-rai ไม่อันตราย

safety pin kěm glùt เข็มกลัด

sail (*noun*) bai reu-a ใบเรือ

sailboard (*noun*) gra-dahn dtôh lom กระดานโตลม

sailboarding gahn lên gra-dahn dtôh lom การเล่นกระดานโต้ลม

salad sa-lùt สลัด

salad dressing náhm sa-lùt น้ำสลัด

sale: for sale kǎi ขาย

salt gleu-a เกลือ

same: the same měu-un gun เหมือนกัน

the same as this měu-un yàhng née เหมือนอย่างนี้

the same again, please kǒr yàhng derm ขออย่างเดิม

it's all the same to me a-rai gôr dâi อะไรก็ได้

sand sai ทราย

sandals rorng táo dtàir รองเท้าแตะ

sandwich sairn-wít แซนด์วิช

sanitary napkins, sanitary towels pâh un-nah-mai ผ้าอนามัย

Saturday wun sǎo วันเสาร์

sauce núm jìm น้ำจิ้ม

saucepan môr หม้อ

saucer jahn rorng tôo-ay จานรองถ้วย

sauna sao-nah เซานา

sausage sâi gròrk ไส้กรอก

say (*verb*) bòrk, pôot บอก, พูด

how do you say... in Thai? pah-sǎh tai ... pôot wâh yung-ngai? ภาษาไทย ... พูดว่าอย่างไร

what did he say? káo pôot wâh yung-ngai? เขาพูดว่าอย่างไร

she said... káo bòrk wâh... เขาบอกว่า...

could you say that again? pôot èek tee dâi mái? พูดอีกที่ได้ไหม

scarf (for neck) pâh pun kor ผ้าพันคอ

(for head) pâh pôhk sěe-sà ผ้าโพกศีรษะ

scenery poo-mi-bpra-tâyt ภูมิประเทศ

schedule (US) dtah-rahng way-lah ตารางเวลา

scheduled flight dtah-rahng têe-o bin

school rohng ree-un โรงเรียน

scissors: a pair of scissors dta-grai ตะไกร

scooter rót sa-góot-dter รถสกู๊ตเตอร์

scotch lâo wít-sa-gêe เหล้าวิสกี้

Scotch tape sa-górt táyp
สก๊อตเทป

Scotland sa-górt-lairn
สกอตแลนด์

Scottish kon sa-górt คนสกอต
I'm Scottish pǒm (chún)
bpen kon sa-górt ผม(ฉัน)
เป็นคนสกอต

scrambled eggs kài kon ไข่คน

scratch (*noun*) roy kòo-un
รอยขว่น

screw (*noun*) dta-bpoo koo-ung
ตะปูควง

screwdriver kǎi koo-ung ไขควง

sea ta-lay ทะเล
by the sea chai ta-lay
ชายทะเล

seafood ah-hǎhn ta-lay
อาหารทะเล

seafood restaurant pút-
ta-kahn ah-hǎhn ta-lay
ภัตตาคารอาหารทะเล

seafront chai ta-lay ชายทะเล

seagull nók nahng noo-un
นกนางนวล

search (*verb*) hǎh หา

seashell bplèu-uk hǒy
เปลือกหอย

seasick: I feel seasick pǒm
(chún) róo-sèuk mao klêun
ผม(ฉัน)รู้สึกเมาคลื่น
I get seasick pǒm (chún)

mao klêun ngâi ผม(ฉัน)
เมาคลื่นง่าย

seaside: by the seaside chai
ta-lay ชายทะเล

seat têe nûng ที่นั่ง
is this seat taken? têe nêe
wâhng mái? ที่นี่ว่างไหม

seat belt kěm kùt ní-ra-pai
เข็มขัดนิรภัย

sea urchin bpling ta-lay
ปลิงทะเล

seaweed sǎh-rài-ta-lay
สาหร่ายทะเล

secluded dòht dèe-o โดดเดี่ยว

second (*adj*) têe sǒrng ที่สอง
(of time) wí-nah-tee วินาที
just a second! děe-o gòrn!
เดี๋ยวก่อน

second class (travel etc) chún
sǒrng ชั้นสอง

second floor chún nèung
ชั้นหนึ่ง
(US) chún sǒrng ชั้นสอง

see hěn เห็น
can I see? kǒr doo nòy, dâi
mái? ขอดูหน่อยได้ไหม
have you seen...? hěn ... rěu
bplào? เห็น ... หรือเปล่า
I saw him this morning hěn
méu-a cháo née เห็นเมื่อเช้านี้
see you! jer gun mài ná!

เจอกันใหม่นะ

I see (I understand) kâo jai láir-o
เข้าใจแล้ว

self-service bor-rí-gahn
chôo-ay dtoo-a ayng
บริการช่วยตัวเอง

sell kǎi ขาย

do you sell...? mee ... kǎi
mái? มี ... ขายไหม

Sellotape sa-górt táyp
สก็อตเทป

send sòng ส่ง

**I want to send this to
England** pǒm (chún) yàhk ja
sòng nêe bpai ung-grìt ผม(ฉัน)
อยากจะส่งนี้ไปอังกฤษ

senior citizen kon cha-rah
คนชรา

separate dtàhng hàhk ต่างหาก

separated: I'm separated
(male) pǒm yâirk gun gùp pun-
ra-yah ผมแยกกันกับภรรยา
(female) chún yâirk gun gùp
sǎh-mee ฉันแยกกันกับสามี

separately (pay, travel) yâirk gun
แยกกัน

September gun-yah-yon
กันยายน

septic mee chéu-a มีเชื้อ

serious (person) ao jing ao jung
เอาจริงเอาจัง
(situation) dtreung krêe-ut

ตรึงเครียด

(problem, illness) nùk หนัก

service charge (in restaurant)
kâh bor-rí-gahn ค่าบริการ

service station bpúm núm mun
ปั๊มน้ำมัน

serviette pâh chét bpàhk
ผ้าเช็ดปาก

set menu ah-hǎhn chóot
อาหารชุด

several lǎi หลาย

sew yép เย็บ

**could you sew this back
on?** chôo-ay yép hâi nòy dâi
mái? ช่วยเย็บให้หน่อยได้ไหม

sex gahn rôo-um bpra-way-nee
การร่วมประเวณี

sexy sek-sêe เซ็กซี่

shade: in the shade nai rôm
ในร่ม

shake: let's shake hands jùp
meu gun จับมือกัน

shallow (water) dtêun ตื้น

shame: what a shame! nâh
sěe-a dai! น่าเสียดาย

shampoo (noun) chairm-poo
แชมพู

shampoo and set sà sét
สระเซ็ท

share (verb: room, table etc) bàirng
แบ่ง

sharp (knife) kom คม

(taste) bprêe-o เปรี้ยว

(pain) sĕe-o เสียว

shattered (very tired) nèu-ay mâhk เหนื่อยมาก

shaver krêu-ung gohn nòo-ut เครื่องโกนหนวด

shaving foam kreem gohn nòo-ut ครีมโกนหนวด

shaving point bplúk krêu-ung gohn nòo-ut ปลั๊กเครื่องโกนหนวด

she káo เขา

is she here? káo yòo têe nêe mái? เขาอยู่ที่นี่ไหม

sheet (for bed) pâh bpoo têe norn ผ้าปูที่นอน

shelf hîng หิ้ง

shellfish hŏy หอย

ship reu-a เรือ

by ship tahng reu-a ทางเรือ

shirt sêu-a chért เสื้อเชิ้ต

shit! âi hàh! ไอ้ห่า

shock: I got an electric shock from the... pŏm (chún) tòok fai chórk têe... ผม(ฉัน)ถูกไฟช็อคที่ ...

shock-absorber chórk ช็อค

shocked dtòk jai ตกใจ

shocking lĕu-a gern jing jing เหลือเกินจริงๆ

shoe rorng táo รองเท้า

a pair of shoes rorng táo kôo nèung รองเท้าคู่หนึ่ง

shoelaces chêu-uk pòok rorng táo เชือกผูกรองเท้า

shoe polish yah kùt rorng táo ยาขัดรองเท้า

shoe repairer kon sòrm rorng táo คนซ่อมรองเท้า

shop ráhn ร้าน

shopping: I'm going shopping pŏm (chún) bpai séu kŏrng ผม(ฉัน)ไปซื้อของ

shopping centre sŏon gahn káh ศูนย์การค้า

shop window nâh gra-jòk ráhn หน้ากระจกร้าน

shore chai fùng ชายฝั่ง

short (person) dtêe-a เตี้ย

(time) sûn สั้น

shortcut tahng lút ทางลัด

shorts gahng-gayng kăh sûn กางเกงขาสั้น

(US: underwear) gahng gayng nai กางเกงใน

should: what should I do? pŏm (chún) koo-un ja tum yung-ngai? ผม(ฉัน)ควรจะทำอย่างไร

you should... koon koo-un ja... คุณควรจะ ...

you shouldn't... koon mâi

koo-un ja… คุณไม่ควรจะ …

he should be back soon
dĕe-o káo kong glùp mah
เดี๋ยวเขาคงกลับมา

shoulder lài ไหล่

shout (*verb*) dta-gohn ตะโกน

> **Travel tip** Most Thais hate
> raised voices, visible irritation
> and confrontations of any
> kind, so losing one's cool in
> public is much more of a no-no
> than you might be used to.

show (in theatre) gahn sa-dairng

การแสดง **could you
show me?** kŏr doo nòy
ขอดูหน่อย

shower (rain) fŏn bproy bproy
ฝนปรอยๆ

(in bathroom) fùk boo-a ฝักบัว

with shower mee fùk boo-a
มีฝักบัว

shower gel kreem àhp náhm
ครีมอาบน้ำ

shut (*verb*) bpìt ปิด

when do you shut? kOOn
bpìt gèe mohng? คุณปิดกี่โมง

when does it shut? bpìt gèe
mohng? ปิดกี่โมง

they're shut káo bpìt láir-o
เขาปิดแล้ว

I've shut myself out
leum ao gOOn-jair òrk mah
ลืมเอากุญแจออกมา

shut up! yòot pôot ná!
หยุดพูดนะ

shutter (on camera) chút-dter
ชัตเตอร์
(on window) bahn glèt
nâh-dtàhng
บานเกล็ดหน้าต่าง

shy ai อาย

sick (ill) mâi sa-bai ไม่สบาย
I'm going to be sick (vomit)
róo-sèuk wâh klêun sâi
รู้สึกว่าคลื่นไส้

side kâhng ข้าง
the other side of the street
èek fâhk nèung kórng
ta-nǒn อีกฟากหนึ่งของถนน

sidelights fai kâhng ไฟข้าง

side salad sa-lùt สลัด

side street soy ซอย

sidewalk bàht wít-těe บาทวิถี

sight: the sights of...
sa-tǎhn-têe nâh têe-o nai...
สถานที่น่าเที่ยวใน ...

**sightseeing: we're going
sightseeing** rao ja bpai têe-o
เราจะไปเที่ยว

sightseeing tour rai gahn num
têe-o รายการนำเที่ยว

sign (roadsign etc) bpâi
sǔn-yahn ja-rah-jorn
ป้ายสัญญาณจราจร

signal: he didn't give a

signal (driver, cyclist) káo
mâi dâi hâi sǔn-yahn
เขาไม่ได้ให้สัญญาณ

signature lai sen ลายเซ็น

signpost dtìt bpâi ja-rah-jorn
ติดป้ายจราจร

silence kwahm ngêe-up
ความเงียบ

silk mǎi ไหม

silly ngôh โง่

silver (*noun*) ngern เงิน

silver foil gra-dàht dta-gòo-a
กระดาษตะกั่ว

similar měu-un เหมือน

simple (easy) ngâi ง่าย

since: since last week
dtûng dtàir ah-tít gòrn
ตั้งแต่อาทิตย์ก่อน

since I got here dtûng
dtàir pǒm (chún) mah těung
ตั้งแต่ผม(ฉัน)มาถึง

sing rórng playng ร้องเพลง

singer núk rórng นักร้อง

single: a single to... dtǒo-a
bpai... ตั๋วไป ...

I'm single pǒm (chún) bpen
sòht ผม(ฉัน)เป็นโสด

single bed dtee-ung dèe-o
เตียงเดี่ยว

single room hôrng dèe-o
ห้องเดี่ยว

single ticket dtǒo-a bpai ตั๋วไป

sink (in kitchen) àhng อ่าง

sister (older) pêe săo พี่สาว

(younger) nórng săo น้องสาว

sister-in-law (older) pêe sa-pái kŏrng พี่สะใภ้ของ

(younger) nórng sa-pái kŏrng น้องสะใภ้ของ

sit: can I sit here? kŏr nûng têe nêe, dâi mái? ขอนั่งที่นี่ได้ไหม

is anyone sitting here? mee kon nûng têe nêe rĕu bplào? มีคนนั่งที่นี่หรือเปล่า

sit down nûng นั่ง

do sit down chern nûng see เชิญนั่งซิ

size ka-nàht ขนาด

skin pĕw ผิว

skin-diving gahn dum náhm léuk การดำน้ำลึก

skinny pŏrm ผอม

skirt gra-bprohng กระโปรง

sky fáh ฟ้า

sleep (verb) norn lùp นอนหลับ

did you sleep well? lùp dee mái? หลับดีไหม

sleeper (on train) rót norn รถนอน

sleeping bag tŏong norn ถุงนอน

sleeping car rót norn รถนอน

sleeping pill yah norn lùp ยานอนหลับ

sleepy: I'm feeling sleepy pŏm (chún) ngôo-ung norn ผม(ฉัน)ง่วงนอน

sleeve kăirn sêu-a แขนเสื้อ

slide (photographic) sa-lai สไลด์

slip (garment) gra-bprohng chún nai กระโปรงชั้นใน

slippery lêun ลื่น

slow cháh ช้า

slow down! (driving) kùp cháh cháh nòy! ขับช้า ๆ หน่อย

(speaking) pôot cháh cháh nòy! พูดช้า ๆ หน่อย

slowly cháh ช้า

very slowly cháh mâhk ช้ามาก

small lék เล็ก

smell: it smells (smells bad) mĕn เหม็น

smile (verb) yím ยิ้ม

smoke (noun) kwun ควัน

do you mind if I smoke? kŏr sòop bOO-rèe dâi mái? ขอสูบบุหรี่ได้ไหม

I don't smoke pŏm (chún) mâi sòop bOO-rèe ผม(ฉัน) ไม่สูบบุหรี่

do you smoke? kOOn sòop bOO-rèe mái? คุณสูบบุหรี่ไหม

snake ngoo งู

sneeze (*verb*) jahm จาม

snorkel tôr hǎi jai ท่อหายใจ

snow (*noun*) hí-má หิมะ

so: it's so good dee jung ler-ee
ดีจังเลย

it's so expensive pairng jung
ler-ee แพงจังเลย

not so much mâi kôy mâhk
ไม่ค่อยมาก

not so bad mâi kôy lay-o
ไม่ค่อยเลว

so am I pǒm (chún)
gôr měu-un gun
ผม(ฉัน)ก็เหมือนกัน

so do I pǒm (chún) gôr měu-
un gun ผม(ฉัน)ก็เหมือนกัน

so-so rêu-ay rêu-ay เรื่อย ๆ

soap sa-bòo สบู่

soap powder pǒng súk fôrk
ผงซักฟอก

sober mâi mao ไม่เมา

sock tǒong táo ถุงเท้า

socket (electrical) bplúk fai
ปลั๊กไฟ

soda (water) núm soh-dah
น้ำโซดา

sofa têe nûng rúp kàirk
ที่นั่งรับแขก

soft (material etc) nîm นิ่ม

soft drink náhm kòo-ut น้ำขวด

sole (of shoe, of foot) péun rorng
táo พื้นรองเท้า

could you put new soles
on these? sài péun rórng
táo mài hâi nòy, dâi mái?
ใส่พื้นรองเท้าใหม่ให้หน่อย
ได้ไหม

some bahng บาง

some people bahng kon
บางคน

can I have some? kǒr nòy,
dâi mái? ขอหน่อยได้ไหม

somebody, someone krai ใคร

something a-rai อะไร

something to eat kǒrng gin
ของกิน

sometimes bahng tee บางที

somewhere têe nǎi ที่ไหน

son lôok chai ลูกชาย

song playng เพลง

son-in-law lôok kěr-ee ลูกเขย

soon děe-o เดี๋ยว

I'll be back soon děe-o glùp
ná เดี๋ยวกลับนะ

as soon as possible yàhng
ray-o têe sòot têe ja ray-o dâi
อย่างเร็วที่สุดที่จะเร็วได้

sore: it's sore jèp เจ็บ

sore throat jèp kor เจ็บคอ

sorry: (I'm sorry) pǒm (chún)
sěe-a jai ผม(ฉัน)เสียใจ

sorry? (I didn't understand) a-rai

na? อะไรนะ

sort: what sort of...? ...bàirp
nǎi? ...แบบไหน

soup sóop ซุป

sour (taste) bprée-o เปรี้ยว

south dtâi ใต้

in the south nai pâhk dtâi
ในภาคใต้

South Africa ah-fri-gah dtâi
อาฟริกาใต้

South China Sea ta-lay jeen
dtâi ทะเลจีนใต้

southeast dta-wun òrk
chěe-ung dtâi
ตะวันออกเฉียงใต้

southwest dta-wun dtòk
chěe-ung dtâi
ตะวันตกเฉียงใต้

souvenir kǒrng têe ra-léuk
ของที่ระลึก

soy sauce núm see éw น้ำซีอิ๊ว

Spain bpra-tâyt sa-bpayn
ประเทศสเปน

spanner gOOn-jair bpàhk dtai
กุญแจปากตาย

spare part a-lài อะไหล่

spare tyre yahng a-lài
ยางอะไหล่

spark plug hǒo-a tee-un
หัวเทียน

speak: do you speak

English? kOOn pôot pah-
sǎh ung-grìt bpen mái?
คุณพูดภาษาอังกฤษเป็นไหม

I don't speak... pǒm (chún)
pôot ... mâi bpen ผม(ฉัน)พูด
... ไม่เป็น

can I speak to...? kǒr pôot
gùp ... nòy, dâi mái? ขอพูดกับ
... หน่อยได้ไหม

DIALOGUE

can I speak to Tongchai?
kǒr pôot gùp kOOn Tong-
chai nòy, dâi mái ká?
who's calling? krai pôot
krúp?
it's Patricia chún Patricia
pôot kâ
**I'm sorry, he's not in, can I
take a message?** káo mâi
yòo krúp mee a-rai ja fàhk
bòrk mái?
**no thanks, I'll call back
later** mâi mee kâ ja toh
glùp mah dtorn lǔng
please tell him I called
chôo-ay bòrk káo wâh chún
toh mah

spectacles wâirn dtah แว่นตา

speed (noun) kwahm ray-o
ความเร็ว

speed limit ùt-dtrah kwahm
ray-o อัตราความเร็ว

speedometer krêu-
ung wút kwahm ray-o

เครื่องวัดความเร็ว

spell: how do you spell it? sa-gòt yung-ngai?
สะกดอย่างไร

spend chái ngern ใช้เงิน

spider mairng mOOm แมงมุม

spin-dryer krêu-ung bpùn pâh hâi hâirng เครื่องปั่นผ้าให้แห้ง

splinter sa-gèt mái สะเก็ดไม้

spoke (in wheel) sêe lór rót ซี่ล้อรถ

spoon chórn ช้อน

sport gee-lah กีฬา

sprain: I've sprained my... pǒm (chún) tum ... klét
ผม(ฉัน)ทำเคล็ด ...

spring (season) réu-doo bai mái plì ฤดูใบไม้ผลิ
in the spring dtorn réu-doo bai mái plì
ตอนฤดูใบไม้ผลิ

squid bplah-mèuk ปลาหมึก

stairs bun-dai บันได

stale mâi sòt ไม่สด

stall: the engine keeps stalling krêu-ung dùp bòy
เครื่องดับบ่อย

stamp (noun) sa-dtairm แสตมป์

standby 'standby'

star dao ดาว
(in film) dah-rah nǔng
ดาราหนัง

start (verb) rêrm เริ่ม
when does it start? rêrm mêu-rai? เริ่มเมื่อไร
the car won't start rót sa-dtàht mâi dtìt
รถสตาร์ทไม่ติด

starter (of car) bpÒOm sa-dtàht ปุ่มสตาร์ท

starving: I'm starving pǒm (chún) hěw jung ler-ee
ผม(ฉัน)หิวจังเลย

state (country) rút รัฐ
the States (USA) sa-hǎh-rút
สหรัฐ

station sa-tǎh-nee rót fai
สถานีรถไฟ

statue rôop bpûn รูปปั้น

stay: where are you staying? kOOn púk yòo têe nǎi?
คุณพักอยู่ที่ไหน
I'm staying at... pǒm (chún) púk yòo têe...
ผม(ฉัน)พักอยู่ที่ ...

I'd like to stay another two nights pǒm (chún) yàhk ja púk yòo èek sǒrng keun ผม(ฉัน) อยากจะพักอยู่อีกสองคืน

steak néu-a sa-dték เนื้อเสต็ก

steal ka-moy-ee ขโมย

my bag has been stolen gra-bpǎo tòok ka-moy-ee กระเป๋าถูกขโมย

steep (hill) chun ชัน

steering mǒon poo-ung mah-lai หมุนพวงมาลัย

step: on the steps têe kûn bun-dai ที่ขึ้นบันได

stereo sa-dtay-ri-oh สเตริโอ

sterling ngern bporn เงินปอนด์

steward (on plane) pa-núk ngahn krêu-ung bin พนักงานเครื่องบิน

stewardess pa-núk ngahn dtôrn rúp bon krêu-ung bin พนักงานต้อนรับบนเครื่องบิน

sticking plaster bplah-sa-dter พลาสเตอร์

sticky rice kâo něe-o ข้าวเหนียว

still: I'm still here pǒm (chún) yung yòo têe nêe ผม(ฉัน) ยังอยู่ที่นี่

is he still there? káo yung yòo têe nûn mái? เขายังอยู่ที่นั่นไหม

keep still! yòo nìng níng! อยู่นิ่ง ๆ

sting: I've been stung pǒm (chún) tòok ma-lairng dtòy ผม(ฉัน)ถูกแมลงต่อย

Travel tip The best way to minimize the risk of stepping on the toxic spines of sea urchins, stingrays and stonefish is to wear thick-soled shoes in the sea, though these cannot provide total protection. Sea urchin spikes should be removed after softening the skin with ointment; for stingray and stonefish stings, alleviate the pain by immersing the wound in hot water while awaiting help.

stockings tǒong nôrng ถุงน่อง

stomach tórng ท้อง

stomach ache bpòo-ut tórng ปวดท้อง

stone (rock) hǐn หิน

stop (verb) yòot หยุด

please stop here (to taxi driver etc) yòot dtrong née krúp (kâ) หยุดตรงนี้ครับ(ค่ะ)

do you stop near...? koon yòot glâi glâi ... mái? คุณหยุดใกล้ ๆ ... ไหม

stop it! yòot na! หยุดนะ

stopover wáir แวะ

storm pah-yóo พายุ

straight: it's straight ahead
yòo dtrong nâh อยู่ตรงหน้า

a straight whisky wít-sa-gêe
pee-o วิสกี้เพียว

straightaway tun-tee ทันที

strange (odd) bplàirk แปลก

stranger kon bplàirk nâh
คนแปลกหน้า

I'm a stranger here pŏm
(chún) mâi châi kon têe nêe
ผม(ฉัน)ไม่ใช่คนที่นี่

strap săi สาย

strawberry sa-dtor-ber-rêe
สตรอเบอร์รี่

stream lum-tahn ลำธาร

street ta-nŏn ถนน

on the street bon ta-nŏn
บนถนน

streetmap păirn-têe ta-nŏn
แผนที่ถนน

string chêu-uk เชือก

strong kăirng rairng แข็งแรง

stuck dtìt ติด

it's stuck mun dtìt มันติด

student núk-sèuk-săh นักศึกษา

stupid ngôh โง่

suburb bor-ri-wayn chahn meu-
ung บริเวณชานเมือง

suddenly tun-tee ทันที

suede nŭng glùp หนังกลับ

sugar núm dtahn น้ำตาล

suit (*noun*) chóot ชุด

it doesn't suit me (jacket
etc) mâi mòr gùp pŏm (chún)
ไม่เหมาะกับผม(ฉัน)

it suits you mòr gùp kOOn
dâi dee เหมาะกับคุณได้ดี

suitcase gra-bpǎo dern tahng
กระเป๋าเดินทาง

summer nâh rórn หน้าร้อน

in the summer dtorn nâh
rórn ตอนหน้าร้อน

sun prá-ah-tít พระอาทิตย์

in the sun dtàhk dàirt
ตากแดด

out of the sun nai rôm ในร่ม

sunbathe àhp dàirt อาบแดด

sunblock (cream) yah tah gun
dàirt ยาทากันแดด

sunburn tòok dàirt ถูกแดด

sunburnt tòok dàirt mâi
ถูกแดดไหม้

Sunday wun ah-tít วันอาทิตย์

sunglasses wâirn gun dàirt
แว่นกันแดด

sun lounger máh nûng àhp dàirt
ม้านั่งอาบแดด

sunny: it's sunny dàirt òrk
แดดออก

sunroof (in car) lŭng-kah gra-jòk
หลังคากระจก

sunset ah-tít dtòk อาทิตย์ตก

sunshade ngao dàirt เงาแดด

sunshine dàirt òrk แดดออก

sunstroke rôhk páir dàirt โรคแพ้แดด

suntan pěw klúm dàirt ผิวคล้ำแดด

suntan lotion kreem tah àhp dàirt ครีมทาอาบแดด

suntanned mee pěw klúm dàirt มีผิวคล้ำแดด

suntan oil núm mun tah àhp dàirt น้ำมันทาอาบแดด

super yôrt yêe-um ยอดเยี่ยม

supermarket sOO-bper-mah-get ซูเปอร์มาร์เก็ต

supper ah-hăhn yen อาหารเย็น

supplement (extra charge) kâh bor-ri-gahn pi-sàyt ค่าบริการพิเศษ

sure: are you sure? kOOn nâir-jai rěu? คุณแน่ใจหรือ

sure! nâir-norn! แน่นอน

surname nahm sa-gOOn นามสกุล

swearword kum sa-bòt คำสบถ

sweater sêu-a sa-wet-dter สเวตเตอร์

Sweden bpra-tâyt sa-wee-den ประเทศสวีเดน

sweet (taste) wăhn หวาน

(noun: dessert) kŏrng wăhn ของหวาน

sweets tórp-fêe ท๊อฟฟี่

swelling boo-um บวม

swim (verb) wâi náhm ว่ายน้ำ

I'm going for a swim pŏm (chún) bpai wâi náhm ผม(ฉัน)ไปว่ายน้ำ

let's go for a swim bpai wâi náhm mái? ไปว่ายน้ำไหม

swimming costume chóot àhp náhm ชุดอาบน้ำ

swimming pool sà wâi náhm สระว่ายน้ำ

swimming trunks gahng-gayng wâi náhm กางเกงว่ายน้ำ

switch (noun) sa-wít สวิช

switch off bpìt ปิด

switch on bpèrt เปิด

Switzerland bpra-tâyt sa-wìt ประเทศสวิส

swollen boo-um บวม

T

table dtó โต๊ะ

a table for two dtó sŭm-rùp sŏrng kon โต๊ะสำหรับสองคน

tablecloth pâh bpoo dtó ผ้าปูโต๊ะ

table tennis bping bporng ปิงปอง

tailback (of traffic) rót dtìt รถติด

tailor châhng dtùt sêu-a pâh

ช่างตัดเสื้อผ้า

take (lead: something somewhere)
ao … bpai เอา … ไป

(someone somewhere) pah …
bpai พา … ไป

take (accept) rúp รับ

can you take me to the…?
pah bpai … dâi mái? พาไป …
ได้ไหม

do you take credit cards?
rúp bùt kray-dìt rĕu bplào?
รับบัตรเครดิตหรือเปล่า

fine, I'll take it oh kay, pŏm
(chún) ao โอเค ผม(ฉัน)เอา

can I take this? (leaflet
etc) kŏr un née dâi mái?
ขออันนี้ได้ไหม

how long does it take?
chái way-lah nahn tâo-rài?
ใช้เวลานานเท่าไร

it takes three hours chái
way-lah săhm chôo-a mohng
ใช้เวลาสามชั่วโมง

is this seat taken? têe nêe
wâhng mái? ที่นี่ว่างไหม

**can you take a little off
here?** (to hairdresser) dtùt
dtrong née òrk nít-nòy dâi mái?
ตัดตรงนี้ออกนิดหน่อยได้ไหม

talcum powder bpâirng แป้ง

talk (verb) pôot พูด

tall sŏong สูง

tampons tairm-porn แทมพอน

tan (noun) klúm คล้ำ

to get a tan hâi pĕw klúm
ให้ผิวคล้ำ

tank (of car) tŭng núm mun
ถังน้ำมัน

tap górk náhm ก๊อกน้ำ

tape (for cassette) táyp เทป

tape measure săi wút สายวัด

tape recorder krêu-
ung bun-téuk sĕe-ung
เครื่องบันทึกเสียง

taste (noun) rót รส

can I taste it? kŏr
lorng chim nòy, dâi mái?
ขอลองชิมหน่อยได้ไหม

taxi táirk-sêe แท็กซี่

will you get me a taxi?
chôo-ay rêe-uk táirk-
sêe hâi nòy, dâi mái?
ช่วยเรียกแท็กซี่ให้หน่อย
ได้ไหม

taxi-driver kon kùp táirk-sêe
คนขับแท็กซี่

taxi rank têe jòrt rót táirk-sêe
ที่จอดรถแท็กซี่

tea (drink) núm chah น้ำชา

tea for one/two, please kŏr
núm chah têe nèung/sŏrng têe
ขอน้ำชาที่หนึ่ง/สองที่

teabags chah tŏong ชาถุง

**teach: could you teach
me?** sŏrn hâi dâi mái?
สอนให้ได้ไหม

teacher kroo ครู

team teem ทีม

teaspoon chórn chah ช้อนชา

tea towel pâh chét jahn
ผ้าเช็ดจาน

teenager dèk wai rôon
เด็กวัยรุ่น

telephone toh-ra-sùp โทรศัพท์

television toh-ra-tút โทรทัศน์

tell: could you tell him…?
chôo-ay bòrk kǎo wâh … nòy,
dâi mái? ช่วยบอกเขาว่า …
หน่อยได้ไหม

temperature (weather) OOn-na-
ha-poom อุณหภูมิ
(fever) kâi ไข้

temple wút วัด

tennis tay-nít เทนนิส

tennis ball lôok ten-nít
ลูกเทนนิส

tennis court sa-nǎhm ten-nít
สนามเทนนิส

tennis racket mái dtee ten-nít
ไม้ตีเทนนิส

tent dten เต็นท์

term term เทอร์ม

terminus (rail) sa-tǎh-nee
สถานี

terrible yâir แย่

terrific yôrt yêe-um ยอดเยี่ยม

text kôr kwahm ข้อความ
(verb) sòng kôr kwahm ส่ง
ข้อความ

Thai (adj) tai ไทย
(language) pah-sǎh tai ภาษาไทย
a Thai, the Thais kon tai
คนไทย

Thailand (formal) bpra-tâyt tai
ประเทศไทย
(informal) meu-ung tai เมืองไทย

than gwàh กว่า
smaller than lék gwàh
เล็กกว่า

thanks, thank you kòrp-kOOn
ขอบคุณ
thank you very much kòrp-
kOOn mâhk ขอบคุณมาก
thanks for the lift korp-kOOn
tee mah song ขอบคุณที่มาส่ง

no thanks mâi ao kòrp-kOOn
ไม่เอาขอบคุณ

thanks kòrp-kOOn
that's OK, don't mention it
mâi bpen rai

that: that boy pôo-chai kon nún
ผู้ชายคนนั้น

that girl pôo-yĭng kon nún
ผู้หญิงคนนั้น

that one un nún อันนั้น

I hope that… pŏm (chún)
wŭng wâh…
ผม(ฉัน)หวังว่า …

that's nice sŏo-ay สวย

is that…? …châi mái?
…ใช่ไหม

that's it (that's right) châi láir-o
ใช่แล้ว

the (there is no Thai equivalent)

theatre rohng la-korn
โรงละคร

their kŏrng kǎo ของเขา

theirs kŏrng kǎo ของเขา

them kǎo เขา

for them sŭm-rùp kǎo
สำหรับเขา

with them gùp kǎo กับเขา

to them gàir kǎo แก่เขา

who? – them krai? – pôo-uk
kǎo ใคร – พวกเขา

then (at that time) dtorn nún
ตอนนั้น

(after that) lǔng jàhk nún
หลังจากนั้น

there têe nún ที่นั่น

over there têe-nôhn ที่โน่น

up there kâhng bon nún ข้างบนนั้น

is/are there...? mee … mái? มี … ไหม

there is/are... mee… มี …

there you are (giving something) nêe krúp (kà) นี่ครับ(ค่ะ)

thermometer bpròrt ปรอท

Thermos flask gra-dtìk náhm กระติกน้ำ

these: these men pôo-chai pôo-uk lào née ผู้ชายพวกเหล่านี้

these women pôo-yǐng pôo-uk lào née ผู้หญิงพวกเหล่านี้

I'd like these ao pôo-uk lào née เอาพวกเหล่านี้

they káo เขา

thick nǎh หนา

(stupid) ngôh โง่

thief ka-moy-ee ขโมย

thigh nôrng น่อง

thin pǒrm ผอม

thing kǒrng ของ

my things kǒrng pǒm (chún) ของผม(ฉัน)

think kít คิด

I think so pǒm (chún) kít wâh yung-ngún ผม(ฉัน)คิดว่าอย่างนั้น

I don't think so pǒm (chún) kít wâh kong mâi ผม(ฉัน)คิดว่าคงไม่

I'll think about it pǒm (chún) ja lorng kít doo gòrn ผม(ฉัน)จะลองคิดดูก่อน

thirsty: I'm thirsty pǒm (chún) hěw náhm ผม(ฉัน)หิวน้ำ

this: this boy pôo-chai kon née ผู้ชายคนนี้

this girl pôo-yǐng kon née ผู้หญิงคนนี้

this one un née อันนี้

this is my wife nêe pun-ra-yah kǒrng pǒm นี่ภรรยาของผม

is this...? …châi mái? …ใช่ไหม

those: those men pôo chai pôo-uk lào nún ผู้ชายพวกเหล่านั้น

those women pôo yǐng pôo-uk lào nún ผู้หญิงพวกเหล่านั้น

which ones? – those un nâi? – un nún อันไหน – อันนั้น

thread (*noun*) sên dâi เส้นด้าย

throat kor hǒy คอหอย

throat pastilles yah om gâir kor jèp ยาอมแก้คอเจ็บ

through pàhn ผ่าน

does it go through...? (train,

bus) pàhn ... rĕu bplào? ผ่าน ... หรือเปล่า

throw (verb) kwâhng ขว้าง

throw away (verb) tíng ทิ้ง

thumb néw hŏo-a máir meu นิ้วหัวแม่มือ

thunderstorm pah-yóo fŏn พายุฝน

Thursday wun pá-réu-hùt วันพฤหัส

ticket dtŏo-a ตั๋ว

a return to Chiangmai dtŏo-a bpai glùp chee-ung-mài

coming back when? glùp mêu-rai?

today/next Tuesday wun née/wun ung-kahn náh

that will be 200 baht sŏrng róy bàht

ticket office (bus, rail) têe jum-nài dtŏo-a ที่จำหน่ายตั๋ว

tie (necktie) nék-tai เน็คไท

tight (clothes etc) kúp คับ

it's too tight kúp gern bpai คับเกินไป

tights tŏong yai boo-a ถุงใยบัว

till (cash desk) têe gèp ngern ที่เก็บเงิน

time way-lah เวลา

what's the time? gèe mohng

láir-o? กี่โมงแล้ว

this time krúng née ครั้งนี้

last time krúng têe láir-o ครั้งที่แล้ว

next time krúng náh ครั้งหน้า

three times săhm krúng สามครั้ง

timetable dtah-rahng way-lah ตารางเวลา

tin (can) gra-bpŏrng กระป๋อง

tinfoil gra-dàht a-loo-mí-nee-um กระดาษอลูมิเนียม

tin-opener têe bpèrt gra-bpŏrng ที่เปิดกระป๋อง

tiny lék เล็ก

tip (to waiter etc) ngern típ เงินทิป

Travel tip It's usual to tip hotel bellboys and porters, and to round up taxi fares. Most guides, drivers, masseurs, waiters and maids also depend on tips, and although some upmarket hotels and restaurants will add an automatic ten percent service charge to your bill, this is not always shared out.

tired nèu-ay เหนื่อย

I'm tired pŏm (chún) nèu-ay ผม(ฉัน)เหนื่อย

tissues pâh chét meu ผ้าเช็ดมือ

to: to Bangkok bpai groOng-tâyp ไปกรุงเทพฯ

to Thailand bpai meu-ung tai
ไปเมืองไทย

to the post office bpai bprai-
sa-nee ไปไปรษณีย์

toast (bread) ka-nŏm bpung
bping ขนมปังปิ้ง

today wun née วันนี้

toe néw táo นิ้วเท้า

together dôo-ay gun ด้วยกัน

  we're together (in shop
  etc) rao mah dôo-ay gun
  เรามาด้วยกัน

toilet hórng náhm ห้องน้ำ

  where is the toilet?
  hórng náhm yòo têe năi?
  ห้องน้ำอยู่ที่ไหน

  I have to go to the toilet
  pŏm (chún) dtôrng bpai hórng
  náhm ผม(ฉัน)ต้องไปห้องน้ำ

toilet paper gra-dàht chum-rá
กระดาษชำระ

tomato ma-kěu-a tâyt มะเขือเทศ

tomato juice núm ma-kěu-a
tâyt น้ำมะเขือเทศ

tomato ketchup sórt ma-kěu-a
tâyt ซอสมะเขือเทศ

tomorrow prôong née พรุ่งนี้

  tomorrow morning cháo
  prôong née เช้าพรุ่งนี้

  the day after tomorrow wun
  ma-reun née วันมะรืนนี้

toner (cosmetic) toner

tongue lín ลิ้น

tonic water núm toh-ník
น้ำโทนิค

tonight keun née คืนนี้

tonsillitis dtòrm torn-sín
ùk-sàyp ต่อมทอนซิลอักเสบ

too (excessively) …gern bpai
…เกินไป

  (also) dôo-ay ด้วย

  too hot rórn gern bpai
  ร้อนเกินไป

  too much mâhk gern bpai
  มากเกินไป

  me too pŏm (chún) gôr měu-
  un gun ผม(ฉัน)ก็เหมือนกัน

tooth fun ฟัน

toothache bpòo-ut fun ปวดฟัน

toothbrush bprairng sěe fun
แปรงสีฟัน

toothpaste yah sěe fun ยาสีฟัน

top: on top of… yòo bon…
อยู่บน …

  at the top yòo kâhng bon
  อยู่ข้างบน

top floor chún bon ชั้นบน

topless bpleu-ay òk เปลือยอก

torch fai chăi ไฟฉาย

total (noun) roo-um yôrt รวมยอด

tour (noun) rai-gahn num têe-o
รายการนำเที่ยว

is there a tour of…? mee rai-gahn num têe-o bpai … mái? มีรายการนำเที่ยวไป … ไหม

tour guide múk-kOO-tàyt มัคคุเทศก์

tourist núk tôrng têe-o นักท่องเที่ยว

tourist information office sǔm-núk kào sǎhn núk tôrng têe-o สำนักงานข่าวสารนักท่องเที่ยว

tour operator pôo-jùt bor-ri-gahn num têe-o ผู้จัดการบริการนำเที่ยว

towards sòo สู่

towel pàh chét dtoo-a ผ้าเช็ดตัว

town meu-ung เมือง

in town nai meu-ung ในเมือง

just out of town nork meu-ung bpai nòy นอกเมืองไปหน่อย

town centre jai glahng meu-ung ใจกลางเมือง

town hall tàyt-sa-bahn เทศบาล

toy kŏrng lên ของเล่น

track chahn chah-lah ชานชาลา

which track is it for Chiangmai? bpai chee-ung-mài chahn chah-lah a-rai? ไปเชียงใหม่ชานชาลาอะไร

tracksuit chóot gee-lah ชุดกีฬา

traditional bpen ka-nòp-tum nee-um เป็นขนบธรรมเนียม

traffic ja-rah-jorn จราจร

traffic jam rót dtìt รถติด

traffic lights fai sǔn-yahn ja-rah-jorn ไฟสัญญาณจราจร

trailer (for carrying tent etc) rót pôo-ung รถพ่วง

train rót fai รถไฟ

by train doy-ee rót fai โดยรถไฟ

trainers (shoes) rorng táo gee-lah รองเท้ากีฬา

train station sa-tǎhn-nee rót fai สถานีรถไฟ

translate bplair แปล

could you translate that? chôo-ay bplair hâi nòy, dâi mái? ช่วยแปลให้หน่อยได้ไหม

translation gahn bplair การแปล

translator pôo bplair ผู้แปล

trash can tǔng ka-yà ถังขยะ

travel gahn dern tahng

การเดินทาง

we're travelling around rao
dern tahng bpai rêu-ay rêu-ay
เราเดินทางไปเรื่อย ๆ

travel agent's trah-wern ay-yen
ทราเวิลเอเยนต์

traveller's cheque chék dern
tahng เช็คเดินทาง

tray tàht ถาด

tree dtôn mái ต้นไม้

tremendous wí-sàyt วิเศษ

trendy tun sa-mǎi ทันสมัย

trim: just a trim, please (to
hairdresser) chôo-ay dtùt òrk nít-
nòy tâo-nún krúp (ká) ช่วยตัดอ
อกนิดหน่อยเท่านั้นครับ(คะ)

trip (excursion) têe-o เที่ยว

I'd like to go on a trip to...
pǒm (chún) yàhk ja bpai têe-o...
ผม(ฉัน)อยากจะไปเที่ยว ...

trolley rót kěn รถเข็น

trouble (noun) bpun-hǎh ปัญหา

I'm having trouble with...
pǒm (chún) mee bpun-hǎh
gùp... ผม(ฉัน)มีปัญหากับ ...

trousers gahng-gayng กางเกง

true jing จริง

that's not true mâi jing
ไม่จริง

trunk (US: car) gra-bprohng tái rót
กระโปรงท้ายรถ

trunks (swimming) gahng-gayng

wâi náhm กางเกงว่ายน้ำ

try (verb) pa-yah-yahm พยายาม

can I try it? kǒr lorng nòy, dâi
mái? ขอลองหน่อยได้ไหม

try on lorng sài doo ลองใส่ดู

can I try it on? kǒr lorng
sài doo nòy, dâi mái?
ขอลองใส่ดูหน่อยได้ไหม

T-shirt sêu-a yêut เสื้อยืด

Tuesday wun ung-kahn
วันอังคาร

tuna bplah too-nah ปลาทูน่า

tunnel oo-mohng อุโมงค์

turn: turn left/right lée-o sái/
kwǎh เลี้ยวซ้าย/ขวา

turn off: where do I turn off?
ja lée-o têe nǎi? จะเลี้ยวที่ไหน

**can you turn the air-
conditioning off?** chôo-ay
bpìt krêu-ung bprùp ah-gàht
nòy, dâi mái? ช่วยปิดเครื่องปรั
บอากาศหน่อยได้ไหม

**turn on: can you turn the air-
conditioning on?** chôo-ay
bpèrt krêu-ung bprùp ah-gàht
nòy, dâi mái? ช่วยเปิดเครื่องป
รับอากาศหน่อยได้ไหม

turning (in road) tahng lée-o
ทางเลี้ยว

TV tee-wee ทีวี

tweezers bpàhk kèep ปากคีบ

twice sǒrng krúng สองครั้ง

twice as much mâhk sŏrng tâo มากสองเท่า

twin beds dtee-ung kôo เตียงคู่

twin room hôrng kôo ห้องคู่

twist: I've twisted my ankle kôr táo pŏm (chún) plík ข้อเท้าผม(ฉัน)พลิก

type (*noun*) bàirp แบบ

another type of... ...èek bàirp nèung ...อีกแบบหนึ่ง

typical bàirp cha-bùp แบบฉบับ

tyre yahng rót ยางรถ

U

ugly nâh glèe-ut น่าเกลียด

UK bpra-tâyt ung-grìt ประเทศอังกฤษ

ulcer plăir gra-pór แผลกระเพาะ

umbrella rôm ร่ม

uncle (older brother of mother/ father) loOng ลุง

(younger brother of father) ah อา

(younger brother of mother) náh นา

unconscious mòt sa-dtì หมดสติ

under (in position) dtâi ใต้

(less than) dtùm gwàh ต่ำกว่า

underdone (meat) sòok-sòok

dìp-dìp สุก ๆ ดิบ ๆ

underpants gahng-gayng nai กางเกงใน

understand: I understand pŏm (chún) kâo jai ผม(ฉัน)เข้าใจ

I don't understand pŏm (chún) mâi kâo jai ผม(ฉัน) ไม่เข้าใจ

do you understand? kâo jai mái? เข้าใจไหม

United States sa-hà-rút a-may-ri-gah สหรัฐอเมริกา

university ma-hăh-wít-ta-yah-lai มหาวิทยาลัย

unleaded petrol núm mun rái săhn dta-gòo-a น้ำมันไร้สารตะกั่ว

unlimited mileage mâi jum-gùt ra-ya tahng ไม่จำกัดระยะทาง

unlock kăi gOOn-jair ไขกุญแจ

unpack gâir hòr แก้ห่อ

until jon จน

unusual pìt tum-ma-dah ผิดธรรมดา

up kêun ขึ้น

up there yòo bon nún อยู่บนนั้น

he's not up yet (not out of bed) kăo yung mâi dtèun เขายังไม่ตื่น

what's up? (what's wrong?) bpen a-rai? เป็นอะไร

upmarket rŏo-rǎh หรูหรา

upset stomach tórng sěe-a
ท้องเสีย

upside down kwûm คว่ำ

upstairs kâhng bon ข้างบน

urgent dòo-un ด่วน

us rao เรา

 with us gùp rao กับเรา

 for us sǔm-rùp rao
 สำหรับเรา

USA sa-hà-rút a-may-ri-gah
สหรัฐอเมริกา

use (verb) chái ใช้

 may I use...? kŏr chái … dâi
 mái? ขอใช้ … ได้ไหม

useful mee bpra-yòht
มีประโยชน์

usual tum-ma-dah ธรรมดา

V

**vacancy: do you have any
 vacancies?** (hotel) mee hôrng
 wâhng mái? มีห้องว่างไหม

vacation wun yòot วันหยุด

 on vacation yòot púk pòrn
 หยุดพักผ่อน

vaccination chèet wúk-seen
ฉีดวัคซีน

vacuum cleaner krêu-ung dòot
fòon เครื่องดูดฝุ่น

valid (ticket etc) chái dâi ใช้ได้

 how long is it valid for?
 chái dâi těung mêu-a rài?
 ใช้ได้ถึงเมื่อไร

valley hòop kǎo หุบเขา

valuable (adj) mee kâh มีค่า

 **can I leave my valuables
 here?** ao kào kŏrng tíng
 wái têe nêe, dâi mái?
 เอาข้าวของทิ้งไว้ที่นี่ได้ไหม

value (noun) kâh ค่า

van rót dtôo รถตู้

vanilla wá-ní-lah วานิลา

 a vanilla ice cream ait kreem
 wá-née-lah

vary: it varies láir-o dtàir
แล้วแต่

vase jair-gun แจกัน

vegetables pùk ผัก

vegetarian (noun) kon mâi gin
néu-a คนไม่กินเนื้อ

vending machine dtôo ตู้

very mâhk มาก

 very little for me
 kŏr nít dee-o tâo-nún
 ขอนิดเดียวเท่านั้น

 I like it very much pǒm
 (chún) chôrp mâhk ผม(ฉัน)
 ชอบมาก

vest (under shirt) sêu-a glâhm
เสื้อกล้าม

via pàhn ผ่าน

video (*noun*: film) wee-dee-o วีดีโอ
(recorder) krêu-ung wee-dee-oh
เครื่องวีดีโอ

Vietnam bpra-tâyt wêe-ut-nahm
ประเทศเวียดนาม

Vietnamese (*adj*) wêe-ut-nahm
เวียดนาม

view wew วิว

village mòo bâhn หมู่บ้าน

vinegar núm sôm น้ำส้ม

visa wee-sâh วีซ่า

visit (*verb*: place) têe-o เที่ยว
(person) yêe-um เยี่ยม

I'd like to visit... pǒm (chún)
yàhk ja bpai têe-o/yêe-um...
ผม(ฉัน)อยากจะไปเที่ยว/
เยี่ยม ...

vital: it's vital that... sǔm-
kun mâhk têe ja dtôrng...
สำคัญมากที่จะต้อง...

vodka word-kâh วอร์ดก้า

voice sěe-ung เสียง

voltage rairng fai fáh แรงไฟฟ้า

vomit ah-jee-un อาเจียน

W

waist ay-o เอว

waistcoat sêu-a gúk เสื้อกั๊ก

wait ror รอ

wait for me ror pǒm (chún)
nòy ná รอผม(ฉัน)หน่อยนะ

don't wait for me mâi
dtôrng ror pǒm (chún) ná
ไม่ต้องรอผม(ฉัน)นะ

can I wait until my wife/
partner gets here? ror jon
pun-ra-yah/fairn mah dâi mái?
รอจนภรรยา/แฟนมาได้ไหม

can you do it while I wait?
pǒm (chún) ror ao dâi mái?
ผม(ฉัน)รอเอาได้ไหม

could you wait here for
me? ror pǒm (chún) têe nêe
dâi mái? รอผม(ฉัน)ที่นี่ได้ไหม

waiter kon sérp คนเสิริฟ

waiter! kOOn krúp (kâ)!
คุณครับ(ค่ะ)

waitress kon sérp คนเสิริฟ

waitress! kOOn krúp (kâ)!
คุณครับ(ค่ะ)

wake: can you wake me up at
5.30? chôo-ay bplòok pǒm
(chún) way-lah dtee hâh krêung
dâi mái? ช่วยปลุกผม(ฉัน)
เวลาตีห้าครึ่งได้ไหม

Wales Wales เวลส์

walk: is it a long walk? dern
glai mái? เดินไกลไหม

it's only a short walk dern
mâi glai เดินไม่ไกล

I'll walk pŏm (chún) dern bpai ผม(ฉัน)เดินไป

I'm going for a walk pŏm (chún) bpai dern lên ผม(ฉัน)ไปเดินเล่น

wall (inside) făh ฝา

(outside) gum-pairng กำแพง

wallet gra-bpăo sa-dtahng กระเป๋าสตางค์

wander: I like just wandering around pŏm (chún) chôrp dern lên rêu-ay bpèu-ay bpai ผม(ฉัน)ชอบเดินเล่นเรื่อยเปื่อยไป

want: I want a... pŏm (chún) ao... ผม(ฉัน)เอา...

I don't want any... pŏm (chún) mâi yàhk dâi... ผม(ฉัน)ไม่อยากได้...

I want to go home pŏm (chún) yàhk ja glùp bâhn ผม(ฉัน)อยากจะกลับบ้าน

I don't want to... pŏm (chún) mâi yàhk... ผม(ฉัน)ไม่อยาก ...

he wants to... káo yàhk ja... เขาอยากจะ ...

what do you want? kOOn dtôrng-gahn a-rai? คุณต้องการอะไร

ward (in hospital) hŏr pôo bpòo-ay หอผู้ป่วย

warm rórn ร้อน

I'm so warm pŏm (chún) rórn jung ผม(ฉัน)ร้อนจัง

was: he was káo bpen เขาเป็น

she was káo bpen เขาเป็น

it was (mun) bpen มันเป็น

wash (verb) súk ซัก

(oneself) láhng ล้าง

can you wash these? súk un née hâi nòy dâi mái? ซักอันนี้ให้หน่อยได้ไหม

washer (for bolt etc) wong-wăirn วงแหวน

washhand basin àhng láhng nâh อ่างล้างหน้า

washing machine krêu-ung súk páh เครื่องซักผ้า

washing powder pŏng súk fôrk ผงซักฟอก

washing-up liquid núm yah láhng น้ำยาล้าง

wasp dtairn แตน

watch (wristwatch) nah-li-gah นาฬิกา

will you watch my things for me? chôo-ay fâo kŏrng hâi nòy dâi mái? ช่วยเฝ้าของให้หน่อยได้ไหม

watch out! ra-wung! ระวัง

watch strap săi nah-li-gah สายนาฬิกา

water náhm น้ำ

may I have some water?
kŏr náhm nòy dâi mái?
ขอน้ำหน่อยได้ไหม

waterproof (adj) gun náhm
กันน้ำ

waterskiing sa-gee náhm
สกีน้ำ

wave (in sea) klêun คลื่น

way: it's this way bpai tahng
née ไปทางนี้

it's that way bpai tahng nóhn
ไปทางโน้น

is it a long way to…? bpai
… glai mái? ไป … ไกลไหม

no way! mâi mee tahng!
ไม่มีทาง

DIALOGUE

**could you tell me the way
to…?** chôo-ay bòrk tahng
bpai … hâi nòy, dâi mái?

**go straight on until you
reach the traffic lights**
dern dtrong bpai jon tĕung
fai sŭn-yahn

turn left lée-o sái

take the first on the right
lée-o kwăh têe tahng yâirk
un râirk

see **where**

we rao เรา

weak (person, drink) òrn-air
อ่อนแอ

weather ah-gàht อากาศ

website wép-sái เว็บไซต์

wedding pi-tee dtàirng ngahn
พิธีแต่งงาน

wedding ring wăirn dtàirng
ngahn แหวนแต่งงาน

Wednesday wun póot วันพุธ

week ah-tít อาทิตย์

a week (from) today èek
ah-tít nèung jàhk wun née bpai
อีกอาทิตย์หนึ่งจากวันนี้ไป

a week (from) tomorrow
èek ah-tít nèung jàhk
prôong née bpai
อีกอาทิตย์หนึ่งจากพรุ่งนี้ไป

weekend wun săo wun ah-tít
วันเสาร์วันอาทิตย์

at the weekend wun săo
ah-tít วันเสาร์อาทิตย์

weight núm-nùk น้ำหนัก

weird bplàirk แปลก

weirdo kon bplàirk คนแปลก

welcome: welcome to… kŏr
dtôrn rúp… ขอต้อนรับ…

you're welcome (don't mention
it) mâi bpen rai ไม่เป็นไร

well: I don't feel well pŏm
(chún) róo-sèuk mâi kôy sa-bai
ผม(ฉัน)รู้สึกไม่ค่อยสบาย

she's not well káo mâi sa-bai
เขาไม่สบาย

you speak English very well kOOn pôot pah-sǎh ung-grìt dâi dee mâhk
คุณพูดภาษาอังกฤษได้ดีมาก

well done! dee mâhk! ดีมาก

this one as well un née dôo-ay อันนี้ด้วย

well well! (surprise) mǎir! แหม

how are you? bpen yung-ngai bâhng?

very well, thanks, and you? sa-bai dee kòrp-kOOn, láir-o kOOn lâ?

well-done (meat) sÒOk sÒOk สุก ๆ

Welsh: I'm Welsh pǒm (chún) bpen kon Wales ผม(ฉัน) เป็นคนเวลส์

were: we were rao bpen เราเป็น

you were kOOn bpen คุณเป็น

they were káo bpen เขาเป็น

west dta-wun dtòk ตะวันตก

in the west dta-wun dtòk ตะวันตก

West Indian (*adj*) mah jàhk mòo gòr in-dee-a dta-wun dtòk มาจากหมู่เกาะอินเดียตะวันตก

wet bpèe-uk เปียก

what? a-rai? อะไร

what's that? nûn a-rai? นี่นอะไร

what should I do? ja tum yung-ngai dee? จะทำอย่างไรดี

what a view! wew sŏo-ay jung ler-ee! วิวสวยจังเลย

what bus do I take? kêun rót may săi năi? ขึ้นรถเมล์สายไหน

wheel lór ล้อ

wheelchair rót kĕn sŭm-rùp kon bpòo-ay รถเข็นสำหรับคนป่วย

when? mêu-rai? เมื่อไร

when we get back mêu-a rao glùp mah/bpai เมื่อเรากลับมา/ไป

when's the train/ferry? rót fai/reu-a òrk gèe mohng? รถไฟ/เรือออกกี่โมง

where? têe-năi? ที่ไหน

I don't know where it is pŏm (chún) mâi sâhp wâh yòo têe-năi ผม(ฉัน) ไม่ทราบว่าอยู่ที่ไหน

where is the temple? wút yòo têe năi?

it's over there yòo têe-nóhn

could you show me where it is on the map? chôo-ay chée hâi hĕn wâh yòo têe năi nai păirn-têe

it's just here yòo dtrong née

see **way**

which: which bus? rót may săi năi? รถเมล์สายไหน

which one? un năi?

that one un nún

this one? un née, châi mái?

no, that one mâi châi un nún

while: while I'm here ka-nà têe pŏm (chún) yòo têe nêe ขณะที่ผม(ฉัน)อยู่ที่นี่

whisky lâo wít-sa-gêe เหล้าวิสกี้

white sĕe kăo สีขาว

white wine lâo wai kăo เหล้าไวน์ขาว

who? krai? ใคร

who is it? nún krai lâ? นั่นใครล่ะ

the man who... kon têe... คนที่...

whole: the whole week dta-lòrt ah-tít ตลอดอาทิตย์

the whole lot túng mòt ทั้งหมด

whose: whose is this? née kŏrng krai? นี่ของใคร

why? tum-mai? ทำไม

wide gwâhng กว้าง

wife: my wife pun-ra-yah kŏrng pŏm ภรรยาของผม

Wi-Fi wai-fai วายฟาย

will: will you do it for me? chôo-ay tum hâi nòy dâi mái?

ช่วยทำให้หน่อยได้ไหม

wind (*noun*) lom ลม

window nâh-dtàhng หน้าต่าง

   near the window glâi nâh-dtàhng ใกล้หน้าต่าง

   in the window (of shop) têe nâh-dtàhng ที่หน้าต่าง

window seat têe nûng dtìt nâh-dtàhng ที่นั่งติดหน้าต่าง

windscreen gra-jòk nâh rót yon กระจกหน้ารถยนต์

windscreen wiper têe bpùt núm fŏn ที่ปัดน้ำฝน

windsurfing gahn lên gra-dahn dtôh lom การเล่นกระดานโต้ลม

windy: it's so windy lom rairng jung ลมแรงจัง

wine wai ไวน์

   can we have some more wine? kŏr wai èek dâi mái? ขอไวน์อีกได้ไหม

wine list rai-gahn wai รายการไวน์

winter nâh nǎo หน้าหนาว

   in the winter nai nâh nǎo ในหน้าหนาว

wire lôo-ut ลวด

   (electric) sǎi fai fáh สายไฟฟ้า

wish: best wishes dôo-ay kwahm bprah-ta-nǎh dee ด้วยความปรารถนาดี

with gùp กับ

   I'm staying with... pŏm (chún) púk yòo gùp... ผม(ฉัน)พักอยู่กับ...

without doy-ee mâi โดยไม่

witness pa-yahn พยาน

   will you be a witness for me? chôo-ay bpen pa-yahn hâi pŏm (chún) dâi mái? ช่วยเป็นพยานให้ผม(ฉัน)ได้ไหม

woman pôo-yĭng ผู้หญิง

wonderful yôrt yêe-um ยอดเยี่ยม

won't: it won't start mâi yorm dtìt ไม่ยอมติด

wood (material) mái ไม้

woods (forest) bpàh ป่า

wool kŏn sùt ขนสัตว์

word kum คำ

work (*noun*) ngahn งาน

   it's not working mun sĕe-a มันเสีย

   I work in... pŏm (chún) tum ngahn têe … ผม(ฉัน)ทำงานที่ …

world lôhk โลก

worry: I'm worried pŏm (chún) bpen hòo-ung ผม(ฉัน)เป็นห่วง

worse: it's worse yâir gwàh แย่กว่า

worst yâir têe sòot แย่ที่สุด

worth: is it worth a visit? nâh têe-o mái? น่าเที่ยวไหม

would: would you give this to...? chôo-ay ao nêe bpai hâi... dâi mái? ช่วยเอานี่ไปให้ ... ได้ไหม

wrap: could you wrap it up? chôo-ay hòr hâi nòy, dâi mái? ช่วยห่อให้หน่อยได้ไหม

wrapping paper gra-dàht hòr kŏrng kwǔn กระดาษห่อของขวัญ

wrist kôr meu ข้อมือ

write kěe-un เขียน

could you write it down? hôo-ay kěe-un long hâi nòy, dâi mái? ช่วยเขียนลงให้หน่อยได้ไหม

how do you write it? kěe-un yung-ngai? เขียนอย่างไร

writing paper gra-dàht kěe-un jòt-mǎi กระดาษเขียนจดหมาย

wrong: it's the wrong key gOOn-jair pìt กุญแจผิด

this is the wrong train rót fai pìt ka-boo-un รถไฟผิดขบวน

the bill's wrong kít bin pìt คิดบิลผิด

sorry, wrong number kŏr-tôht dtòr ber pìt ขอโทษ ต่อเบอร์ผิด

sorry, wrong room kŏr-tôht, pìt hôrng ขอโทษ ผิดห้อง

there's something wrong with... ...mee a-rai pìt ...มีอะไรผิด

what's wrong? bpen a-rai? เป็นอะไร

X

X-ray 'X-ray' เอ็กซ์เรย์

Y

yacht reu-a yórt เรือยอชท์

yard

year bpee ปี

yellow sěe lěu-ung สีเหลือง

yes krúp (kâ); châi ครับ(ค่ะ); ใช่

yesterday mêu-a wahn née เมื่อวานนี้

yesterday morning cháo wahn née เช้าวานนี้

the day before yesterday wun seun née วันซืนนี้

yet yung ยัง

is it here yet? mah láir-o rěu yung?

no, not yet yung

you'll have to wait a little longer yet koOn dtôrng koy èek sùk nòy

yoghurt yoh-gut โยกัด

you koOn คุณ

this is for you nêe sǔm-rùp koOn นี่สำหรับคุณ

with you gùp koOn กับคุณ

young (*male*) nòOm หนุ่ม

(*female*) sǎo สาว

young (child) dèk lék เด็กเล็ก

your kǒrng koOn ของคุณ

your camera glôrng tài rôop kǒrng koOn กล้องถ่ายรูปของคุณ

yours kǒrng koOn ของคุณ

Z

zero sǒon ศูนย์

zip sìp ซิป

could you put a new zip on? chôo-ay sài sìp mài dâi mái? ช่วยใส่ซิบใหม่ได้ไหม

zip code ra-hùt bprai-sa-nee รหัสไปรษณีย์

zoo sǒo-un sùt สวนสัตว์

THAI

→ ENGLISH

Entries are listed alphabetically according to the first complete word, for example, entries beginning with **bâhn** precede those beginning with **bahng**.

Colloquialisms

You might well hear the following expressions but you shouldn't be tempted to use any of the stronger ones – local people will not be amused or impressed by your efforts.

âi hàh! shit!

bpai (hâi pón)! go away!

bpai nǎi! hi!

chìp-hǎi! damn!

dtai hàh! oh hell!

dtai jing! oh no!

mâi chêu-a! come on!, I don't believe you!

mâi mee tahng! no chance!, no way!

mǎir! goodness!

òrk bpai hâi pón! get out!

tôh! good heavens!

yòot pôot ná! shut up!

yôrt! great!

A

ah uncle (younger brother of father); aunt (younger sister of father)

ah-fri-gah Africa; African

ah-gahn klêun hěe-un nausea

ah-gahn ùk-sàyp infection

ah-gàht air; weather

ah-hǎhn meal; food; cuisine; cooking

ah-hǎhn bpen pít food poisoning

ah-hǎhn cháo breakfast

ah-hǎhn glahng wun lunch

ah-hǎhn kao savoury

ah-hǎhn mâi yôy indigestion

ah-hǎhn pí-sàyt speciality

ah-hǎhn yen evening meal; supper; dinner

ah-jahn teacher

ah-kahn building

àhn read

àhng sink, basin

àhng àhp náhm bath

àhng láhng nâh washbasin

àhp dàirt sunbathe

ah-tít week

ah-tít dtòk sunset

ah-tít kêun sunrise

ah-yóo age

    koon ah-yóo tâo-rài? how old are you?

ai cough; shy

âi hàh! shit!

ai-lairn Ireland

ai-lairn něu-a Northern Ireland

air hóht-tet air stewardess

ai-rít Irish

airm amp

àirt @, at sign

airt-pai-rin aspirin

a-lài spare part(s)

a-may-ri-gah America; American (person)

a-may-ri-gun American (*adj*)

a-nah-kót future

a-nóo-săh-wa-ree monument; statue

ao like; want

ào bay

ao ... bpai take; remove

ao jing ao jung serious

ao krúp (kâ) yes please

ao lá! right!, OK!

ao ... mah fetch; bring

ao ... mái? do you want...?

ào tai Gulf of Siam

a-páht-mén flat, apartment

a-rai something
a-rai? what?

a-rai èek something else
a-rai eèk? what else?

a-rai gôr dâi anything

a-rai ná? pardon (me)?, sorry?; excuse me?

a-ròy nice, delicious

àyk-ga-săhn document; leaflet

ay-o waist

ay-see-a Asia

ay-see-a ah-ka-nay South East Asia

B

bâh mad, crazy

bâhn house; home

têe bâhn at home

bâhn tùt bpai nextdoor

bahng thin; some

bâhng a few; some

bahng krúng bahng krao occasionally

bahng tee sometimes; maybe; perhaps

bàht baht (unit of currency)

bàht jèp injured

bàht plăir wound

bàht wít-tĕe pavement, sidewalk

bài afternoon
bài ... mohng ... pm (in the afternoon)
bài née this afternoon
bài prôong née tomorrow afternoon
bài wahn née yesterday afternoon

bai bai ná cheerio, bye

bai báirng banknote, (US) bill

bai bplew leaflet

bai bpra-gàht kôht-sa-nah poster

bai kùp kèe driving licence

bai kùp kèe săh-gon international driving licence

bai mái leaf

bai mêet gohn razor blade(s)

bai reu-a sail

bai rúp bpra-gun guarantee

bai rúp-rorng guarantee; certificate

bai sèt rúp ngern receipt

bai sùng yah prescription

bai ùn-nóo-yâht licence, permit

bair-dta-rêe battery

bàirk carry

bairn flat (adj)

bàirng share; divide

bàirp sort, kind, type; pattern

bàirp cha-bùp typical

bàirp fa-rùng European-style

bàirp form form

bàirp ree-un pah-sǎh
  language course

bàirp yàhng pattern

bao light (not heavy)

ber toh-ra-sùp phone number

bèu-a bored

bin bill, (US) check; fly (verb)

bòhk rót hitchhike, hitch

boh-rahn ancient

boh-rahn wút-thóo antique

bon on; on top of
  bon péun din on the ground

bòn complain

bóop-fay buffet

boo-rèe cigarette(s)

boo-rèe gôn grorng
  tipped cigarettes

boo-ròot gents' toilet,
  men's room

bòo-uk plus

boo-um swollen

bòrk say; tell

bòrk wâh say

bor-ri-gahn service

bor-ri-gahn ngern dòo-un
  cashpoint, ATM

bor-ri-gahn num têe-o
  excursion

bor-ri-gahn rót châo car rental

bor-ri-gahn rúp chái nai
  hôrng púk room service

bor-ri-gahn sòrp tǎhm
  ber toh-ra-sùp directory
  enquiries

bor-ri-sòot innocent

bor-ri-sùt company, firm

bor-ri-wayn bâhn backyard

bor-ri-wayn chahn meu-ung
  suburb

bòt ree-un lesson

bòy bòy often

bpà-dti-tin calendar

bpâh aunt (elder sister of mother/
  father)

bpàh jungle; forest

bpàh cháh cemetery

bpàh dong dìp forest, jungle

bpàh mái sùk teak forest

bpah-gee-sa-tǎhn Pakistan

bpàhk mouth

bpàhk-gah pen

bpàhk-gah lôok lêun
  ballpoint pen

bpai to; go; go away
  bpai (hâi pón)! go away!
  bpai tèr let's go

bpâi label

bpai glùp wun dee-o day trip

bpai gùp pǒm (chún)
  come with me

bpai nǎi! hi!

bpâi rót may bus stop

bpai séu kǒrng go shopping

bpâi ta-bee-un rót
  licence plates

bpâirng powder; face powder; talcum powder

bpàirt eight

bpan-hăh sĭn-chêu credit crunch

bpa-rin-yah degree

bpây lŭng rucksack

bpee year

   bpee têe láir-o last year; a year ago

bpee mài New Year

bpèek wing

bpèe-uk wet

bpen be; is; in; can; be capable of

   bpen... it is...; it was...

   bpen a-rai? what's up?, what's wrong?

bpen bâi dumb (can't speak)

bpen bpai dâi possible

bpen bpai mâi dâi impossible

bpen bpra-yòht beneficial

bpen gun ayng informal

bpen hòo-ung worry

bpen ìt-sa-rá independent

bpen ka-nòp-tum nee-um traditional

bpen lom faint (verb); stroke; attack

bpen mun greasy

bpen nêe bOOn-kOOn grateful

bpen nern hilly

bpen pèun heat rash

bpen pêu-un friendly

bpen pít poisonous; polluted

bpen sai sandy

bpen sòht single, unmarried

bpen tahng gahn formal

bpen têe nâh por jai satisfactory

bpen têe nee-yom popular

bpen yung-ngai bâhng? how are you?

bper-sen per cent

bpèrt open (adj); on

bpèt duck

bpeun gun

bpeun pók pistol

bpeun yao rifle

bpìt close, shut; closed

bplah fish

bplah cha-lăhm shark

bplah-sa-dter plaster, Elastoplast, Bandaid

bplah-sa-dtìk plastic

bplair interpret; translate

bplàirk strange, odd, funny, weird

bplàirk bpra-làht strange

bplay cot

bplèe-un change

   bplèe-un rót fai change trains

bpleu-ay naked

bplòrk condom

bplòrk mŏrn pillow case

bplòrt-pai safe

bplúk plug; adaptor

bplúk fai power point

bplúk krêu-ung gohn nòo-ut shaving point

bpoh-sa-dter poster

bpóht-gáht postcard

bpoo crab

bpòo grandfather (paternal)

bpòOm dtìt krêu-ung ignition

bpòOm sa-dtàht starter (of car)

bpòo-ut it aches

bpòo-ut fun toothache

bpòo-ut hŏo-a headache; hangover

bpòo-ut lŭng backache

bpòo-ut tórng stomach ache

bpòrt lungs; nervous

bpra-chah-chon public; population

bpra-chOOm meeting

> **Travel tip** Thais use the *wai* as a greeting and to acknowledge respect, gratitude or apology. A prayer-like gesture made with raised hands, the "stranger's" *wai* requires that your hands be raised close to your chest with your fingertips just below your chin. If someone makes a *wai* at you, you should *wai* back, but it's safer not to initiate.

---

bpra-chót sarcastic

bpra-dtoo door; gate; goal

bpra-gun insurance

bprah-sàht castle

bprairng brush

bprairng pŏm hairbrush

bprairng sĕe fun toothbrush

bprairng tah kreem gohn nòo-ut shaving brush

bprairng tŏo lép nailbrush

bprai-sa-nee post office; mail

bprai-sa-nee dòo-un express mail

bprai-sa-nee glahng central post office

bpra-jum deu-un period (menstruation)

bpra-làht jai suprised

bpra-mahn roughly, about, approximately

bpra-pay-nee custom

bpra-tahn director, president (of company)

bpra-tah-nah-tí-bor-dee president (of country)

bpra-tâyt country

bpra-tâyt bayl-yee-um Belgium

bpra-tâyt fa-rùng-sàyt France

bpra-tâyt fi-líp-bpin Philippines

bpra-tâyt gao-lĕe Korea

bpra-tâyt gum-poo-chah Cambodia

bpra-tâyt hor-lairn Holland

bpra-tâyt ì-dtah-lee Italy

bpra-tâyt in-dee-a India

bpra-tâyt in-don-nee-see-a Indonesia

bpra-tâyt jeen China

bpra-tâyt kairn-nah-dah Canada

bpra-tâyt lao Laos

bpra-tâyt mah-lay-see-a Malaysia

bpra-tâyt new see-láirn New Zealand

bpra-tâyt pa-mâh Burma

bpra-tâyt sa-bpayn Spain

bpra-tâyt sa-górt-lairn Scotland

bpra-tâyt tai Thailand (formal)

bpra-tâyt ung-grìt England; Britain

bpra-tâyt wêe-ut-nahm Vietnam

bpra-tâyt yêe-bpÒOn Japan

bpra-tâyt yer-ra-mun Germany

bpra-wùt-sàht history

bprêe-o sour; sharp (taste)

bprèe-up têe-up compare

bpròht favourite

bpròrt thermometer

bpúm núm mun petrol station, gas station

bpun-hăh problem; trouble

bpùt-joo-bun-née nowadays

brayk meu handbrake

bum-nahn pension

bun-dai ladder; stairs

bun-dai lêu-un escalator

bun-dai sŭm-rùp nĕe fai fire escape

bung-ern quite by chance

bun-yai describe

bùt bpra-jum dtoo-a identity card

bùt chern invitation

bùt kray-dìt credit card

bùt têe-nûng boarding pass

C

cháh late; slow; slowly

cháh cháh slowly

chahm dish, bowl

chahn chah-lah platform, (US) track

chahn meu-ung outskirts

cháhng elephant

châhng bpra-bpah plumber

châhng dtùt pŏm hairdresser; barber

châhng dtùt sêu-a pâh tailor

châhng fai fáh electrician

châhng ngern silversmith

châhng tài rôop photographer

châhng torng goldsmith

chai man; male

chái use

chái dâi valid

chai dairn border

chai hàht beach

châi láir-o that's it, that's right

châi láir-o! exactly!

châi mái? isn't it?

chái ngern spend

chái … rôo-um gun share

chai ta-lay seaside; coast

châir kăirng deep-freeze; frozen

cha-làht clever, intelligent

cha-ná win

châo rent, hire

cháo morning

cháo née this morning

cháo prÔOng née tomorrow morning

cháo wahn née yesterday morning

chao bâhn villager

chao dtàhng bpra-tâyt

foreigner
chao kǎo hill tribe
chao nah rice farmer
chao yóo-rôhp European
chèet yah injection
chee-wít life
chék cheque, (US) check
chék dern tahng traveller's cheque
chék doo check (*verb*)
chên for example
chern choo-un invite
chern gòrn after you
chern kâo mah! come in!
chern krúp (kâ)... please...
cherng kǎo hillside
chêu first name
   kOOn chêu a-rai?
   what's your name?
chêu lên nickname
chêu-a believe
chéu-a châht race (ethnic)
chéun humid; damp

chêu-uk rope; string
chêu-uk rorng táo shoelaces
chim taste
chín piece
   chín yài a big bit
chìp-hǎi! damn!
chôhk luck
chôhk dee fortunately; good luck!
chôhk rái unfortunately; hard luck!
chon glÒom nói ethnic minority
chon-na-bòt countryside
choo chêep lifebelt
chôo-a krao temporary
chôo-a mohng hour
chôo-a rá-yá period (of time)
chôo-ay help
   chôo-ay...? please...?, would you please...?
   chôo-ay dôo-ay! help!
chÒOk chěrn emergency
chÒOk-la-hòok hectic

chóot suit

chóot ah-hǎhn course (of meal)

chóot àhp náhm
swimming costume

chóot bpa-thǒm pa-yah-bahn
first-aid kit

chóot fun tee-um false teeth

chóot norn nightdress

chórk shock-absorber

chórn spoon

chórn sôrm cutlery

chôrng lane (on motorway)

chôrng kâo gate

chôrng kǎo mountain pass

chôrp like

chôrp … mâhk gwàh prefer

chun steep

chún I; me; myself (said by a woman); floor, storey

chún nèung first class; ground floor, (US) first floor

chún sǎhm third class; second floor, (US) third floor

chún sǒrng second class; first floor, (US) second floor

D

dâhm handle

dahw-lòht download

dâi get, obtain; may; might; be able

dâi glìn smell

… dâi mái? can I/you… ?

dâi yin hear

dàirt òrk sunny; sunshine

dao star

dee good; fine; nice

dee! good!

dee gwàh better

dee jai happy; pleased

dee kêun mâhk much better

dee láir-o! good!;
that'll do nicely!

dee mâhk! well done!;
magnificent!

dee têe sòot (the) best

dee wee dee DVD

dee-chún I; me (said by a woman)

dee-o just, only

děe-o soon

děe-o, děe-o just a minute

děe-o gòrn! just a second!

děe-o née now; at present

dèk child; children

dèk chai boy

dèk òrn baby; young child

dèk wai rôOn teenager

dèk yǐng girl

dern walk

dern bpai on foot

dern tahng travel

dern tahng bpai tóo-rá gìt
business trip

dèuk late

dèum drink (verb)

deung pull

deu-un in; month

din earth; land

din-sǒr pencil

dìp raw

dòht dèe-o secluded

don-dtree music

don-dtree péun meu-ung folk music

don-dtree pórp pop music

don-dtree tai derm Thai classical music

doo look (at); watch

doo lair take care of

doo měu-un look, seem; look like

dôo-ay too, also

dôo-ay gun together

dôo-ay kwahm bprah-ta-nah dee with best wishes

dòo-un urgent

dòrk gOO-làhp rose

dòrk-mái flower

doy-ee by

doy-ee rót yon by car

doy-ee cha-pòr especially

doy-ee jay-dta-nah deliberately

doy-ee mâi without

dta-bai (fǒn) lép nailfile

dta-gèe-up chopsticks

dta-gla greedy

dta-gohn shout

dta-grâh basket

dta-grâh ka-yà wastepaper basket

dta-grai scissors

dtah eye; grandfather (maternal)

dtah bòrt blind

dtahm follow

dtahm tum-ma-dah as usual

dtàhng different

dtàhng bpra-tâyt abroad; foreign

dtàhng dtàhng various

dtàhng hàhk separate

dtàhng jung-wùt up-country (outside Bangkok)

dtah-rahng têe-o bin scheduled flight

dtah-rahng way-lah timetable, (US) schedule

dtai die; dead; kidneys (in body)

dtâi south; under, below

dtai hàh! oh hell!

dtai jing! oh no!

dtàir but

dtàir la kon each of them (people)

dtàir la krúng each time

dtàir la un each of them (things)

dtàirk break

dtàirk láir-o broken

dtàirk ngâi fragile

dtâirm score

dtàirng ngahn láir-o married

dta-làht market

dta-làht náhm floating market

dta-làht yen night market

dta-lòk funny, amusing; joke

dta-lòrt throughout; whole

dtao cooker

dtào turtle; tortoise

dtao òp oven

dtao rêet iron

dta-wun dtòk west

dta-wun dtòk chěe-ung dtâi southwest

dta-wun dtòk chěe-ung něu-a northwest

dta-wun òrk east

dta-wun òrk chěe-ung dtâi southeast

dta-wun òrk chěe-ung něu-a northeast

dtee hit

dtêe-a short

dteen bottom (of hill)

dtee-ung bed

dtee-ung dèe-o single bed

dtee-ung kôo twin beds

dtem, dtem láir-o full

dten tent

dtên rum dance

dterm fill

dtèuk block of flats, apartment block

dtèun shallow

dtèun awake; wake up; get up

dtèun-dtên excited; nervous

dtìt stuck

dtìt dtòr contact

dtìt gùp next to

dtó table

dtó jài ngern cash desk, cashier

dtòk miss (bus etc)

dtòk jai shock

dtôn bpahm palm tree

dtôn mái plant; tree

dtôo cupboard, closet; compartment; kiosk

dtôo bprai-sa-nee letterbox, mailbox

dtôo châir kǎirng freezer

dtôo gèp gra-bpǎo locker

dtôo jòt-mǎi letterbox, mailbox

dtôo norn sleeper, sleeping car

dtôo núng-sěu pim newsstand

dtôo toh-ra-sùp phone box, phone booth

dtôo yen fridge; refrigerator

dtǒo-a ticket

dtǒo-a bpai single ticket, one-way ticket

dtǒo-a bpai glùp return ticket, round trip ticket

dtoo-a yàhng example

dtóok-ga-dtah doll

dtoo-lah-kom October

dtôom hǒo earring(s)

dtòr connection

dtòr rah-kah bargain (verb)

dtòr wâh complain

dtorn bài afternoon

dtorn cháo morning

dtorn glahng keun evening; night

dtorn yen late afternoon

dtôrng must; have to

dtôrng-gahn need

dtòy sting (verb)

dtrah brand

dtreung krêe-ut serious

dtrong direct

dtrong dtrong straight

dtrong kâhm opposite

dtrong nâh straight ahead

dtrong née right here, just here

dtrong way-lah on time

dtròòt jeen Chinese New Year

dtròo-ut examine

dtròo-ut chûng núm-nùk check-in

dtròrk lane (off a soi)

dtúk-dtúk tuk-tuk (motorized three-wheeled taxi)

> **Travel tip** Many tuk-tuk drivers earn most of their living through commissions from tourist-oriented shops. The most common scam is for drivers to pretend that the sight you intended to visit is closed for the day and to offer to take you on a city tour instead. The easiest way to avoid this is to take a metered taxi, but if you're set on taking a tuk-tuk, ignore any that are parked up or loitering and be firm about where you want to go.

dtùm low
dtùm gwàh under, less than
dtum-ròo-ut police; policeman
dtun blocked
dtûng-dtàir since (time)
dtùp liver
dtùp ùk-sàyp hepatitis
dtùt cut
dtùt fai power cut
dtùt pǒm haircut
dum dark (*adj*)
dum náhm dive
dung loud

E

èek more; again
èek bpra-děe-o in a minute
èek kon nèung the other one (person)

èek mâhk a lot more
èek ... nèung another... ; the other...
èek un nèung the other one (thing)
ee-mayl email
èun other; others; another

F

fáh sky
fǎh wall; lid
fah-ee file
fáh lâirp lightning
fáh rórng thunder
fai fire; light
fâi cotton
fai chǎi torch, flashlight
fai cháirk cigarette lighter
fai fáh electric; electricity
fai kâhng sidelights
fai krêu-ung yon ignition
fai lée-o indicator
fai lǔng rót rear lights
fai mâl fire (blaze)
   fai mâi! fire!, it's on fire!
fai mòrk fog lights
fai nâh rót headlights
fairn boyfriend; girlfriend; partner
fàirt twins
fa-rùng European; Caucasian; Westerner; foreigner
fa-rùng-sàyt France; French
feem film (for camera); negative
feem sěe colour film

fláirt flat, apartment; flash
fók-chúm bruise
fǒn rain
  fǒn dtòk it's raining
fǒong kon crowd
fóot-born football
for-mairt em pee sǎhm
  MP3 format
fùk boo-a shower
fun tooth
fung listen (to)
  fung si! listen!
fùng shore; bank
... fùng dtrong kâhm
  across the...

G

gah núm chah teapot
gahn bpa-tǒm pa-yah-bahn
  first aid
gahn bplair translation
gahn bpra-gun pai insurance
gahn chók dtòy fight
gahn dern tahng journey; travel
gahn dtai death
gahn dtôrn rúp kùp sôo
  hospitality
gahn dum náhm léuk
  skin-diving
gahn fórn rum péun meu-ung
  folk dancing
gahn jùp bplah fishing

gahn kàirng kǔn match; race
gahn lót rah-kah reduction
gahn meu-ung politics
gahn pàh dtùt operation
gahn rôo-um bpra-way-nee sex
gahn sa-dairng don-dtree concert
gahn sòrp exam
gahn sùng ngót cancellation
gahn ta-hǎhn military
gahn wâi náhm swimming
gahng-gayng trousers, (US) pants
gahng-gayng kǎh sûn shorts
gahng-gayng nai underpants, underwear
gahng-gayng nai sa-dtree pants, panties
gahng-gayng wâi náhm swimming trunks
gahng-gayng yeen jeans
gàir strong; dark; old
gâir hòr unpack
gâirm cheek (on face)
gâir-o glass
gáirt gas
gao glue; scratch
gào old
gâo nine
gâo êe chair
gâo êe pâh bai deckchair
gâo êe rúp kàirk sofa
gâo êe sǒong highchair
ga-rúk-ga-dah-kom July
ga-see-un retired

gǎy gǎi smart
gáyt háot guesthouse

> **Travel tip** At the busiest times of year, the best-known guesthouses in popular tourist centres are often full night after night. Some will take bookings via their websites, but for those that don't it's usually a question of turning up and waiting for a vacancy. At most guesthouses, checkout time is either 11a.m. or noon.

gèe? how many?
  gèe mohng láir-o? what time is it?
gee-a tǒy lǔng reverse gear
gee-lah sport
gee-lah náhm water sports
gèng well
... gern bpai too...
gèrt kêun happen
  gèrt a-rai kêun? what's happening?
gèu-up nearly, almost
gin dâi edible
gin (kâo) eat
gin yòo prórm full board
glâh hǎhn brave
glahng medium; middle
glahng jâirng outdoors
glahng keun night; overnight
glahng meu-ung central
glai far (away)
  glai gwàh farther (than)

glâi near; near here

  ... têe glâi têe sòot
  the nearest...

glèe-ut hate

gler pal, mate

glom round

gloo-a afraid; fear

glòom group

glòom jai depressed

glòom kon party, group

glòrng carton

glòrng gee-a gearbox

glôrng tài nǔng movie camera

glôrng tài pâhp-pa-yon
  camcorder

glôrng tài rôop camera

**glôrng yah sên, glôrng yah
  sòop** pipe (for smoking)

glùp get back

glùp bâhn go home

glùp bpai go back

glùp mah come back

  glùp mah nêe! come back!

goh-hòk lie (tell untruth)

gohn shave

goh-roh-goh-sǒh junk, rubbish

gôn bottom (of body)

gôn grorng filter-tipped

gOOm-pah-pun February

gOOn-jair key; lock

gôr then

gòr island

gòr ai-lairn Ireland

gôr měu-un gun too, also

gôr yàhng nún làir so-so

górk náhm tap, faucet

gòrn ago; before

  sǎhm wun gòrn three days ago

**gorng dtum-ròo-ut dùp
  plerng** fire brigade

górp golf

gòt-mǎi law

gra-bpǎo bag; briefcase; luggage,
  baggage; pocket

gra-bpǎo dern tahng suitcase;
  baggage

gra-bpǎo kwâi lǔng backpack

gra-bpǎo sa-dtahng purse;
  wallet, billfold

gra-bpǎo těu handbag, (US)
  purse; hand luggage, hand
  baggage

gra-bpǒrng can, tin

gra-bprohng skirt

gra-bprohng rót bonnet (of car),
  (US) hood

gra-bprohng tái (rót) boot (of
  car), (US) trunk

gra-dàht paper

**gra-dàht chét meu, gra-dàht
  chét nâh** paper handkerchiefs,
  Kleenex

gra-dàht chum-rá toilet paper

gra-dàht hòr kǒrng kwǔn
  wrapping paper

gra-dàht kěe-un jòt-mǎi
  writing paper

gra-dìng bell

gra-dòok bone

gra-dòok hùk fracture

gra-dOOm button

gra-dtìk náhm vacuum flask

gra-jòk nâh rót yon

windscreen

gra-jòk ngao mirror
gra-ter-ee gay, homosexual
grìng bell
gròht angry
grom dtròo-ut kon kâo meu-ung Immigration Department
grOOng-tâyp Bangkok
grum gramme
gum-lai meu bracelet
...gum-lung pôot speaking
gum-pairng wall
gun chon bumper, (US) fender
gun-chah marijuana
gun-grai scissors
gun-yah-yon September
gùp with
gùp kâo dish; meal
gùt insect bite
gwàh than; more; over, more than
gwâhng wide

H

hâh five
hǎh look for
hǎh yâhk rare
hâhm prohibited, forbidden; prohibit
hâhm sòop bOO-rèe non-smoking
hâhng department store
hàhng glai remote
hâhng kǎi yah pharmacy

> **Travel tip** Thai pharmacies are typically open daily between 8.30 a.m. and 8 p.m. They are well-stocked with local and international branded medicines and are nearly all run by trained English-speaking pharmacists, who are usually the best people to talk to if your symptoms aren't acute enough to warrant seeing a doctor.

hàht beach
hâi give; for
hǎi lose
hǎi bpai disappear
hâi châo for hire, to rent
hǎir fishing net
hâirng dry
hàirng châht national
hǎi-ya-ná disaster
hàyt cause
hèep box
hěn see
hěn dôo-ay agree
hěw hungry
hêw carry
hěw kâo hungry
hěw náhm thirsty
hi-má snow
hǐn stone, rock
hîng shelf
hòk six
hǒo ear
hǒo nòo-uk deaf
hǒo-a head; corner
hǒo-a jai heart

hŏo-a jai wai heart attack
hŏo-a kào knee
hŏo-a láhn bald
hŏo-a mOOm corner
hŏo-a nom lòrk dummy
hŏo-a rór laugh
hŏo-a tee-un spark plug
hòop kăo valley
hòr package, parcel
hŏr sa-mòot library
hôrng room
hôrng ah-hăhn dining room
hôrng air air-conditioned room
hôrng bprùp ah-gàht air-conditioned room
hôrng dèe-o single room
hôrng kôo twin-bedded room
hôrng kórk-tayn cocktail bar
hôrng kroo-a kitchen
hôrng náhm bathroom; toilet, restroom
hôrng náhm pôo-chai gents' toilet, men's room
hôrng náhm pôo-yĭng ladies' toilet, ladies' room
hôrng náhm sòo-un dtoo-a private bathroom
hôrng norn bedroom
hôrng pôo doy-ee săhn kăh òrk departure lounge
hôrng púk waiting room
hôrng rúp kàirk living room
hôrng rúp-bpra-tahn ah-hăhn dining room
hôrng sa-mòot library
hôrng tŏhng lounge

hŏy shell
hùk break; deduct
hŭn bpai tahng… facing the…
hun-loh hello

I

in-dter-nèt Internet
ì-sa-rá free

J

jàhk from
jàhk … bpai … from… to…
jàhk bpai leave, go away
jàhk meu-ung 'Wales' Welsh
jahn dish; plate
jahn rorng tôo-ay saucer
jahn sĕe-ung record
jài pay
jai dee kind, generous
jai glahng meu-ung city centre
jair-gun vase
jàirm săi pleasant
ja-mòok nose
jâo-bào bridegroom
jâo-fáh chai prince
jâo-fáh yĭng princess
jâo-kŏrng owner
jâo kŏrng bâhn landlord
jâo nai boss
jâo-săo bride
ja-rah-jorn traffic
jay-dee pagoda
jeen China; Chinese

jèp sore; hurt
jèp bpòo-ut painful
jer find
jèt seven
jing true; real
jing jai sincere
jing jing lěr? honestly?
jîng-jòk lizard
jìt-dta-gum fǎh pa-nǔng murals
jon until; poor
jòop kiss
jòot-mǎi bplai tahng destination
jòp finish, end
jor-jair busy
jorng reservation; reserve
jor-ra-kây crocodile
jòrt park (*verb*)
jòt-mǎi letter; mail
jòt-mǎi ah-gàht aerogramme
jòt-mǎi long ta-bee-un registered letter
jùk-gra-yahn bicycle
jùk-sòo pâlrt optician
jum dâi remember; recognize
jum-bpen necessary
jung ler-ee so
jung-wùt changwat, province
jùp catch; arrest
jùp bplah fishing
jùt arrange; bright; strong
jùt gahn organize

K

kǎh leg
kâh kill; value
kǎh kâo arrival
kâh bor-ri-gahn service charge
kâh bor-ri-gahn pi-sàyt supplement (extra charge)
kâh châo rent
kâh doy-ee sǎhn fare
kâh mút-jum deposit
kǎh òrk departure
kâh pàhn tahng toll
kǎh-gun-grai jaw
kâhm ta-lay crossing
kahng chin
kâhng beside; side
kâhng bon above, over; upstairs
kâhng lâhng downstairs
kâhng lǔng back; behind; rear
kâhng nâh in front (of); at the front
kâhng nai indoors; inside
kâhng nôrk outside
kahng toom mumps
kài egg
kâi temperature, fever; feverish
kǎi sell
kâi gOOn-jair unlock
kâi jùp sùn malaria
kài móok pearl
kâi wùt flu
kàirk Indian; guest
kǎirn arm
kǎirn sêu-a sleeve

kair-nah-dah Canada; Canadian
kăirng solid; hard
kăirng rairng strong
kâirp narrow
ka-măyn Cambodian
ka-moy-ee steal; thief; burglar
ka-nà têe while
ka-nàht size; measurements
ka-nàht glahng medium-sized
ka-nòp-tum-nee-um tradition
káo he; him; she; her; they; them
kâo rice
kăo hill; mountain
kào message; news
kâo bpai go in
kâo jai understand
  kâo jai láir-o I understand
kào-săhn information
ka-yà rubbish, litter, trash
kàyt district
kêe fòon dirt
kêe gèe-ut lazy
kèet sŏong sòot maximum
kĕe-un write
kem salty
kĕm needle
kĕm glùt sêu-a brooch
kĕm kùt belt
kĕm kùt ni-ra-pai seatbelt
kĕm mòot pin
kĕm-tít compass
ker-ee ever
kĕrn embarrassed; embarrassing
keun night; give back
  keun la... ... per night
kêun up

kêun bpai go up
keun née tonight; this evening
keun ngern refund
kêun rót may catch a bus
kew queue, line
kít think
klohn mud
klorng canal
kohm fai (fáh) lamp
koh-ték tampon
kŏhn classical masked drama
kòht hĭn rocky
kom sharp
kŏm bitter
kòm-kĕun rape
kon person; people
kŏn hair (on the body)
kon bâh idiot
kon bpah-gee-sa-tăhn
  a Pakistani; Pakistanis
kon bplàirk nâh stranger
kon châo tenant
kon cha-rah senior citizen
kon dee-o just, only; alone,
  by oneself
kon dern táo pedestrian
kon fâo bpra-dtoo doorman;
  porter
kon fa-rùng-sàyt a French
  person; the French
kon hŏo-a sŏong snob
kon jai yen calm
kon jeen a Chinese person;
  the Chinese
kon jùp bplah fisherman
kon ka-măyn a Cambodian;
  the Cambodians

kon kùp (rót) driver
kon kùp táirk-sêe taxi-driver
kon lao a Lao; the Laos
kon lée-ung doo dèk
child minder
kon mâi gin néu-a vegetarian
kon nâirn crowded
kon new see-láirn a New
Zealander; New Zealanders
kon ngôh fool
kon nún chap
kon pa-mâh a Burmese person;
the Burmese
kon sa-górt a Scot; the Scots
kon sérp waiter; waitress
kon sèrp yǐng waitress
kon sôrm rorng táo
shoe repairer
kǒn sùt wool
kon tai a Thai person; the Thais
kon tèep jùk-ra-yahn cyclist
kon tum ka-nǒm-bpung baker
kon tum kwahm sa-àht maid
kon ung-grìt an English person;
the English; a Briton; the
British
kon yêe-bpòon a Japanese
person; the Japanese
kon yer-ra-mun a German
person; the Germans
kong (ja) probably
kôo pair
kôo meu num têe-o guidebook
kôo meu sǒn-ta-nah
phrasebook
kôo mûn fiancé; fiancée
koo-ee chat

kóok prison
koon you
koon krúp (kâ) excuse me
koon-na-pâhp quality
koo-un ja should
kòo-ut bottle
kor neck; collar
kǒr please
   pǒm (chún) kǒr I would like
kor bpòk sêu-a collar
kôr glào hǎh complaint
kǒr hâi dern tahng doy-
ee bplòrt-pai! have a safe
journey!
kor hǒy throat
kôr meu wrist
kǒr … nòy can I have…?
kǒr rórng request
kǒr sa-dairng kwahm yin dee!
congratulations!
kôr sòrk elbow
kôr táo ankle
kôr tét jing fact
kórn hammer
kórng gong
kǒrng thing; of
kǒrng bplorm fake
kǒrng bpròht favourite
kǒrng fôom feu-ay luxury
kǒrng káo his; her; hers; their;
theirs
kǒrng koon your; yours
kǒrng kwǔn present, gift
kǒrng lên toy
kǒrng pǒm (chún) my; mine
   …kǒrng pǒm (chún) ayng

my own…

kŏrng rao our; ours

kŏrng têe ra-léuk souvenir

kôrn-kâhng ja… rather…

kòrp-kOOn thank; thanks, thank you

  kòrp-kOOn mâhk thank you very much

kŏr-tôht excuse me; sorry; I beg your pardon?

krai somebody

  krai? who?

krai gôr dâi anybody

krao beard

kreem bum-rOOng pĕw moisturizer

kreem gohn nòo-ut shaving foam

kreem nôo-ut pŏm conditioner

kreem rorng péun foundation cream

kreem sa-măhn pĕw cold cream

kreem tah àhp dàirt suntan lotion

kreem tah nŭng dtah eye shadow

krêung half

krêung chôo-a mohng half an hour

krêung lŏh half a dozen

krêu-ung air air-conditioning

krêu-ung bàirp uniform

krêu-ung bin plane, airplane

krêu-ung bpào pŏm hairdryer

krêu-ung bplairng fai fáh adaptor (for voltage)

krêu-ung bpra-dùp ornament

krêu-ung bprùp ah-gàht air-conditioning

krêu-ung bpûn din păo pottery, earthenware

krêu-ung bun-téuk sĕe-ung tape recorder

krêu-ung chái sŏy equipment

krêu-ung cháht toh-ra-sùp phone charger

krêu-ung chôo-ay fung hearing aid

krêu-ung dèum drink

krêu-ung dòot fòon vacuum cleaner

krêu-ung dùp plerng fire extinguisher

krêu-ung gohn nòo-ut shaver

krêu-ung kít lâyk calculator

krêu-ung kOOm gum-nèrt contraceptive

krêu-ung lên pàirn sĕe-ung record player

krêu-ung lên tâyp kah-set cassette player

krêu-ung reu-un furniture

krêu-ung súk pâh washing machine

krêu-ung sŭm-ahng make-up

krêu-ung wee-dee-oh videorecorder

krêu-ung wút OOn-na-ha-poom thermometer

krêu-ung yon motor; engine

krít Protestant

krít-dtung Roman Catholic

krít-sa-maht Christmas

kroo teacher
krôrp-kroo-a family
krúng time
krúng nèung once
krúp (kâ) yes
kum word
kûm dark
kum chern invitation
kum dtòrp answer
kum tǎhm question
kun itch
kûn bun-dai step
kun gee-a gear lever
kun rêng accelerator
kun yôhk lever
kúp tight
kùp drive
kwǎh right (not left)
kwahm bpra-préut behaviour
kwahm bun-terng entertainment
kwahm chéun humidity
kwahm chôo-ay lěu-a help
kwahm dtai death
kwahm dtàirk dtàhng difference
kwahm fǔn dream
kwahm jèp bpòo-ay illness
kwahm jèp bpòo-ut pain
kwahm jing truth
kwahm kâo jai pìt misunderstanding
kwahm kít idea
kwahm lúp secret
kwahm ngêe-up silence
kwahm pìt fault; mistake

kwahm ray-o speed
kwahm rórn heat
kwahm rúk love
kwahm sǒong height
kwâhng throw
kwai water buffalo
kwûm upside down
kwun smoke

L

lah gòrn bye
láh sa-mǎi old-fashioned
lâhm interpreter
lǎhn chai grandson; nephew
lǎhn sǎo niece; granddaughter
láhng wash; develop (film)
lǎi several
lâi shoulder
lai sen signature
láir and
lâirk bplèe-un exchange (verb: money)
... láir-o already
láir-o dtàir it depends (on); it's up to you
láirp-tòrp laptop
la-korn play
lâo alcohol
lay-kǎh-nóo-gahn secretary
layn glôrng lens (of camera)
lée-o kwǎh turn right
lée-o sái turn left
lèe-um sǒong cheeky
lék small, little, tiny**

lèk iron
lék nóy only a few
lên play
lép meu fingernail
ler-ee bpai further; beyond
  ler-ee bpai èek further on
lěu-a gern jing jing shocking
léuk deep
leum forget
lêun slippery
lêu-ut blood
líf lift, elevator
likay popular folk theatre

> **Travel tip** The most
> spectacular form of traditional
> Thai theatre is *khon*, a
> stylized drama performed
> by highly trained classical
> dancers wearing masks and
> elaborate costumes. You can
> see it performed with English
> subtitles at Bangkok's Sala
> Chalermkrung, and it also
> features in the various cultural
> shows staged for tourists in
> Bangkok, Phuket and Pattaya.

lín tongue
lít litre
lŏh dozen
loh-hà metal
loh-hà sŭm-rít bronze
lôhk world; earth
lom wind
lom òrn òrn breeze
long get off
long bpai go down

long bpai! get down!
long mah! get down!
long ta-bee-un register
lôok child; children (one's own)
lôok born ball
lôok bpùt beads
lôok chai son
lôok gwàht sweets, candies
lôok kěr-ee son-in-law
lôok ra-bèrt bomb
lôok sǎo daughter
lôok sa-pâi daughter-in-law
loong uncle (older brother of father or mother)
lôo-ung nâh in advance
lóp minus
lòr good-looking
lór wheel
lorng try; try out, test
lòrt fai fáh lightbulb
lum-tahn stream
lǔng after; back (of body)
lǔng jàhk nún then, after that
lǔng-kah roof

M

mah come
mǎh dog
máh horse
mah gèp... collect
máh glàirp pony
mah nêe come here
mah těung arrive

ma-hăh-wít-ta-yah-lai
university

mah-dtra-tăhn standard

mâhk a lot, lots; many; much;
very; very much

… mâhk plenty of…

mâhk (gern) bpai too much;
excessive

màhk fa-rùng chewing gum

mâhk lĕu-a gern extremely

mâhk por sŏm-koo-un
quite a lot

màhk róok chess

mâhn curtain

mai mile

măi silk

mái wood

mài new

mâi no; not

mâi ao… no…

mâi (ao) … èek no
more…

mâi ao năi poor (quality);
disgusting

mâi bòy seldom

mâi bpen rai don't mention it;
it doesn't matter; never mind;
that's all right

mâi bpen rêu-ung nonsense

mâi chêu-a! come on!, I don't
believe you!

mâi dàirt sunburn

mâi dee bad

mái dtee racket (tennis)

mâi dtông sĕe-a pah-sĕe
duty-free goods

mâi gin néu-a vegetarian

mái gwàht brush

mâi jing false

mâi jum-gùt ra-ya tahng
unlimited mileage

mái kèet match

mâi ker-ee never

mâi kôy hardly

mâi lay-o it's not bad

mâi ler-ee not in the least

mâi mâhk not a lot, not much

mâi mâhk gwàh…
no more than…

mâi mâhk tâo-rài
not so much

mâi mao sober

mâi mee… there isn't/aren't…;
no…

mâi mee a-rai nothing

mâi mee bpra-sìt-ti-pâhp
inefficient

mâi mee krai nobody, no-one

mâi mee lôo-ut lai plain

mâi mee mah-ra-yâht rude

mâi mee tahng! no chance!,
no way!

mâi nâh chêu-a amazing

mái nèep (pâh) clothes peg

mái pài bamboo

mâi pèt mild

mâi rêe-up bumpy

mâi rôrk! certainly not!

mâi sài without

mái sùk teak

mâi tĕung... less than...
mâi wâhng engaged, occupied
măi-lâyk number, figure
măir! well well!
máir dtàir... even the...
mâir (kŏrng) mother
mâir mái widow
mâir náhm river
máir wâh although
  máir wâh... even if...
mâir-náhm kŏhng
  Mekhong River
mairng ga-prOOn jellyfish
mair-o cat
ma-lairng insect
ma-lairng gùt insect bite

ma-lairng sàhp cockroach
ma-lairng wun fly
mao drunk
ma-reun-née the day after
  tomorrow
mâyk kréum cloudy
may-săh-yon April
máyt metre
mee have
  mee... there is/are...
  mee... mái? have you got...?;
  is/are there...?
mee bpra-sìt-ti-pâhp efficient
mee bpra-yòht useful
mee chee-wít chee-wah lively
mee chee-wít yòo alive
mee chêu sěe-ung famous
mee fùk boo-a with shower
mee hàyt-pŏn sensible
mee kâh valuable
mee kwahm pìt guilty
mee lom òrn òrn breezy
mee-nah-kom March
mee pĕw klúm dàirt suntanned
mee sa-này charming
mee sòOk-ka-pâhp dee
  healthy
mee tórng pregnant
mêet knife
mêet gohn razor
mêet púp penknife
mem-moh-rêe sa-dtík
  memory stick
měn smell, stink

meu hand

mêu-a gòrn née once, formerly

mêu-a keun née last night

mêu-a rài? when?

mêu-a ray-o ray-o née lately, recently

mêu-a wahn née yesterday

měu-un similar, like

měu-un gun same

meu-ung city; town; country

meu-ung boh-rahn Ancient City

meu-ung gào old town

meu-ung lǒo-ung capital city

meu-ung tai Thailand (informal)

mí-cha-nún otherwise

mí-tOO-nah-yon June

mók-ga-rah-kom January

mǒo pig

moo-ay (sǎh-gon) boxing (international)

moo-ay tai Thai-style boxing

> **Travel tip** The best place to see Thai boxing is at one of Bangkok's two main stadiums, which between them hold bouts every night of the week. But you'll come across local matches in the provinces too. The sport enjoys a following similar to football in the West and you can be sure that large noisy crowds will gather whenever it's shown on TV.

mòo-bâhn village

mòo-bâhn bon poo-kǎo mountain village

mòo bâhn bpra-mong fishing village

mòo gòr in-dee-a dta-wun dtòk West Indies

môo-lêe blinds

móOng mosquito net

mòo-uk hat; cap

móo-un tâyp kah-set cassette

mǒr doctor

mòr ideal

môr saucepan

mǒr fun dentist

mòr sǒm suitable, appropriate

mòrk mist

mòrk long foggy

mǒrn pillow; cushion

mor-ra-sOOm monsoon

mor-sor scruffy

mòt láir-o empty

mòt sa-dtì unconscious

múk-kOO-tâyt guide, courier

mun it; it is; they; fat (on meat); rich

mun bpen it's

mûn engaged (to be married)

mun fa-rùng tôrt chips, French fries; crisps, (US) chips

mùt flea

N

năh thick

nah paddy field

náh uncle (younger brother of mother); aunt (younger sister of mother)

nâh face; front (part); page; season; next

nâh bèu-a boring

nâh dtèun dtên exciting

nâh fŏn rainy season

nâh glèe-ut ugly; horrible; disgusting

nâh năo winter

nâh nèu-ay nài tiring

nâh òk chest; bust

nâh rórn summer

nâh rung-gèe-ut unpleasant; revolting

nâh sĕe-a dai! what a shame!

nâh sêet pale

nâh sŏn jai interesting

nâh sŏng-săhn! what a pity!

nâh têung impressive

nâh tOO-râyt nasty

nâh-dtàhng window

nah-li-gah clock; watch

nah-li-gah bplòok alarm clock

nah-li-gah kôr meu watch

náhm water

nahm bùt business card

náhm dèum drinking water

nahm sa-gOOn surname, last name

nahm sa-gOOn derm

maiden name

nahn a long time

nahng Mrs

nahng pa-yah-bahn nurse

nahng-săo Miss

nah-tee minute

nah-yók director, president

nah-yók rút-ta-mon-dtree prime minister

nai on; in; into; Mr

năi? which?

nai a-nah-kót in future

nai bpra-tâyt rao at home

nai lŏo-ung king

Travel tip It's a criminal offence to make critical or defamatory remarks about the Thai royal family, and you should be prepared to stop in your tracks if the town, train station or airport you're in plays the national anthem over its PA system (many small towns do this twice a day at 8 a.m. and 6 p.m.).

---

nai ra-wàhng during; among

nai têe sòot eventually, at last

nâir jai certain, sure

nâir norn of course, certainly, definitely

nâirn crowded, busy

năo cold; feel cold

née this; these

nêe... this is...

nêe a-rai? what's this?

nêe kŏrng krai? whose is this?

nêe krúp (kâ) there you are
nêe ngai here you are
nĕe-o sticky; sultry
nék-tai tie, necktie
nĕu-a north
nèu-ay tired
nèung one
nèung nai sèe quarter
néw inch
néw hŏo-a mâir meu thumb
néw meu finger
néw táo toe
ngah cháhng tusk
ngahm sa-ngàh elegant
ngahn job; work; carnival; festival
ngahn lée-ung party
ngahn sa-dairng sĭn-káh trade fair
ngahn sòp funeral
ngâi easy; simple
ngao shadow
ngăo lonely
ngao dàirt sunshade
ngêe-up quiet; silent
ngêe-up ngêe-up nòy! be quiet!
ngern money; silver
ngern bporn sterling
ngern deu-un salary
ngern dorn-lâh dollar
ngern dtàhng bpra-tâyt foreign exchange
ngern rĕe-un coin
ngern sòt cash
ngern típ tip

ngèu-uk gum
ngêu-un kăi bpra-gun insurance policy
ngôh stupid, silly, dumb
ngoo snake
ngoo hào cobra
ngôo-ung norn sleepy
ngót cancel
nîm soft
nít dee-o tâo-nún just a little
ní-tahn story
ní-tá-sa-gahn exhibition
nít-nòy a little bit
nít-ta-ya-săhn magazine
nók bird
nom milk
nŏo mouse; rat
nòom young; young man
nòom nòom săo săo young people
nòo-uk hŏo noisy
nôo-ut massage
nòo-ut moustache
nôrk jàhk apart from
norn lie down
norn lùp sleep
norn lùp yòo asleep
nôrng thigh
nŏrng swamp
nórng chai younger brother
nórng săo younger sister
nórng sa-pái younger sister-in-law
nòy some
nóy few
nóy gwàh... less than...

nóy têe sòot minimum
nùk heavy; serious
núk don-dtree musician
núk moo-ay boxer
núk rórng singer
núk sa-dairng chai actor
núk sa-dairng yǐng actress
núk sèuk-sǎh student
núk tôrng têe-o tourist
núm dtòk waterfall
núm hǒrm perfume
núm kǎirng ice
núm mun oil; petrol, (US) gas
núm mun gáht petrol, (US) gas
núm mun krêu-ung
  oil (motor oil)
núm mun rót dee-sen
  diesel (fuel)
núm mun tah àhp dàirt
  suntan oil

núm nùk weight
núm nùk gern excess baggage
núm póo fountain
núm tôo-um flood
núm yah àhp náhm
  bubble bath
núm yah láhng chahm
  washing-up liquid
nún that
nûn a-rai? what's that?
nûng sit
nǔng leather; film, movie
nǔng glùp suede
nûng si sit down!
núng-sěu book
núng-sěu dern tahng passport
núng-sěu num têe-o
  guidebook
núng-sěu pim newspaper
nút appointment

O

oh-gàht chance, opportunity
ong-sǎh degree
òo sôrm rót garage
oo-bùt-dti-hàyt accident
ôo-ee! ouch!
ÔOm carry
oo-mohng tunnel
oon-na-ha-poom temperature
òop-bpa-gorn equipment
òot fun filling
òot-sǎh-ha-gum industry
ôo-un fat
òrk bpai go out
   òrk bpai hâi pón! get out!
òrk sěe-ung pronounce
òrn weak (drink)
òrn-air weak (person)
orn-lai online

P

pâh material, cloth
pah bpai take
pâh bpòo têe norn sheet; bed linen
pâh chét bpàhk napkin
pâh chét dtoo-a towel
pâh chét jahn tea towel
pâh chét meu napkin, serviette; tissues, Kleenex
pâh chét nâh handkerchief; flannel
pâh hòm blanket

pâh kêe réw cloth, rag
pâh ôrm nappy, diaper

> **Travel tip** Although most Thai babies don't wear them, disposable nappies (diapers) are sold at convenience stores, pharmacies and supermarkets in big resorts and sizeable towns; for stays on lonely islands, consider bringing some washable ones as back-up.

pâh pôhk sěe-sà headscarf
pâh pun kor scarf (for neck)
pâh pun plǎir bandage; dressing
pâh un-nah-mai sanitary towel, sanitary napkin
pâhk region
pâhk bung-kúp compulsory
pâhk dtâi southern region of Thailand
pâhk ee-sǎhn north-eastern region of Thailand
pâhk glahng central region of Thailand
pàhn through; via
pàhn bpai go through
pâhp kěe-un painting; picture
pah-sǎh language
pah-sǎh tai Thai (language)
pah-sǎh tìn dialect
pah-sǎh ung-grìt English (language)
pah-sěe duty; tax
pah-sěe sa-nǎhm bin airport tax

pah-yóo storm

pah-yóo fǒn thunderstorm

pâi cards

páir goat; allergic to

páir dàirt heat stroke

pàirn slice

pàirn sěe-ung record

pairng expensive

pǎirn-têe map

pǎirn-têe ta-nǒn road map, streetmap

pa-mâh Burma; Burmese

pa-nàirk dtôrn rúp reception; reception desk

pa-núk ngahn dtôrn rúp receptionist

pa-núk ngahn krêu-ung bin steward

pa-núk ngahn toh-ra-sùp operator

pa-nun gamble

pa-yah-yahm try; persevere

pay-dahn ceiling

pêe older brother/sister

pêe chai older brother

pêe sǎo older sister

pêe sa-pái older sister-in-law

pêrm increase

pèt hot, spicy

pét diamond

pét ploy jewellery

péun floor

   yòo bon péun on the floor

pèun rash (on skin)

péun din ground

péun rorng táo sole (of shoe)

pêu-un friend

pêu-un bâhn neighbour

pêu-un rôo-um ngahn partner (in business)

pêu-un tahng jòt-mǎi penfriend

pěw skin

pěw klúm dàirt suntan

pěw nǔng skin

pí-gahn disabled

pí-pít-ta-pun museum

pí-pít-ta-pun hàirng châht National Museum

pi-sàyt special; de luxe

pìt wrong; faulty

pìt gòt-mǎi illegal

pìt tum-ma-dah unusual

pìt wǔng disappointed

pi-tee dtàirng ngahn wedding

plǎir bàht jèp injury

plǎir gra-pór ulcer

plǎir mâi burn

plǎir porng blister

plǎir wèr nasty

plǎirng eccentric

playng song

playng póp pop song

plùk push

pǒm I; me; myself (said by a man); hair

pǒng súk fôrk soap powder

pǒn-la-mái fruit

pôo bplair translator

pôo doy-ee sǎhn passenger

pôo-chai boy; man

poo-gèt Phuket

pôo-jùt-gahn manager

poo-kǎo mountain

poo-mi-bpra-tâyt scenery; landscape

pôot speak; talk

pôot èek tee repeat

pôot lên joke

pôo-uk group

pôo-uk née these

pôo-uk nún those

pôo-uk pôo-yǐng women

poo-ung mah-lai sái left-hand drive

poo-ung ma-lai kwǎh right-hand drive

pôo-yài adult

pôo-yài bâhn village headman

pôo-yǐng woman; lady; girl

pôo-yǐng bah hostess (in bar)

pôo-yǐng ung-grìt English girl/woman

por enough

pôr father

pôr dtah father-in-law (of a man)

pôr dtah mâir yai parents-in-law (wife's parents)

por jai satisfied

por láir-o no more; that's enough

pôr mái widower

pôr mâir parents

pôr pǒo-a father-in-law (of a woman)

pôr pǒo-a mâir pǒo-a parents-in-law (husband's parents)

por sǒm-koo-un quite, fairly

pǒrm thin, skinny

pòt prickly heat

pót-ja-nah-nóo-grom dictionary

prá monk; priest

prá-ah-tít sun

prá-jâo God

prá-jun moon

prá-póot-ta-jâo Buddha

prá-póot-ta-rôop Buddha image

prá-rah-chi-nee queen

prá-râht-cha-wung palace

prá-tóo-dong mendicant monk

pree-o slim

préut-sa-jìk-gah-yon November

préut-sa-pah-kom May

prom carpet; rug

prôong née tomorrow

prór because

prórm ready

púk stay

pùk vegetables

púk krêung interval

púk pòrn rest

pun-ra-yah wife

pút fan (handheld)

pùt stir-fry

pút lom fan (mechanical)

R

ra-bee-ung patio; terrace; balcony

rah-kah cost; price

rah-kah tòok downmarket

ráhn shop, store

ráhn ah-hǎhn restaurant

ráhn ah-hǎhn jeen Chinese restaurant

ráhn gǒo-ay dtěe-o café; noodle shop

ráhn kǎi dòrk-mái florist

ráhn kǎi kǒrng chum food store

ráhn kǎi kǒrng gào antique shop

ráhn kǎi krêu-ung lèk hardware store

ráhn kǎi krêu-ung pét ploy jeweller's

ráhn kǎi lâo liquor store, shop selling wines and spirits

ráhn kǎi núng-sěu bookshop, bookstore

ráhn kǎi pâhp kěe-un art gallery

ráhn kǎi pùk greengrocer's

ráhn kǎi yah chemist's, pharmacy

ráhn kǎi yah sòop tobacconist's, tobacco store

ráhn néu-a butcher's

ráhn sěrm sǒo-ay beauty salon

ráhn súk hâirng dry-cleaner's

ráhn súk (sêu-a) pâh laundry

ráhn tum ka-nǒm-bpung bakery

râhng-gai body

rahng-wun prize

ra-hùt pàhn password

ra-hùt toh-ra-sùp dialling code

rai-gahn schedule

rai-gahn num têe-o tour

râirk first

rairng fai fáh voltage

ra-kung bell

rao we; us

ra-wàhng between

ra-wung! be careful!; look out!
  ra-wung ná! look out!

ra-yá tahng distance

ray-o early; quick, fast; quickly

ray-o ray-o kâo! hurry up!

ray-o ray-o nòy! come on!

rêep rêep nòy! hurry up!

rêe-uk call; be called

ree-un learn

rêe-up smooth

rêe-up róy neat

rêrm begin, start

rěu or
  … rěu … either… or…

reu-a ship; boat

reu-a bpra-mong fishing boat

reu-a choo chêep lifeboat

reu-a hǎhng yao long-tailed boat

reu-a kâhm fâhk ferry

reu-a pai rowing boat

reu-a ray-o speedboat

reu-a sǔm-bpûn sampan

reu-a sǔm-pao junk

reu-a yon motorboat

reu-a yórt yacht

rêu-ay rêu-ay so-so

reu-doo season

reu-doo bai mái plì spring

réu-doo bai-mái rô-ung autumn, (US) fall

rêu-ung story

  rêu-ung a-rai gun?
  what's going on?

rim fěe bpàhk lip

rôhk disease

rôhk áyd Aids

rôhk bìt dysentery

rôhk bpòo-ut nai kôr
  rheumatism

rôhk gloo-a náhm rabies

rôhk hèut hay fever; asthma

rôhk hùt measles

rôhk hùt yer-ra-mun
  German measles

rôhk páir dàirt sunstroke

rôhk sâi dtìng appendicitis

rohng la-korn theatre

rohng ngahn factory

rohng nǔng cinema, movie
  theater

rohng pa-yah-bahn hospital

rohng rairm hotel

rohng ree-un school

rohng rót garage

rohng rúp jum-num pawnshop

rohng yim gym

rôm umbrella; parasol

  nai rôm in the shade

rôm gun dàirt beach umbrella

roo hole

róo know

róo-a fence

rôo-a leak

roo-ay rich

róo-jùk know

rôong dawn

rôong cháo at dawn

rôop picture

rôop gàir sa-lùk carving

rôop lòr handsome

rôop-song figure

rôop tài photograph

rǒo-rǎh posh; luxurious;
  upmarket

róo-sèuk feel

róo-sèuk ja ah-jee-un feel sick

róo-sèuk kòrp-kOOn
  feel grateful

róo-sèuk mâi sa-bai
  feel unwell

roo-um include

roo-um yòo dôo-ay included

roo-um yôrt total

róp-goo-un disturb

ror wait

rórn hot; warm

rórng hâi cry

rórng playng sing

rorng táo shoe(s); boot(s)

rorng táo dtàir sandal(s)

rorng táo gee-lah trainer(s)

rorng táo ma-nóot gòp
  flipper(s)

rót car; taste; flavour

rót air air-conditioned bus

rót bprùp ah-gàht
  air-conditioned bus

rót bun-tóok lorry, truck

rót châo rented car

rót dtôo van

rót fai train

rót fai dòo-un express train

rót kĕn pushchair

rót kĕn sŭm-rùp kon bpòo-ay wheelchair

rót may bus

rót may bprùp ah-gàht air-conditioned bus

rót mor-dter-sai motorbike; moped

rót norn sleeping car

rót num têe-o coach trip

rót pa-yah-bahn ambulance

rót sa-bee-ung dining car

rót sa-góot-dter scooter

rót sǎhm lór trishaw

rót sa-nǎhm bin airport bus

rót too-a tour bus

rót yon car

rúk love

rûm roo-ay wealthy

rum tai Thai classical dancing

rum-kahn annoying; annoy

rum-wong ramwong dance (popular Thai folk dance)

rúp accept; receive

rút state

rút-ta-bahn government

S

sà pond; wash

sà pŏm wash one's hair

sà wâi náhm swimming pool

sa-àht clean

sa-bai well, in good health

    sa-bai dee OK, all right

sa-bòo soap

sa-bòo gohn nòo-ut shaving soap

sa-bpay chèet pŏm hairspray

sa-dòo-uk convenient; comfortable

sa-dtahng satang (unit of currency)

sa-dtairm stamp

sa-dtree ladies' toilet, ladies' room

sa-gee náhm waterskiing

sa-górt táyp Sellotape, Scotch tape

sa-hà-rút a-may-ri-gah United States

sǎh-gon international

sâhk sa-lùk hùk pung remains, ruins

sǎh-lah pavilion

sǎhm three

sǎhm lèe-um torng kum Golden Triangle

sǎh-mee husband

sâhp know

sàh-sa-nǎh religion

sàh-sa-nǎh póot Buddhism; Buddhist

> **Travel tip** Buddhism plays a fundamental role in Thai culture, and Buddhist monuments should be treated with respect – which basically means wearing long trousers or knee-length skirts, covering your arms and removing your shoes whenever you visit one.

sǎh-tah-ra-ná public

sai sand
sài put
sái left
săi late; telephone line; strap
săi fai fáh wire; lead
sài gOOn-jair lock
săi pahn fanbelt
săi rút fastener
săi yahng yêut elastic
sairng overtake
sa-lai slide
sa-lĕung salung (unit of currency)
sa-lùk nâh-dtàhng shutter
sa-mĕr always
sa-moh-sŏrn club, clubhouse
sa-mOOn prai herbs (medicinal)
sa-mòot notebook
sa-mòot bun-téuk bpra-jum wun diary
sa-móot măi lâyk toh-ra-sùp phone book
sa-mòot yay-loh páyt yellow pages
sa-năhm playing field; pitch
sa-năhm bin airport
sa-năhm gee-lah hàirng châht National Stadium
sa-năhm górp golf course
sa-năhm ten-nít tennis court
sa-năhm yâh lawn
sa-ngòp calm
sa-nòok pleasant
sa-nòok dee enjoyable, fun
sâo sad
săo young (girl)
sa-pahn bridge
sa-tăhn bor-ri-gahn rót châo car rental company
sa-tăhn gong-sOOn consulate
sa-tăhn lée-ung dèk lék nursery

sa-tǎhn sùk-gah-rá shrine
sa-tǎhn tôot embassy
sa-tǎhn-na-gahn situation
sa-tǎh-nee terminus; station
sa-tǎh-nee dtum-ròo-ut
  police station
sa-tǎh-nee rót fai
  railway station
sa-tǎh-nee rót may bus
  station
sa-tǎhn-têe place
sa-wàhng bright
sa-wít switch
sa-wít fai switch
sa-wùt dee hello
sa-wùt dee bpee mài!
  happy New Year!
sa-wùt dee kâ hello
sa-wùt dee krúp hello
sàyt sa-dtahng small change
sèe four
sěe colour; paint
sěe chom-poo pink
sěe dairng red
sěe dum black
sěe kǎo white
sěe kěe-o green
sěe krohng rib
sěe lěu-ung yellow
sěe lêu-ut mǒo scarlet
sěe môo-ung purple
sěe néu-a beige
sěe núm dtahn brown
sěe núm ngern blue
sěe òrn pale
sěe sôm orange

sěe tao grey
sěe tao gairm lěu-ung fawn
sèe yâirk crossroads,
  intersection
sěe-a broken, faulty, out of
  order; polluted
sěe-a jai sorry
sěe-a láir-o damage; damaged
sěe-o sharp
sèe-ung risky
sěe-ung sound, noise; voice
sên line
sên dâi thread, cotton
sên lôo-ut wire
sèt ready; over, finished
séu buy
sêu dtrong honest
sêu-a ohért shirt
sêu-a choo chêep lifejacket
sêu-a chóot dress

> **Travel tip** Clothing – or the
> lack of it – is what bothers
> Thais most about tourist
> behaviour. Keep short shorts
> and vests for the real tourist
> resorts, and be especially
> diligent about covering up in
> rural areas. Baring your flesh
> on beaches is also very much
> a Western practice: Thais find
> topless and nude bathing
> offensive.

sêu-a fǒn raincoat
sêu-a gahng-gayng norn
  pyjamas
sêu-a glâhm vest (under shirt)
sêu-a gúk waistcoat

sêu-a kloom coat, overcoat
sêu-a kloom chóot norn
  dressing gown
sêu-a nôrk jacket
sêu-a pâh clothes
sêu-a pâh chún nai underwear
sêu-a pôo-yǐng blouse
sêu-a sa-wet-dter sweater;
  sweatshirt
sêu-a yêut T-shirt
sêu-a yók song bra
si-gah cigar
sîn sòot end
sǐng-hǎh-kom August
sǐn-la-bpà art
sǐn-la-bpà sa-mǎi mài
  modern art
sǐn-la-bpin artist
sìp ten; zip
sìp-hâh nah-tee
  quarter of an hour
sǒh-pay-nee prostitute
sòht single (unmarried)
sòk-ga-bpròk dirty
sôn rorng táo heel (of shoe)
sôn táo heel (of foot)
sòng send
sòng dtòr forward
sòng jòt-mǎi post, mail
sòng jòt-mǎi dtahm bâhn
  delivery
sòng kôr kwahm text message
sòng tahng ah-gàht by airmail
sǒng-grahn Thai New Year
sǒng-krahm war
sòo towards
sǒo-ay beautiful

sòok ripe
sòok sòok well-done (steak)
sòok sòok dìp dìp rare (steak)
sòok-ka-pâhp health
sòok-ka-pâhp mâi dee
  unhealthy
sòok-ka-pâhp sǒm-boon
  fit, healthy
sôom sǎhm clumsy
sǒon zero
sǒon glahng centre
sǒong tall; high
soon-la-gah-gorn Customs
soo-pâhp polite
soo-pâhp boo-ròot gentleman
soo-pâhp sa-dtree lady
sòop boo-rèe smoke
sòot bottom (of road)
sòot tái last
sôo-um sǎh-tah-ra-ná
  public convenience
sòo-un part
sǒo-un garden
sòo-un dtoo-a private
sòo-un mâhk most (of)
sòo-un pa-sǒm mixture
sǒo-un sǎh-tah-ra-ná park
sǒo-un sùt zoo
sòo-ut mon pray
sôrm repair, mend; fork
sǒrn teach
sôrn hide
sorng pack, packet
sǒrng two
sǒrng ah-tít fortnight
sorng jòt-mǎi envelope
sǒrng krúng twice

sŏrng tâir-o van with two benches, used as a bus

sòt fresh

sòt chêun refreshing

soy side street; lane; soi

sôy kor necklace, chain

súk wash

... sùk nít nèung a little...

súk pâh wash clothes; laundry

sŭm-kun important; main

sŭm-lee cotton wool, absorbent cotton

sŭm-núk kào sǎhn núk tôrng têe-o tourist information office

sŭm-núk ngahn office

sŭm-núk ngahn kào sǎhn information office

sŭm-rùp for

   sŭm-rùp koOn for you

sûn short

sŭn-châht nationality

sùng order

sŭn-yah promise

sŭn-yahn fay mâi fire alarm

sùp-sŏn complicated

sùt animal

T

ta-bee-un rót car registration number

tâh if

tâh reu-a docks; harbour; port; jetty; quay(side)

tâh yàhng nún then, in that case

tǎhm ask

tahn (kâo) eat

tahng direction; path; route; way

tahng ah-gàht by air

tahng dern corridor

tahng dòo-un motorway, highway, freeway

tahng kâo entrance

tahng kóhng bend

tahng kwǎh on the right

tahng lée-o turning

tahng lŏo-ung highway

tahng máh-lai pedestrian crossing

tahng òrk exit

tahng ôrm detour

tahng rót fai railway

tahng rót fai pàhn level crossing

tahng sái on the left

tahng yâirk junction; fork

tàht tray

tai Thai (*adj*)

tái tights, pantyhose

tài rôop photograph

táir genuine; original

tairm-porn tampon

tairn instead

   tairn têe ja... instead of...

tǎir-o queue, line

ta-lay sea

ta-lay sàhp lake

ta-nah-kahn bank

ta-nai kwahm lawyer

ta-nǒn street; road

ta-nǒn yài main road

ta-nùt meu sái left-handed

táo foot

tâo-nún just; only

tâo-rài? how much?

tâyp nĕe-o Sellotape, Scotch tape

tee time

têe at

têe bâhn at home

têe bpèrt gra-bpŏrng can-opener

têe bpèrt kòo-ut bottle-opener; corkscrew

têe bpùt núm fŏn windscreen wipers

têe èun somewhere else

têe fàhk gra-bpăo left luggage, baggage check

têe fàhk kŏrng cloakroom

têe hâhm rót kâo pedestrian precinct

têe jâirng kŏrng hăi lost property office

têe jòrt rót car park, parking lot

têe jòrt rót táirk-sêe taxi rank

têe jum-nài dtŏo-a ticket office

têe kèe-a bOO-rèe ashtray

têe láir-o last, previous

tee la nóy gradually

têe lĕu-a rest

tee lŭng afterwards; later, later on

têe năi somewhere

têe năi? where?

têe nêe here; over here

têe nôhn there; over there

têe norn mattress; berth

têe nûn there

têe nûng seat

têe nûng dtìt nâh-dtàhng window seat

têe nûng kâhng lŭng back seat

têe nûng rúp kàirk couch

têe pìt error

têe púk accommodation(s)

têe râhp lôom plain

tee râirk at first

têe rúk darling

têe rút kĕm kùt seatbelt

têe sŏrng second (*adj*)

têe sòrp tăhm information desk

têe tum ngahn office

têe yòo address

têe-o visit; trip

têe-o bin flight

têe-o bin măo charter flight

têe-o hâi sa-nòok! enjoy yourself!

têe-o sa-nòok ná! have fun!; have a good journey!

tee-um imitation

tee-un candle

têe-ung keun at midnight

têe-ung wun midday

tee-wee TV

tén tent

ter you

tĕu carry

tĕung reach

tíng throw away

tíng wái leave behind

tôh! good heavens!

toh tahng glai long-distance call

toh-ra-lâyk telegram
toh-ra-sùp phone
toh-ra-sùp gèp ngern bplai tahng reverse-charge call, collect call
toh-ra-sùp săh-tah-ra-ná payphone
toh-ra-tút television
tong flag
too-a bus tour
tòo-a peanuts; peas; beans
tôo-a bpai everywhere
tôo-ay cup
tôo-ay chahm crockery
tóok every
tòok right, correct; cheap, inexpensive
tòok dàirt mâi sunburnt
tòok gòt-măi legal
tòok ka-moy-ee robbed; stolen
tóok kon everyone
tòok láir-o that's right
tóok yàhng everything
tòok-dtôrng accurate
... tôom ... pm (in the evening)
tŏong bag
tŏong bplah-sa-dtìk plastic bag
tŏong gra-dàht paper bag
tŏong meu gloves
tŏong norn sleeping bag
tŏong nôrng stocking(s)
tŏong táo sock(s)
tŏong yahng condom
tŏong yai boo-a tights, pantyhose

tóo-rá business
tóo-ra-gìt deal
tôr pipe
torng gold
tórng stomach
tórng pòok constipated
tórng sĕe-a diarrhoea; upset stomach
tórp-fêe sweet(s), candy
tôrt deep-fry
trah-wern ay-yen travel agency
tum make; do
tûm cave
tum dôo-ay meu handmade
tum hâi cause
tum hâi ôo-un fattening
tum kwahm sa-àht clean
tum lép manicure

tum ngahn work
tum têe bâhn home-made
tum-ma-châht nature; natural
tum-ma-dah normal; usually, normally; ordinary; plain
tum-mai? why?
tûn you
tun sa-mǎi fashionable; modern
tǔng bucket
tǔng dtàirk broke
tǔng ka-yà dustbin, trashcan
túng mòt all; altogether; completely
tǔng núm mun petrol tank, gas tank
túng sǒrng both of them
tun-tee at once, immediately; suddenly
tun-wah-kom December

U

um-per amphoe (sub-division of province)
un thing
un nǎi? which one?
un née this one
un nún that one
un-dta-rai harm; danger; dangerous
ung-grìt English (*adj*); British
un-nóo-yâht allowed
ùt-dta-noh-mút automatic
ùt-dtrah rate
ùt-dtrah lâirk bplèe-un exchange rate

ùt-ta-noh-mút automatic
ùt-ti-bai explain

W

wâh say
wǎhn sweet
wahn seun née the day before yesterday
wahng put
wâhng empty; deserted
wâhng bplào empty, vacant
wâhng ngahn unemployed
wâi náhm swim
wai-fai Wi-Fi
wáir stopover
wǎirn ring
wǎirn dtah glasses, (US) eyeglasses
wǎirn dtàirng ngahn wedding ring
wǎirn gun dàirt sunglasses
wǎirn mûn engagement ring
wai-yah-gorn grammar
wâo kite
way-lah time
way-lah sòo-un mâhk most of the time
way-lah-nún then, at that time
wěe comb
wee-sah visa
wèet rórng scream
wép-sái website
wew view
wí-nah-tee second (in time)
wîng run

wí-sàyt incredible, tremendous

wí-sàyt jung ler-ee fantastic

wít-ta-yah-lai college

wít-ta-yah-sàht science

wít-ta-yóo radio

wít-tee method

wong don-dtree orchestra

wong glom circle

woo-a cow

wun day

wun ah-tít Sunday

wun gèrt birthday

wun gòrn... the day before...

wun jun Monday

wun lǔng jàhk têe...
  the day after...

wun ma-reun née
  the day after tomorrow

wun née today

wun pa-réu-hùt Thursday

wun póot Wednesday

wun prá Buddhist holy day

wun sǎo Saturday

wun sǎo ah-tít weekend

Travel tip You may only
notice national holidays
because the trains and buses
suddenly get extraordinarily
crowded: although banks
and government offices shut,
most shops and tourist-
oriented businesses carry
on regardless. The only time
an inconvenient number of
restaurants, shops and hotels
close is during Chinese New
Year.

---

wun seun née
  the day before yesterday

wun sîn bpee New Year's Eve

wun sòok Friday

wun têe date

wun ung-kahn Tuesday

wun yòot holiday, vacation

wun yòot râht-cha-gahn
  public holiday

wung palace

wǔng hope

wút temple; monastery

wùt cold (illness)

wút-ta-na-tum culture

Y

yah medicine

yâh grandmother (paternal); grass

yàh! don't!

yah dùp glìn dtoo-a deodorant

yah glôrng pipe tobacco

yàh gun láir-o divorced

yah gun ma-lairng
  insect repellent

yah kâh chéu-a antiseptic

yah kâh chéu-a rôhk
  disinfectant

yah koom gum-nèrt
  contraceptive pill

yah kùt polish

yah kùt rorng táo shoe polish

yah kwin-neen quinine

yah láhng make-up remover

yah mét tablet

yah pít poison

yah ra-ngúp bpòo-ut painkiller
yah sà pǒm shampoo
yah sàyp-dtìt drug, narcotic
yah sěe fun toothpaste
yah sòop tobacco
yah tah lotion; ointment
yah tah gun dàirt sunblock
yah tah lǔng àhp dàirt
   aftersun cream
yah tah lǔng gohn nòo-ut
   aftershave
yah tài laxative
yâhk hard, difficult
yàhk dâi want
yàhk (ja) I'd like to
yahng rubber
yahng a-lài spare tyre

yahng dtàirk puncture
yahng lóp rubber, eraser
yahng nai inner tube
yàhng née this way, like this
yàhng nóy at least
yahng rót tyre
yahng rút rubber band
yâht relatives
yai grandmother (maternal)
yài big, large
yài bêr-rêr enormous
yai sǔng-krór synthetic
yâir terrible, dreadful
yâir jung! too bad!
yâir long worse
yâir mâhk awful, terrible
yâir têe sòot worst

yâirk gun separate; separately

yao long

yêe hôr brand

yêe-bpòOn Japan; Japanese

yeen jeans

yêe-um excellent, brilliant; visit

yêe-um ler-ee lovely, excellent

yêe-um yôrt fantastic

yen cold; cool

yen née this afternoon

yen prôOng née
  tomorrow evening

yép sew

yer-ra-mun Germany; German

yeun stand

yèu-uk jug

yím smile

yin dee glad

yĭng rúp chái maid,
  chambermaid

yók wáyn except

yòo live; still; in, at home
  káo mâi yòo he/she's not in
  ... yòo têe nǎi? where is...?

yòo bon... on top of...;
  at the top of...

yòo dtrong glahng
  in the middle

yòo dtrong nâh straight ahead

yòo glâi nearby

yòo kâhng bon at the top

yOOng mosquito

yOO-rohp Europe; European

yòot stop

yòot pôot ná! shut up!

yóot-dti-tum fair, just

yôrt smashing, fabulous
  yôrt! great!

yôrt yêe-um splendid, super

yung still; not yet

yung mâi sèt finish

yung-ngai? how?

THAI → ENGLISH: SIGNS

Abbreviations

ป.อ. **bprùp ah-gàht**
air-conditioned

อ. **um-per** Amphoe, district

ก.ท.ม. **grOOng-tâyp-ma-hǎh-na-korn** Bangkok

พ.ศ. **póot-ta-sùk-ga-ràht**
Buddhist Era (BE) (543 years ahead of AD)

ค.ศ. **krít-dta-sùk-ga-ràht**
Christian Era (AD)

ช.ม. **chôo-a mohng** hours

น. **nah-li-gah** hours

ก.ม. **gi-loh-mét** kilometre

ช. **chai** men

จ. **jung-wùt** province

ถ. **ta-nǒn** road

ต. **dtum-bon** Tambon,
sub-district

ญ. **yǐng** women

General signs

ระวัง **ra-wung** caution

อันตราย **un-dta-rai** danger

ห้าม... **hâhm...** ... forbidden

อย่า **yàh...** do not...

สอบถาม **sòrp tǎhm** enquiries

โรงพยาบาลห้ามใช้เสียง **rohng pa-yah-bahn: hâhm chái sěe-ung** hospital: no noise

ห้ามผ่าน **hâhm pàhn**
no admission

ห้ามเข้า **hâhm kâo** no entry

ห้ามทิ้งขยะ **hâhm tíng ka-yà**
no litter

ห้ามจอด **hâhm jòrt** no parking

ห้ามถ่ายรูป **hâhm tài rôop**
no photographs

ห้ามสูบบุหรี่ **hâhm sòop boo-rèe** no smoking

กรุณาอย่าส่งเสียงดัง **ga-roo-nah yàh sòng sěe-ung dung**
please don't make a noise

โปรดถอดรองเท้า **bpròht tòrt rorng táo** please remove shoes

ตำรวจ **dtum-ròo-ut** police

โปรดเงียบ **bpròht ngêe-up**
silence, please

Airport, planes

ที่ทำการบริษัทการบิน **têe tum gahn bor-ri-sùt gahn bin**
airline company offices

ท่าอากาศยาน **tâh ah-gàht-sa-yahn** airport

ถึง **těung** arrives

ประชาสัมพันธ์
ท่าอากาศยานกรุงเทพฯ
bpra-chah sǔm-pun tâh-ah-gàht-sa-yǎhn grOOng-tâyp public relations, Bangkok Airport

ศุลกากร **soon-la-gah-gorn**
Customs

สุขาชาย **sŏo-kăh chai**
gents' toilets, men's room

ชาย **chai** gents

ตรวจคนเข้าเมือง **dtròo-ut kon
kâo meu-ung** immigration

ประชาสัมพันธ์ **bpra-chah
sŭm-pun** information

สุขาหญิง **sŏo-kăh yĭng**
ladies' toilets, ladies' room

หญิง **yĭng** ladies

ออก **òrk** leaves, departs

ฝากกระเป๋า **fàhk gra-bpăo** left
luggage, baggage checkroom

ลิฟท์ **líf** lift, elevator

จุดนัดพบ **jòot nút póp**
meeting point

ห้ามสูบบุหรี่ **hâhm sòop
boo-rèe** no smoking

จุดตรวจค้นผู้โดยสาร **jòot
dtròo-ut kón pôo doy-ee
săhn** passenger check-point

เฉพาะผู้โดยสารและลูกเรือเท่
านั้น **cha-pòr pôo-doy-ee
săhn láir lôok reu-a tâo-nún**
passengers and crew only

ตรวจหนังสือเดินทาง **dtròo-
ut núng-sěu dern tahng**
passport control

ภัตตาคาร **pút-dtah-khan**
restaurant

ตรวจสอบบัตรผู้โดยสารและ
กระเป๋า **dtròo-ut sòrp bùt
pôo-doy-ee-săhn láir gra-
bpăo** ticket and baggage check

ที่จำหน่ายตั๋ว **têe jum-nài
dtŏo-a** ticket office

เวลา **way-lah** time

ผู้มาส่งผู้โดยสาร **pôo mah
sòng pôo-doy-ee-săhn**
visitors

ที่พักผู้มาส่งผู้โดยสาร **têe púk
pôo mah sòng pôo-doy-ee-
sahn** visitors' waiting area

ทางเข้า **tahng kâo**
way in, entrance

ทางออก **tahng òrk** way out, exit

Banks, money

บาท **bàht** baht

ธนาคาร **ta-nah-kahn** bank

ฝากประจำ **fàhk bpra-jum**
deposit account, savings
account

ฝากเงิน **fàhk ngern** deposits

อัตราแลกเปลี่ยนเงิน **ùt-dtrah
lâirk bplèe-un ngern**
exchange rate

อัตราแลกเปลี่ยนเงินตราต่างป
ระเทศ **ùt-dtrah lâirk bplèe-
un ngern dtrah dtàhng
bpra-tâyt** foreign exchange
rate

สอบถาม **sòrp tǎhm** enquiries

ลกเปลี่ยนเงินตราต่างประเทศ **lâirk bplèe-un ngern dtrah dtàhng bpra-tâyt** bureau de change

เปิดบัญชีใหม่ **bpèrt bun-chee mài** new accounts

ถอนเงิน **tǒrn ngern** withdrawals

ตั๋ว **tĕu dtǒo-a doy-ee sǎhn** passengers with tickets only

ที่จำหน่ายตั๋ว **têe jum-nài dtǒo-a** ticket office

กำหนดเวลาเดินรถ **gum-nòt way-lah dern rót** timetable, (US) schedule

รถทัวร์ **rót too-a** tour bus

Bus travel

รถปรับอากาศ **rót bprùp ah-gàht** air-conditioned bus

ถึง **tĕung** arrives

ออก **òrk** departs

สุขาชาย **sòo-kǎh chai** gents' toilets, men's room

ประชาสัมพันธ์ **bpra-chah sǔm-pun** information

สอบถาม **sòrp tǎhm** information, enquiries

สุขาหญิง **sòo-kǎh yǐng** ladies' toilets, ladies' room

รับฝากของ **rúp fàhk kǒrng** left luggage, baggage checkroom

ห้ามสูบบุหรี่ **hâhm sòop boo-rèe** no smoking

ห้องพักผู้โดยสาร **hôrng púk pôo doy-ee sǎhn** passengers' waiting room

ทางเข้าเฉพาะผู้ถือตั๋วโดยสาร **tahng kâo cha-pòr pôo**

Countries, nationalities

อาฟริกา **ah-fri-gah** Africa; African

อีก้อ **ee-gôr** Akha (hill tribe)

อเมริกา **a-may-ri-gah** America; American

เอเชีย **ay-see-a** Asia

ออสเตรเลีย **òrt-sa-dtray-lee-a** Australia; Australian

พม่า **pa-mâh** Burma, Myanmar; Burmese

กัมพูชา **gum-poo-chah** Cambodia

แคนาดา **kair-nah-dah** Canada; Canadian

จีน **jeen** China; Chinese

ประเทศ **bpra-tâyt** country

อังกฤษ **ung-grìt** England; Britain; UK; English; British

ยุโรป **yoo-rôhp** Europe; European

ฝรั่งเศส **a-rùng-sàyt** France; French

ประเทศเยอรมัน **bpra-tâyt yer-ra-mun** Germany; German

ชาวเขา **chao kǎo** hill-tribe person; hill-tribe people

แม้ว **máy-o** Hmong, Meo (hill tribe)

ฮอลแลนด์ **horn-lairn** Holland; Dutch

อินเดีย **in-dee-a** India; Indian

แขก **kàirk** Indian; Malaysian

อินโดนีเซีย **in-doh-nee-see-a** Indonesia; Indonesian

ไอร์แลนด์ **ai-lairn** Ireland

ประเทศอิตาลี **bpra-tâyt ì-dtah-lee** Italy

ญี่ปุ่น **yêe-bpòon** Japan; Japanese

กะเหรี่ยง **ga-rèe-ung** Karen (hill tribe)

เขมร **ka-mǎyn** Khmer; Cambodian

เกาหลี **gao-lěe** Korea; Korean

ลาว **lao** Laos; Lao

มาเลเซีย **mah-lay-see-a** Malaysia; Malaysian

นิวซีแลนด์ **new see-lairn** New Zealand

ไอร์แลนด์เหนือ **ai-lairn něu-a** Northern Ireland

ปากิสถาน **bpah-gi-sa-tǎhn** Pakistan

ฟิลิปปินส์ **fin-lip-bpin** Philippines; Filipino

สกอตแลนด์ **sa-gort-lairn** Scotland

สิงคโปร์ **sǐng-ka-bpoh** Singapore

ประเทศสเปน **bpra-tâyt sa-bpayn** Spain

ไทย **tai** Thai

เมืองไทย **meu-ung tai** Thailand (informal)

ประเทศไทย **bpra-tâyt tai** Thailand (formal)

สหรัฐอเมริกา **sa-hà-rút a-may-ri-gah** United States of America

เวียดนาม **wêe-ut-nahm** Vietnam; Vietnamese

เย้า **yáo** Yao (hill tribe)

Customs

ศุลกากร **sǒon-la-gah-gorn** Customs

มีของต้องสำแดง **mee kǒrng dtôrng sǔm-dairng** goods to declare

ตรวจคนเข้าเมือง **dtròo-ut kon kâo meu-ung** immigration

ไม่มีของต้องสำแดง **mâi mee**

กอง dtôrng sǔm-dairng
nothing to declare

เฉพาะหนังสือเดินทางไทย **cha-pòr núng-sěu dern-tahng tai** Thai passport holders only

Days

วัน **wun** day

อาทิตย์ **ah-tít** week

วันเสาร์อาทิตย์
wun sǎo ah-tít weekend

วันจันทร์ **wun jun** Monday

วันอังคาร **wun ung-kahn**
Tuesday

วันพุธ **wun póot** Wednesday

วันพฤหัส **wun pa-réu-hùt**
Thursday

วันศุกร์ **wun sòok** Friday

วันเสาร์ **wun sǎo** Saturday

วันอาทิตย์ **wun ah-tít** Sunday

Entertainment

... บาท **... bàht** ... baht

ถุงละ ... บาท **tǒong la ... bàht**
... baht per bag

ถ้วยละ ... บาท **tôo-ay la ... bàht** ... baht per cup

ชิ้นละ ... บาท **chín la ... bàht**
... baht per piece

บริการ ๒๔ ช.ม. **bor-ri-gahn yêe-sìp sèe chǒo-a mohng**
24-hour service

รอบ ๑๗.๐๐ น. **rôrp 17.00 n(ah-li-gah)** 5pm show

บาร์ **bah** bar

โบว์ลิ่ง **bohn-lîng** bowling

ที่จำหน่ายตั๋ว **têe jum-nài dtǒo-a** box office

โรงภาพยนตร์ **rohng pâhp-pa-yon** cinema, movie theater

เร็วๆนี้ **ray-o ray-o née**
coming soon

ดิสโก้ **dít-sa-gôh** disco

ทางเข้า **tahng kâo** entrance

ทางออก **tahng òrk** exit

เต็ม **dtem** full

อาบอบนวด **àhp òp nôo-ut**
massage

รายการหน้า **rai-gahn nâh**
next programme

อาทิตย์หน้า **ah-tít nâh**
next week

ไนท์คลับ **náit klùp** nightclub

ฉายวันนี้ **chǎi wun née**
now showing

ราคา **rah-kah** price

รอบ **rôrp** showing

Forms

ที่อยู่ **têe yòo** address

อายุ **ah-yóo** age

พ.ศ. **por sŏr** (year) … BE (543
   years later than AD)

สีตา **sĕe dtah** colour of eyes

สีผม **sĕe pŏm** colour of hair

เกิดวันที่ **gèrt wun-têe**
   date of birth

ชื่อ **chêu** first name

ตั้งแต่ … ถึง … **dtûng-dtàir …
   tĕung …** from … until …

ความสูง **kwahm sŏong** height

บ้านเลขที่ **bâhn lâyk têe**
   house number

ตรอก **dtròrk** lane

ซอย **soy** lane, soi

บันทึก **bun-téuk** memo

เดือน **deu-un** month

สัญชาติ **sŭn-châht** nationality

หมายเหตุ **măi-hàyt** note, n.b.

อาชีพ **ah-chêep** occupation

หนังสือเดินทางหมายเลข **núng-
   sĕu dern tahng măi-lâyk**
   passport number

จังหวัด **jung-wùt** province

เชื้อชาติ **chéu-a châht** race

อยู่ที่ **yòo têe** residing at

ถนน **ta-nŏn** road

เพศ **pâyt** sex

ลายเซ็น **lai sen** signature

ลงชื่อ **long chêu** signed

พักที่ **púk têe** staying at

นามสกุล **nahm sa-gOOn**
   surname

ตำบล **dtum-bon** Tambon,
   sub-district

หมู่บ้าน **mòo-bâhn** village

น้ำหนัก **núm nùk** weight

พยาน **pa-yahn** witness

Garages

บริการ ๒๔ ช.ม. **bor-ri-gahn
   yêe-sìp sèe chôo-a mohng**
   24-hour service

บริการซ่อมรถ **bor-ri-gahn
   sôrm rót** car repairs

บริการล้างรถ **bor-ri-gahn
   láhng rót** car wash

ดีเซล **dee-sen** diesel

เปลี่ยนหม้อกรอง **bplèe-un môr
   grorng** filters changed

อู่ **òo** garage

ห้ามสูบบุหรี่ **hâhm sòop
   bOO-rèe** no smoking

เปลี่ยนน้ำมันเครื่อง **bplèe-un
   núm mun krêu-ung**
   oil changed

บริการอัดฉีด **bor-ri-gahn ùt
   chèet** pressurized air

ปะยาง **bpà yahng**
   punctures repaired

เครื่องอะไหล่ **krêu-ung a-lài**
   spare parts

Geographical terms

คลอง **klorng** canal

เมืองหลวง **meu-ung lŏo-ung**
capital city

ชนบท **chon-na-bòt**
countryside

ป่าดงดิบ **bpàh dong dìp**
forest, jungle

เขา **kǎo** hill

เกาะ **gòr** island

ป่า **bpàh** jungle, forest

ที่ราบลุ่ม **têe râhp lôom** plain

แม่น้ำ **mâir-náhm** river

ทะเล **ta-lay** sea

ชายทะเล **chai ta-lay** seaside

เมือง **meu-ung** town; city;
country

หมู่บ้าน **mòo-bâhn** village

Hairdresser's, beauty salons

เสริมสวย **sěrm sǒo-ay**
beauty care

เครื่องสำอาง **krêu-ung sǔm-ahng** cosmetics

นวดหน้า **nôo-ut nâh**
facial massage

ตัดผม **dtùt pǒm** hair cut

เป่าผม **bpào pôm** hair drying

ไดผม **dai pǒm** hair drying

สระผม **sà pǒm** wash

ตัดเล็บ **dtùt lép** manicure

ดัดผม **dùt pǒm** perm

เซทผม **sét pǒm** set

โกนหนวด **gohn nòo-ut** shave

Health

รถพยาบาล **rót pa-yah-bahn**
ambulance

คุมกำเนิด **koom gum-nèrt**
birth control, contraception

คลีนิค **klee-ník** clinic

ห้องคลอด **hôrng klôrt**
delivery room

ทันตแพทย์ **tun-dta-pâirt**
dentist

ทำฟัน **tum fun** dentist's

จำหน่ายยา **jum-nài yah**
dispensary

แพทย์หญิง **pâirt yǐng** doctor
(female)

พ.ญ. **pâirt yǐng** doctor (female)

น.พ. **nai pâirt** doctor (male)

นายแพทย์ **nai pâirt** doctor
(male)

ตรวจสายตา **dtròo-ut sǎi dtah**
eye test

ตรวจสายตา **dtròo-ut sǎi dtah**
dtròo-ut sǎi-dtah eye-testing

โรงพยาบาล **rohng pa-yah-bahn** hospital

ฉีดยา **chèet yah** injections

นางพยาบาล **nahng pa-yah-bahn** nurse

ห้างขายยา **hâhng kǎi yah** pharmacy, drugstore

ตรวจปัสสาวะ **dtròo-ut bpùt-sǎh-wá** urine test

เอ็กซเรย์ **X-ray** X-ray

Hiring, renting

ชั่วโมงละ ... บาท **chôo-a mohng la ... bàht** ... baht per hour

เดือนละ ... บาท **deu-un la ... bàht** ...baht per month

วันละ ... บาท **wun la ... bàht** ... baht per month

อพาร์ตเม้นท์ให้เช่า **ah-paht-mén hâi châo** apartment for rent

บาท **bàht** baht (unit of currency)

รถให้เช่า **rót hâi châo** car for hire, car to rent

เงินมัดจำ **ngern mút-jum** deposit

แฟลตให้เช่า **flàirt hâi châo** apartment for rent

ให้เช่า **hâi châo** for hire, to let, to rent

บ้านให้เช่า **bâhn hâi châo** house to let, house for rent

รถมอเตอร์ไซค์/ รถจักรยานให้เช่า **rót mor-dter-sai/rót jùk-ra-yahn hâi châo** motorcycle/bicycle for hire, to rent

จ่ายล่วงหน้า **jài lôo-ung nâh** pay in advance

ค่าเช่า **kâh châo** rental, fee

ห้องให้เช่า **hôrng hâi châo** room for rent

Hotels

คอฟฟี่ช็อบ **kòrp-fêe chórp** café serving coffees, alcoholic drinks, snacks and meals

ห้องคู่ **hôrng kôo** double room

ห้องคู่ปรับอากาศ **hôrng kôo bprùp ah-gàht** double room with air-conditioning

ทางออก **tahng òrk** exit

ชั้น **chún** floor

เกสท์เฮาส์ **gàyt háot** guesthouse

สอบถาม **sòrp tǎhm** enquiries

ห้องน้ำสตรี **hôrng náhm sa-dtree** ladies' toilet, ladies' room

หญิง **yǐng** ladies

ลิฟท์ **líf** lift, elevator

บริการรถรับส่ง **bor-ri-gahn rót rúp sòng** limousine service

ห้องน้ำบุรุษ **hôrng náhm boo-ròot** men's toilet, men's room

ชาย **chai** men

ห้ามสูบบุหรี่ **hâhm sòop boo-rèe** no smoking

แผนกต้อนรับ **pa-nàirk dtôrn rúp** reception

ห้องอาหาร **hôrng ah-hǎhn** restaurant

ห้อง **hôrng** room

ห้องให้เช่า **hôrng hâi châo** rooms to let

บริการนำเที่ยว **bor-ri-gahn num têe-o** sightseeing tours

ห้องเดี่ยว **hôrng dèe-o** single room

ห้องเดี่ยวปรับอากาศ **hôrng dèe-o bprùp ah-gàht** single room with air-conditioning

สระว่ายน้ำ **sà wâi náhm** swimming pool

สุขา **sòo-kǎh** toilet

ห้องน้ำ **hôrng náhm** toilets

ห้องว่าง **hôrng wâhng** vacancies

ยินดีต้อนรับ **yin dee dtôrn rúp** welcome

Lifts, elevators

ลง **long** down

ขึ้น **chún** floor

ลิฟท์ **lif** lift, elevator

ไม่เกิน ... คน **mâi gern ... kon** maximum load … people

ห้ามสูบบุหรี่ **hâhm sòop boo-rèe** no smoking

ขึ้น **kêun** up

Medicines

หลังอาหาร **lǔng ah-hǎhn** after meals

ทา **tah** apply (ointments)

ก่อนนอน **gòrn norn** before going to bed

ก่อนอาหาร **gòrn ah-hǎhn** before meals

ยาอันตราย **yah un-dta-rai** dangerous medicine

วิธีใช้ **wí-tee chái** instructions for use

กินเกินขนาดเป็นอันตราย **gin gern ka-nàht bpen un-dta-rai** it is dangerous to exceed the stated dose

ยา **yah** medicine

เม็ด **mét** tablet, pill

รับประทาน **rúp-bpra-tahn** take (orally)

ช้อนชา **chórn chah** teaspoon

วันละ … ครั้ง **wun la … krúng**
times … times per day

วันละ … เม็ด **wun la … mét**
tablets … tablets per day

Months

เดือน **deu-un** month

มกราคม **mók-ga-rah-kom**
January

กุมภาพันธ์ **goom-pah-pun**
February

มีนาคม **mee-nah-kom** March

เมษายน **may-săh-yon** April

พฤษภาคม **préut-sa-pah-kom**
May

มิถุนายน **mí-too-nah-yon** June

กรกฎาคม **ga-rúk-ga-dah-**
kom July

สิงหาคม **sĭng-hăh-kom** August

กันยายน **gun-yah-yon**
September

ตุลาคม **dtoo-lah-kom** October

พฤศจิกายน **préut-sa-jìk-gah-**
yon November

ธันวาคม **tun-wah-kom**
December

Notices on doors

เฉพาะเจ้าหน้าที่ **cha-pór jâo-**
nâh-têe authorized personnel
only

กริ่ง **grìng** bell

หมาดุ **măh dòo**
beware of the dog

ปิด **bpìt** closed

ทางเข้า **tahng kâo** entry

ทางออก **tahng òrk** exit

ห้ามจอดรถขวางประตู **hâhm**
jòrt rót kwăhng bpra-dtoo
no parking in front of the gate

เข้า **kâo** in

ห้ามเข้า **hâhm kâo** no entry

ไม่มีกิจห้ามเข้า **mâi mee**
gìt hâhm kâo no entry to
unauthorized persons

ห้ามจอด **hâhm jòrt** no parking

ห้ามกลับรถ **hâhm glùp rót**
no turning

เปิด **bpèrt** open

ออก **òrk** out

กรุณาถอดรองเท้า **ga-roo-nah**
tòrt rorng táo please remove
your shoes

กรุณากดกริ่ง **ga-roo-nah gòt**
grìng please ring

กด **gòt** press

ถนนส่วนบุคคล **ta-nŏn sòo-un**
bòòk-kon private road

ดึง **deung** pull

ผลัก **plùk** push

ระวังสุนัขดุ **ra-wung sŏo-núk**
dòo beware of the dog

Numbers

ศูนย์ **sŏon** zero
หนึ่ง **nèung** one
สอง **sŏrng** two
สาม **săhm** three
สี่ **sèe** four
ห้า **hâh** five
หก **hòk** six
เจ็ด **jèt** seven
แปด **bpàirt** eight
เก้า **gâo** nine
สิบ **sìp** ten
สิบเอ็ด **sìp-èt** eleven
สิบสอง **sìp-sŏrng** twelve
สิบสาม **sìp-săhm** thirteen
สิบสี่ **sìp-sèe** fourteen
สิบห้า **sìp-hâh** fifteen
สิบหก **sìp-hòk** sixteen
สิบเจ็ด **sìp-jèt** seventeen
สิบแปด **sìp-bpàirt** eighteen
สิบเก้า **sìp-gâo** nineteen
ยี่สิบ **yêe-sìp** twenty
ยี่สิบเอ็ด **yêe-sìp-èt** twenty-one
สามสิบ **săhm-sìp** thirty
สามสิบเอ็ด **săhm-sìp-èt**
  thirty-one
สี่สิบ **sèe-sìp** forty
ห้าสิบ **hâh-sìp** fifty

หกสิบ **hòk-sìp** sixty
เจ็ดสิบ **jèt-sìp** seventy
แปดสิบ **bpàirt-sìp** eighty
เก้าสิบ **gâo-sìp** ninety
หนึ่งร้อย **nèung róy**
  one hundred
หนึ่งพัน **nèung pun**
  one thousand
สองพัน **sŏrng pun**
  two thousand
หนึ่งหมื่น **nèung mèun**
  ten thousand
สองหมื่น **sŏrng mèun**
  twenty thousand
หนึ่งแสน **nèung săirn**
  one hundred thousand
สองแสน **sŏrng săirn**
  two hundred thousand
หนึ่งล้าน **nèung láhn**
  one million
หนึ่งร้อยล้าน **nèung róy láhn**
  one hundred million
๐ **sŏon** 0
๑ **nèung** 1
๒ **sŏrng** 2
๓ **săhm** 3
๔ **sèe** 4
๕ **hâh** 5
๖ **hòk** 6
๗ **jèt** 7

๘ **bpàirt** 8

๙ **gâo** 9

๑๐ **sìp** 10

๑๑ **sìp-èt** 11

๑๒ **sìp-sǒrng** 12

๑๓ **sìp-sǎhm** 13

๑๔ **sìp-sèe** 14

๑๕ **sìp-hâh** 15

๑๖ **sìp-hòk** 16

๑๗ **sìp-jèt** 17

๑๘ **sìp-bpàirt** 18

๑๙ **sìp-gâo** 19

๒๐ **yêe-sìp** 20

๒๑ **yêe-sìp-èt** 21

๓๐ **sǎhm-sìp** 30

๓๑ **sǎhm-sìp-èt** 31

๔๐ **sèe-sìp** 40

๕๐ **hâh-sìp** 50

๖๐ **hòk-sìp** 60

๗๐ **jèt-sìp** 70

๘๐ **bpàirt-sìp** 80

๙๐ **gâo-sìp** 90

๑๐๐ **nèung róy** 100

๑๐๐๐ **nèung pun** 1,000

๒๐๐๐ **sǒrng pun** 2,000

๑๐๐๐๐ **nèung mèun** 10,000

๒๐๐๐๐ **sǒrng mèun** 20,000

๑๐๐๐๐๐ **nèung sǎirn** 100,000

๒๐๐๐๐๐ **sǒrng sǎirn** 200,000

๑๐๐๐๐๐๐ **nèung láhn**
1,000,000

๑๐๐๐๐๐๐๐๐ **nèung róy láhn**
100,000,000

Phones

บาท **bàht** baht

รหัส **ra-hùt** code

เหรียญ **rěe-un** coin

ต่อ **dtòr** extension

โทรศัพท์ทางไกล
toh-ra-sùp tahng glai
long distance telephone

เสีย **sěe-a** out of order

ตำรวจ **dtum-ròo-ut** police

ตู้โทรศัพท์สาธารณะ
**dtôo toh-ra-sùp sǎh-tah-
ra-ná** public telephone box

โทร. **toh** tel.

โทรศัพท์ **toh-ra-sùp** telephone

สมุดเบอร์โทรศัพท์
sa-mòot ber toh-ra-sùp
telephone directory

เบอร์โทรศัพท์ **ber toh-ra-sùp**
telephone number

Place names

อยุธยา **a-yóot-ta-yah**
Ayutthaya

บางปะอิน **bahng-bpà-in**
Bang Pa-In

กรุงเทพฯ **groong-tâyp**
Bangkok

บางลำภู **bahng-lum-poo**
Banglamphu

เชียงใหม่ **chee-ung-mài**
Chiangmai

อนุสาวรีย์ประชาธิปไตย
**a-nóo-săh-wa-ree
bpra-chah-típ-bpa-dtai**
Democracy Monument

หาดใหญ่ **hàht yài** Hat Yai

หัวหิน **hŏo-a hin** Hua Hin

หัวลำโพง **hŏo-a lum-pohng**
Hua Lampong

กาญจนบุรี **gahn-ja-na-boo-
ree** Kanjanaburi

ขอนแก่น **kŏrn-gàirn** Khonkaen

เกาะสมุย **gòr sa-mŏo-ee**
Koh Samui

สวนลุมพินี **sŏo-un loom-pi-
nee** Lumpini Park

นครปฐม **na-korn bpa-tŏm**
Nakhorn Pathom

พัทยา **pút-ta-yah** Pattaya

ภูเก็ต **poo-gèt** Phuket

ประตูน้ำ **bpra-dtoo náhm**
Pratu Nam

แม่น้ำแคว **mâir-náhm kwair**
River Kwai

สนามหลวง **sa-năhm lŏo-ung**
Sanam Luang

สยามแสควร์ **sa-yăhm
sa-kwair** Siam Square

สงขลา **sŏng-klăh** Songkhla

สุโขทัย **sòo-kŏh-tai** Sukhothai

ธนบุรี **ton-boo-ree** Thonburi

อุบลราชธานี **oo-bon
râht-cha-tah-nee**
Ubonratchathani

อนุสาวรีย์ชัยสมรภูมิ **a-nóo-
săh-wa-ree chai sa-mŏr-ra-
poom** Victory Monument

เยาวราช **yao-wa-râht** Yaowarat
(Chinatown area of Bangkok)

Post office

ผู้รับ **pôo rúp** addressee

ทางอากาศ **tahng ah-gàht**
airmail

กรุงเทพฯ **groong-tâyp**
Bangkok

ตู้จดหมาย **dtôo jòt-măi**
letter box, mail box

ที่อื่น **têe èun** other places

พัสดุ **pút-sa-dòo** parcels

รหัสไปรษณีย์ **ra-hùt bprai-sa-
nee** postcode

ที่ทำการไปรษณีย์ **têe tum
gahn bprai-sa-nee**
post office

ลงทะเบียน **long ta-bee-un**
registered mail

ผู้ส่ง **pôo sòng** sender

ไปรษณียากร **bprai-sa-nee-yah-gorn** stamps

ทางเรือ **tahng reu-a** surface mail

โทรเลข **toh-ra-lâyk** telegrams

โทรศัพท์ **toh-ra-sùp** telephone

Public buildings

สนามบิน **sa-năhm bin** airport

ธนาคาร **ta-nah-kahn** bank

สนามมวย **sa-năhm moo-ay** boxing stadium

สถานีรถเมล์ **sa-tăhn-nee rót may** bus station

โรงภาพยนตร์ **rohng pâhp-pa-yon** cinema, movie theater

คลีนิค **klee-ník** clinic

วิทยาลัย **wít-ta-yah-lai** college

กรมศุลกากร **grom sŏon-la-gah-gorn** Customs Department

กรม **grom** department (government)

ที่ว่าการอำเภอ **têe wâh gahn um-per** district office

กอง **gorng** division (government)

สถานทูต **sa-tăhn tôot** embassy

โรงพยาบาล **rohng pa-yah-bahn** hospital

โรงแรม **rohng rairm** hotel

กองตรวจคนเข้าเมือง **gorng dtròo-ut kon kâo meu-ung** Immigration Department

กรมแรงงาน **grom rairng ngahn** Labour Department

ศาล **săhn** law court

ห้องสมุด **hôrng sa-mòot** library

ตลาด **dta-làht** market

กระทรวง **gra-soo-ung** ministry

พิพิธภัณฑ์ **pí-pít-ta-pun** museum

สนามกีฬาแห่งชาติ **sa-năhm gee-lah hàirng châht** National Stadium

ร้านขายยา **ráhn kăi yah** pharmacy

สถานีตำรวจ **sa-tăhn-nee dtum-ròo-ut** police station

ไปรษณีย์ **bprai-sa-nee** post office

โรงเรียน **rohng ree-un** school

ร้าน **ráhn** shop, store

ศูนย์การค้า **sŏon gahn káh** shopping centre

ห้าง **hâhng** store, shop

องค์การส่งเสริมการท่องเที่ยวแห่งประเทศไทย **ong-gahn sòng sĕrm gahn tôrng têe-o hàirng bpra-tâyt** TAT (Tourist Organization of Thailand)

กรมสรรพากร **grom sŭn-pah-gorn** Tax Department

วัด **wút** temple

โรงละคร **rohng la-korn** theatre

สถานีรถไฟ **sa-tăhn-nee rót fai** train station

มหาวิทยาลัย **ma-hăh-wít-ta-yah-lai** university

Public holidays

วันพระ **wun prá** Buddhist holy day

วันหยุดราชการ **wun yòot râht-cha-gahn** official public holiday

วันขึ้นปีใหม่ **wun kêun bpee mài** New Year's Day

วันสงกรานต์ **wun sŏng-grahn** Songkran Day (Thai New Year)

Rail travel

จองตั๋วล่วงหน้า **jorng dtŏo-a lôo-ung nâh** advance bookings

ถึง **tĕung** arrives

ออก **òrk** departs

แผนกสอบถาม **pa-nàirk sòrp tăhm** enquiries

สุขาชาย **sòo-kăh chai** gents' toilets, men's room

สถานีหัวหิน

HUA HIN STATION

สุขาหญิง **sòo-kǎh yǐng**
ladies' toilets, ladies' room

รับฝากของ **rúp fàhk kǒrng** left
luggage, baggage checkroom

ชานชาลา **chahn-chah-lah**
platform, (US) track

ประชาสัมพันธ์ **bpra-chah**
sǔm-pun public relations

สถานีรถไฟ **sa-tǎh-nee rót fai**
railway station, train station

ที่จำหน่ายตั๋ว **têe jum-nài**
dtǒo-a ticket office

กำหนดเวลาเดินรถ **gum-nòt**
way-lah dern ròt timetable,
(US) schedule

รถไฟ **rót fai** train

ห้องพักผู้โดยสาร **hông púk**
pôo doy-ee sǎhn
waiting room

Regions, provinces
etc

ชายแดน **chai dairn** border

เขต **kàyt** boundary; area

ภาคกลาง **pâhk glahng**
central region

แม่น้ำเจ้าพระยา
mâir-náhm jâo pra-yah
Chao Phraya River

ประเทศ **bpra-tâyt** country

อำเภอ **um-per** Amphoe, district

แม่โขง **mâir-kǒhng**
Mekhong River

ภาคอีสาน **pâhk ee-sǎhn**
north-eastern region

ภาคเหนือ **pâhk něu-a**
northern region

จังหวัด **jung-wùt** province

ภาคใต้ **pâhk dtâi**
southern region

ตำบล **dtum-bon**
Tambon, sub-district

บ้านนอก **bâhn-nôrk** up-country

ต่างจังหวัด **dtàhng jung-wùt**
up-country

Restaurants, bars

บริการ ๒๔ ชั่วโมง **bor-ri-gahn**
24 chôo-a mohng
24-hour service

ห้องแอร์ **hông-air**
air-conditioned room

ร้านอาหารโต้รุ่ง **ráhn ah-hǎhn**
dtôh rôong all-night
restaurant

บาร์ **bah** bar

ชาม **chahm** bowl, dish

อาหารเช้า **ah-hǎhn cháo**
breakfast

คอฟฟี่ช็อบ **kórp-fêe chórp**
café serving coffees, alcoholic
drinks, snacks and meals

อาหารจีน **ah-hǎhn jeen**
Chinese food

อาหารเย็น **ah-hǎhn yen**
evening meal

อาหาร **ah-hǎhn** food

อาหารญี่ปุ่น **ah-hǎhn yêe-bpòOn** Japanese food

อาหารกลางวัน **ah-hǎhn glahng wun** lunch

อาหารมุสลิม **ah-hǎhn móO-sa-lim** Muslim food

อาหารอีสาน **ah-hǎhn ee-sǎhn**
North-Eastern food

สวนอาหาร **sǒo-un ah-hǎhn**
open-air restaurant

ชามละ… **chahm la…**
…per bowl/dish

จานละ … **jahn la…**
…per plate/dish

จาน **jahn** plate, dish

ราคา **rah-kah** price

ภัตตาคาร **pút-dtah-kahn**
restaurant

ร้านอาหาร **ráhn ah-hǎhn**
restaurant

ห้องอาหาร **hôrng ah-hǎhn**
restaurant

อาหารทะเล **ah-hǎhn ta-lay**
seafood

เชลล์ชวนชิม **chen choo-un chim** Shell recommended, seal of approval, equivalent to Good Food Guide

อาหารปักษ์ใต้ **ah-hǎhn bpùk dtâi** Southern food

อาหารไทย **ah-hǎhn tai** Thai food

อาหารฝรั่ง **ah-hǎhn fa-rùng**
Western food

Road signs

ทางโค้ง **tahng kóhng** bend

ระวังทางข้างหน้าเป็นทางเอก **ra-wung tahng kâhng nâh bpen tahng àyk** caution: major road ahead

ระวัง **ra-wung** caution

อันตราย **un-dta-rai** danger

ทางเบี่ยง **tahng bèe-ung**
diversion

ขับช้าๆ **kùp cháh cháh**
drive slowly

๔๐ ก.ม. **sèe sìp gi-loh-mét**
40 kilometres

๔ ตัน **sìi dtun** 4 tons

หยุด ตรวจ **yòot – dtròo-ut**
halt – checkpoint

โรงพยาบาลห้ามใช้เสียง **rohng pa-yah-bahn hâhm chái sěe-ung** hospital: no sounding horns

ชิดซ้าย **chít sái** keep left

ห้ามเข้า **hâhm kâo** no entry

ห้ามแซง **hâhm sairng**
no overtaking, no passing

ห้ามจอดรถ **hâhm jòrt rót**
no parking

ห้ามเลี้ยว **hâhm lée-o**
no turning

ห้ามกลับรถ **hâhm glùp rót**
no U-turns

ห้ามรถทุกชนิด **hâhm rót tóok cha-nít** no vehicles

ทางรถไฟ **tahng rót fai** railway

โรงเรียน **rohng ree-un** school

หยุด **yòot** stop

๓ ม. **sahm mét** 3 metres

Shopping

บาท **bàht** baht (unit of currency)

ลูกละ ... บาท **lôok la ... bàht**
... baht each (e.g. for large fruit)

ใบละ ... บาท **bai la ... bàht**
... baht each (e.g. for eggs, fruit)

ตัวละ ... บาท **dtoo-a la ... bàht** ... baht each (e.g. items of clothing)

โลละ ... บาท **loh la ... bàht**
... baht per kilo

คู่ละ ... บาท **kôo la ... baht**
... baht per pair (e.g. shoes)

ชิ้นละ ... บาท **chín la ... bàht**
... baht per piece/portion

สุขภัณฑ์ **sòok-ka-pun**
bathroom accessories

ที่จ่ายเงิน **têe jài ngern**
cash desk, cashier

พนักงานเก็บเงิน **pa-núk ngahn gèp ngern** cashier

แผนกเด็ก **pa-nàirk dèk**
children's department

แผนกไฟฟ้า **pa-nàirk fai fáh**
electrical goods

เครื่องเรือน **krêu-ung reu-un**
furniture

ราคา **rah-kah** price

วิทยุทีวี **wít-ta-yóo – tee-wee**
radio – TV

ลดราคา **lót rah-kah**
sale; reduced

รองเท้า **rorng-táo** shoes

ลดพิเศษ **lót pi-sàyt**
special reductions

อุปกรณ์กีฬา **òo-bpa-gorn gee-lah** sports equipment

ของเล่น **kŏrng lên** toys

นาฬิกา **nah-li-gah** watches

Sport

กรีฑา **gree-tah** athletics

มวย **moo-ay** boxing

ฟุตบอล **fóot-born** football

ประตู **bpra-dtoo** goal

กอล์ฟ **górp** golf

สนามกอล์ฟ **sa-năhm górp**
golf course

สนามม้า **sa-năhm máh**
race course

กีฬา **gee-lah** sport

สนามกีฬา **sa-năhm gee-lah** stadium

ว่ายน้ำ **wâi náhm** swimming

ทีม **teem** team

เทนนิส **ten-nít** tennis

สนามเทนนิส **sa-năhm ten-nít** tennis court

มวยไทย **moo-ay tai** Thai boxing

Streets and roads

ตรอก **dtròrk** lane (off a soi)

ซอย **soy** lane, soi

ถนน **ta-nŏn** road

Thai culture

เมืองโบราณ **meu-ung boh-rahn** Ancient City

กรมศิลปากร **grom sĭn-la-bpa-korn** Department of Fine Arts

ตลาดน้ำ **dta-làht náhm** Floating Market

พิพิธภัณฑ์ **pi-pít-ta-pun** museum

พิพิธภัณฑ์สถานแห่งชาติ **pi-pít-ta-pun sa-tăhn hàirng châht** National Museum

โรงละครแห่งชาติ **rohng la-korn hàirng châht** National Theatre

พระปฐมเจดีย์ **prá-bpa-tŏm jay-dee** Pra Pathom Jedi (Buddhist monument)

พระบรมมหาราชวัง **prá-ba-rom-ma-hăh-râtch-a-wung** Royal Palace

วังสวนผักกาด **wung sŏo-un pùk-gàht** Suan Pakkard Palace

วัด **wút** temple

วัดพระแก้ว **wút pra-kâir-o** Temple of the Emerald Buddha

มวยไทย **moo-ay tai** Thai boxing

รำไทย **rum tai** Thai dancing

วัดโพธิ์ **wút poh** Wat Po

Timetables

ถึง **tĕung** arrives

วันที่ **wun-têe** date

วัน **wun** day

ออก **òrk** departs

วันหยุด **wun yòot** holiday

นาฬิกา **nah-li-gah** hours

เวลา **way-lah** time

กำหนดเวลาเดินรถ **gum-nòt way-lah dern rót** timetable, (US) schedule

วันนี้ **wun née** today

พรุ่งนี้ **prôong née** tomorrow

วันเสาร์อาทิตย์ **wun săo ah-tít**
  weekend
เมื่อวานนี้ **mêu-a wahn née**
  yesterday

Toilets

ไม่ว่าง **mâi wâhng** engaged
บุรุษ **boo-ròot** gentlemen
ชาย **chai** gents
หญิง **yĭng** ladies

สตรี **sa-dtree** ladies
ผู้ชาย **pôo-chai** men
ช. **chor** men
ห้องน้ำ **hôrng náhm**
  toilet, rest room
สุขา **sòo-kăh** toilet, rest room
ว่าง **wâhng** vacant
ญ. **yor** women
ผู้หญิง **pôo-yĭng** women

MENU READER

Food

Essential terms

bowl chahm ชาม

chopsticks dta-gèe-up ตะเกียบ

cup tôo-ay ถ้วย

dessert kǒrng wǎhn ของหวาน

fish bplah ปลา

fork sôrm ส้อม

glass gâir-o แก้ว

knife mêet มีด

meat néu-a เนื้อ

menu may-noo เมนู

noodles gǒo-ay dtěe-o ก๋วยเตี๋ยว

pepper prìk tai พริกไทย

plate jahn จาน

rice kâo ข้าว

salt gleu-a เกลือ

set menu ah-hǎhn chóot อาหารชุด

soup sóop ซุป

spoon chórn ช้อน

table dtó โต๊ะ

another... èek... nèung อีก ... หนึ่ง

excuse me! (to call waiter/ waitress) koon krúp (kâ)! คุณครับ(ค่ะ)

could I have the bill, please? chék bin เช็คบิล

Travel tip Thai food is eaten with a fork (left hand) and a spoon (right hand); there is no need for a knife as it's served in bite-sized chunks. Chopsticks are provided only for noodle dishes, and northeastern sticky-rice dishes are eaten with the fingers of your right hand (never eat with the fingers of your left hand, which is used for washing after going to the toilet).

Basic foods

เนยสด **ner-ee sòt** butter

เนยแข็ง **ner-ee kǎirng** cheese

น้ำพริก **núm prík** chilli paste

กะทิ **ga-tí** coconut milk

น้ำปลา **núm bplah** fish sauce

แป้งสาลี **bpâirng sǎh-lee** flour

น้ำผึ้ง **núm pêung** honey

แยม **yairm** jam; marmalade

น้ำมันพืช **núm mun pêut** oil

น้ำมันมะกอก **núm mun ma-gòrk** olive oil

น้ำมันหอย **núm mun hǒy** oyster sauce

น้ำจิ้ม **núm jîm** sauce

น้ำซีอิ๊ว **núm see éw** soy sauce

น้ำตาล **núm dtahn** sugar

น้ำส้ม **núm sôm** vinegar

โยกัต **yoh-gut** yoghurt

Basic main meals

ข้าวผัดไก่ **kâo pùt gài** chicken fried rice

ข้าวมันไก่ **kâo mun gài** chicken rice

ข้าวผัดปู **kâo pùt bpoo** crab fried rice

บะหมี่แห้ง **ba-mèe hâirng** 'dry' egg noodles, served without soup

ก๋วยเตี๋ยวแห้ง **gǒo-ay dtěe-o hâirng** 'dry' noodles, served without soup

ข้าวหน้าเป็ด **kâo nâh bpèt** duck rice

บะหมี่น้ำ **ba-mèe náhm** egg noodle soup

ก๋วยเตี๋ยวผัดซีอิ๊ว **gǒo-ay dtěe-o pùt see éw** noodles fried in soy sauce

ก๋วยเตี๋ยวผัดราดหน้า **gǒo-ay dtěe-o pùt râht nâh** noodles with fried meat, vegetables and thick gravy

ก๋วยเตี๋ยวน้ำ **gǒo-ay dtěe-o náhm** noodle soup

ข้าวผัดหมู **kâo pùt mǒo** pork fried rice

ข้าวหมูแดง **kâo mǒo dairng** 'red' pork rice (pork soaked in a red marinade)

ข้าวคลุกกะปิ **kâo klóok ga-bpì** rice and shrimp paste fried together and served with pork and shredded omelette

ข้าวผัดกุ้ง **kâo pùt gôong** shrimp fried rice

ผัดไทย **pùt tai** Thai-style fried noodles

ขนมจีนแกงไก่ **ka-nŏm jeen gairng gài** Thai vermicelli with chicken curry

Beef and beef dishes

เนื้อผัดน้ำมันหอย **néu-a pùt núm mun hŏy** beef fried in oyster sauce

เนื้อผัดพริก **néu-a pùt prík** beef fried with chillies

เนื้อผัดกระเทียมพริกไทย **néu-a pùt gra-tee-um prík tai** beef fried with garlic and pepper

เนื้อผัดขิง **néu-a pùt kĭng** beef fried with ginger

เนื้อสับผัดพริกกระเพรา **néu-a sùp pùt prík gra-prao** minced beef fried with chillies and basil

เนื้อเสต๊ก **néu-a sa-dték** steak

Bread

ขนมปัง **ka-nŏm-bpung** bread; roll

ปอนด์ **bporn** loaf

ขนมปังปิ้ง **ka-nŏm bpung bpîng** toast

Cakes and biscuits, sweet pastries

คุกกี้ **kóok-gêe** biscuit, cookie

ขนมเค้ก **ka-nŏm káyk** cake

แป้งขนม **bpâirng ka-nŏm** pastry (dough)

ขนม **ka-nŏm** pastry, small cake

Condiments and seasonings, herbs and spices

ใบกระเพรา **bai gra-prao** basil

พริก **prík** chilli

ผักชี **pùk chee** coriander

ข่า **kàh** galangal (similar to ginger)

> **Travel tip** Bland food is anathema to Thais, and restaurant tables everywhere are decked out with condiment sets featuring the four basic flavours (salty, sour, sweet and spicy). If you bite into a chilli, combat the searing heat with a mouthful of plain rice or beer: swigging water just exacerbates the sensation.

ขิง **kǐng** ginger

เครื่องเทศ **krêu-ung tâyt** herbs

ตะไคร้ **dta-krái** lemon grass

พริกไทย **prík tai** pepper

เกลือ **gleu-a** salt

Cooking methods and typical combinations

... ต้ม ... **dtôm** boiled...

... ย่าง ... **yâhng** charcoal-grilled...

... ทอด ... **tôrt** deep-fried...

... ผัดหน่อไม้ ... **pùt nòr-mái** ... fried with bamboo shoots

... ผัดใบกระเพรา ... **pùt bai gra-prao** ... fried with basil leaves

... ผัดพริก ... **pùt prík** ... fried with chillies

... ทอดกระเทียมพริกไทย ... **tôrt gra-tee-um prík tai** ... fried with garlic and pepper

... ผัดขิง ... **pùt kǐng** ... fried with ginger

... อบ ... **òp** oven-cooked...

... ผัด ... **pùt** stir-fried...

... เปรี้ยวหวาน ... **bprêe-o wǎhn** sweet and sour...

ปิ้ง **bpîng** toasted

Curries

แกงเนื้อ **gairng néu-a** beef curry

แกงเขียวหวาน **gairng kěe-o wǎhn** beef curry made using green curry paste, made from green chilli peppers

ข้าวแกง **kâo gairng** curry and rice

แกงไก่ **gairng gài** chicken curry

พะแนง **pa-nairng** 'dry' curry (in thick curry sauce)

พะแนงเนื้อ **pa-nairng néu-a** 'dry' beef curry (in thick curry sauce)

พะแนงไก่ pa-nairng gài 'dry'
chicken curry (in thick curry
sauce)

พะแนงหมู pa-nairng mŏo 'dry'
pork curry (in thick curry sauce)

แกงกาหรี่ gairng ga-rèe Indian-
style curry made with beef and
potatoes cooked in coconut
milk with yellow curry paste

แกงมัสหมั่น gairng mút-sa-
mùn 'Muslim' curry containing
beef, potatoes and peanuts

แกงเผ็ด gairng pèt spicy curry

แกงจืด gairng jèut
vegetable soup or stock
(an accompaniment to curries)

แกง gairng 'wet' curry – meat
cooked in coconut milk and
served in a bowl full of liquid

Desserts

กล้วยบวชชี glôo-ay bòo-ut
chee banana in sweet coconut-
milk sauce

ของหวาน kŏrng wăhn dessert

ไอศครีม ai-sa- kreem
ice cream

ข้าวเหนียวมะม่วง kăo nĕe-o
ma-môo-ung sweet sticky
rice, mango and coconut cream

ตะโก้ dta-gôh Thai-style jelly
with coconut cream

Eggs and egg dishes

ไข่ต้ม kài dtôm boiled egg

ไข่ kài egg

ไข่พะโล้ kài pa-lóh egg stewed
in soy sauce and spices

ไข่ยัดไส้ kài yút sâi
filled omelette

ไข่ดาว kài dao fried egg

ไข่เจียว kài jee-o omelette

ไข่ลูกเขย kài lôok kĕr-ee
'son-in-law' eggs (hard-boiled
eggs with various condiments)

ไข่ลวก kài lôo-uk very soft
boiled egg (eaten, or rather
'drunk' almost raw)

Fish and seafood

ปู bpoo crab

ปลา bplah fish

กุ้งใหญ่ gôong yài lobster

หอยแมงภู่ hŏy mairng pôo
mussels

ปลาหมึกยักษ์ bplah-mèuk yúk
octopus

หอยนางรม hŏy nahng rom
oyster

อาหารทะเล ah-hăhn ta-lay
seafood

หอย hŏy shellfish

กุ้ง **gôong** shrimp, prawn

ปลาหมึก **bplah-mèuk** squid

Fish and seafood dishes

กุ้งเผา **gôong păo**
barbecued prawns

กุ้งทอดกระเทียมพริกไทย
gôong tôrt gra-tee-um prík tai prawns fried with garlic and pepper

กุ้งผัดใบกระเพรา
gôong pùt bai gra-prao shrimps fried with basil leaves

กุ้งผัดพริก **gôong pùt prík** shrimps fried with chillies

ทอดมันกุ้ง **tôrt mun gôong** shrimp 'tort mun', finely minced shrimps, fried in batter with spices

ปลาหมึกผัดพริก **bplah-mèuk pùt prík** squid fried with chillies

> **Travel tip** Hygiene is a consideration when eating anywhere in Thailand, but being too cautious means you'll spend a lot of money and miss out on some real local treats. Wean your stomach gently by avoiding excessive amounts of chillies and too much fresh fruit in the first few days.

ปลาหมึกทอดกระเทียมพริกไทย
bplah-mèuk tôrt gra-tee-um prík tai squid fried with garlic and pepper

ปลาเปรี้ยวหวาน
bplah bprêe-o wăhn sweet and sour fish

Fruit

แอปเปิล **air-bpêrn** apple

กล้วย **glôo-ay** banana

มะพร้าว **ma-práo** coconut

น้อยหน่า **nóy-nàh**
custard apple (green heart-shaped fruit with white flesh)

อินทผาลัม **in-ta-păh-lum**
dates

ทุเรียน **too-ree-un** durian (large green fruit with spiny skin, yellow flesh and a pungent smell)

ผลไม้ **pŏn-la-mái** fruit

องุ่น **a-ngòon** grapes

ฝรั่ง **fa-rùng** guava (green-skinned fruit with white flesh)

ขนุน **ka-nŏon** jackfruit (large melon-shaped fruit with thick, green skin and yellow flesh)

มะนาว **ma-nao** lemon; lime

ลำใย **lum-yai** longan (like a lychee)

ลิ้นจี่ **lín-jèe** lychee

มะม่วง **ma-môo-ung** mango

มังคุด **mung-kóot** mangosteen (round fruit with a thick, purplish-brown skin and white flesh)

แตงไทย **dtairng tai** melon

ส้ม **sôm** orange

มะละกอ **ma-la-gor** papaya (green or yellow-skinned oblong-shaped fruit with reddish-orange flesh)

ลูกพีช **lôok pêech** peach

ลูกแพร์ **lôok pair** pear

สับปะรด **sùp-bpa-rót** pineapple

ลูกพลัม **lôok plum** plum

ส้มโอ **sôm oh** pomelo (similar to grapefruit)

เงาะ **ngór** rambutan (small fruit with reddish prickly skin and white flesh)

ชมพู่ **chom-pôo** rose apple (red, pink or white strawberry-shaped fruit)

ละมุด **la-móot** sapodilla (small brown-skinned fruit, similar in taste and texture to a pear)

สตรอเบอรี่ **sa-dtror-ber-rêe** strawberry

แตงโม **dtairng moh** water melon

Meat

เนื้อ **néu-a** beef; meat

ไก่ **gài** chicken

เป็ด **bpèt** duck

เครื่องใน **krêu-ung nai** kidneys

ไต **tai** kidneys

เนื้อแกะ **néu-a gàir** lamb

ตับ **dtùp** liver

หมู **mǒo** pork

เนื้อหมู **néu-a mǒo** pork

Menu terms

อาหารจีน **ah-hǎhn jeen** Chinese food

อาหาร **ah-hǎhn** cuisine, cooking; meal; food

กับข้าว **gùp kâo** dish, meal

เมนู **may-noo** menu

รายการอาหาร **rai gahn ah-hǎhn** menu

ราคา **rah-kah** price

Travel tip When looking for a place to eat, you can be pretty sure that any noodle stall or curry shop that's permanently packed with customers is a safe bet. And, because most Thai dishes can be cooked in less than five minutes, you'll rarely have to contend with stuff that's been left to moulder.

Miscellaneous dishes

ทอดมัน **tôrt mun**
  deep-fried fish-cakes

ขนมจีบ **ka-nŏm jèep**
  'dim-sum' (steamed balls of
  minced pork in dough)

ปอเปี๊ยะทอด **bpor bpêe-a tôrt**
  Thai spring roll

Pork and pork dishes

หมูสับผัดพริกกระเพรา
  mŏo sùp pùt prík gra-prao
  minced pork fried with chillies
  and basil

หมู **mŏo** pork

เนื้อหมู **néu-a mŏo** pork

หมูผัดใบกระเพรา **mŏo pùt bai
  gra-prao** pork fried with basil
  leaves

หมูผัดพริก **mŏo pùt prík**
  pork fried with chillies

หมูทอดกระเทียมพริกไทย **mŏo
  tôrt gra-tee-um prík tai** pork
  fried with garlic and pepper

หมูผัดขิง **mŏo pùt kǐng**
  pork fried with ginger

หมูพะโล้ **môo pa-lóh**
  pork stewed in soy sauce

ซี่โครง **sêe krohng mŏo**
  spare ribs

หมูเปรี้ยวหวาน **mŏo bprêe-o
  wăhn** sweet and sour pork

หมูสะเต๊ะ **mŏo sa-dtáy**
  thin strips of charcoal-grilled
  pork

Poultry and poultry dishes

ไก่ย่าง **gài yâhng** barbecued or
  roast chicken

ไก่ **gài** chicken

ไก่ต้มข่า **gài dtôm kàh**
  chicken boiled in spicy stock

ไก่ผัดหน่อไม้ **gài pùt nòr-mái**
  chicken fried with bamboo
  shoots

ไก่ผัดใบกระเพรา **gài pùt bai
  gra-prao** chicken fried with
  basil leaves

ไก่ผัดเม็ดมะม่วงหิมพานต์
  **gài pùt mét ma-môo-ung
  hǐm-ma-pahn** chicken fried
  with cashew nuts

ไก่ผัดพริก **gài pùt prík**
  chicken fried with chillies

ไก่ทอดกระเทียมพริกไทย
  gài tôrt gra-tee-um prík tai
  chicken fried with garlic and
  pepper

ไก่ผัดขิง **gài pùt kĭng**
chicken fried with ginger

ไก่ผัดหน่อไม้ฝรั่ง
gài pùt nòr-mái fa-rùng
chicken with asparagus

เป็ด **bpèt** duck

เป็ดย่าง **bpèt yâhng** roast duck

ไก่ผัดเปรี้ยวหวาน **gài pùt
brêe-o wăhn** sweet and sour
chicken

Rice and noodles

ข้าวสวย **kâo sŏo-ay** boiled rice

หมี่กรอบ **mèe gròrp**
crispy noodles

บะหมี่ **ba-mèe** egg noodles

ข้าวผัด **kâo pùt** fried rice

เส้นใหญ่ **sên yài** large (width of
noodles)

ผัดราดหน้า **pùt râht nâh**
noodles with fried vegetables
and meat, served with a thick
gravy

ก๋วยเตี๋ยว **gŏo-ay dtĕe-o**
rice-flour noodles

ข้าว **kâo** rice

ข้าวต้ม **kâo dtôm** rice porridge

เส้นเล็ก **sên lék** small (width of
noodles)

ข้าวเหนียว **kâo nĕe-o** sticky rice

ขนมจีน **ka-nŏm jeen**
Thai vermicelli

วุ้นเส้น **wóon-sên**
transparent noodles

เส้นหมี่ **sên mèe** very small
(width of noodles)

Salads

ส้มตำ **sôm dtum** papaya salad
made with unripe green
papaya, chillies, lime juice, fish
sauce and dried shrimps

สลัด **sa-lùt** salad

ยำ **yum** Thai salad

Snacks and sweets

ช็อกโกเลต **chórk-goh-let**
chocolate

มันฝรั่งทอด **mun fa-rùng tôrt**
crisps, (US) potato chips

ไอศครีม **ai-sa-kreem**
ice cream

ไอศครีมแท่ง **ai-sa-kreem
tâirng** ice lolly

อมยิ้ม **om-yím** lollipop

ถั่ว **tòo-a** nuts; peanuts

ถั่วลิสง **tòo-a li-sŏng** peanuts

ท็อฟฟี่ **tórp-fêe** sweets, candies

ลูกกวาด **lôok gwàht**
sweets, candies

Soups

ต้มยำไก่ **dtôm yum gài**
chicken 'tom yam' spicy soup

บะหมี่น้ำ **ba-mèe náhm**
egg noodle soup

ต้มยำปลา **dtôm yum bplah**
fish 'tom yam' spicy soup

ต้มยำโป๊ะแตก **dtôm yum bpó dtàirk** mixed seafood 'tom yam' spicy soup

ก๋วยเตี๋ยวน้ำ **gǒo-ay dtěe-o náhm** noodle soup

ต้มยำกุ้ง **dtôm yum gôong**
shrimp 'tom yam' spicy soup

แกงส้ม **gairng sôm**
spicy vegetable soup

Vegetables and vegetable dishes

หน่อไม้ฝรั่ง **nòr-mái fa-rùng**
asparagus

มะเขือ **ma-kěu-a**
aubergine, eggplant

หน่อไม้ **nòr mái** bamboo shoots

ถั่วงอก **tòo-a ngôrk** bean sprouts

กะหล่ำปลี **ga-lùm-bplee**
cabbage

หัวผักกาดแดง **hǒo-a pùk-gàht dairng** carrot

ดอกกะหล่ำปลี **dòrk ga-lùm-bplee** cauliflower

พริก **prík** chilli

มันฝรั่งทอด **mun fa-rùng tôrt**
chips, French fries

แตงกวา **dtairng-gwah** cucumber

ผัดผักบุ้งไฟแดง **pùt pùk bôong fai dairng** fried morning-glory (type of greens)

กระเทียม **gra-tee-um** garlic

ขิง **kǐng** ginger

พริกหยวก **prík yòo-uk** green pepper

ผักกาด **pùk-gàht** lettuce

ถั่วลันเตา **tòo-a lun-dtao**
mange-tout

ผักบุ้ง **pùk bôong** morning-glory (type of greens)

เห็ด **hèt** mushrooms

หัวหอม **hǒo-a hǒrm** onion

ถั่ว **tòo-a** peas; beans; lentils

มันฝรั่ง **mun fa-rùng** potato

พริกหยวกแดง **prík yòo-uk dairng** red pepper

ผักคะน้า **pùk ka-náh**
spring greens

ต้นหอม **dtôn hǒrm**
spring onions

ข้าวโพด **kâo pôht** sweetcorn, maize

มะเขือเทศ **ma-kěu-a tâyt**
tomato

ผัก **pùk** vegetables

Drink

Essential terms

beer bee-a เบียร์

bottle kòo-ut ขวด

  another bottle of..., please
  kǒr... èek kòo-ut nèung
  ขอ ... อีกขวดหนึ่ง

coconut juice núm ma-práo
น้ำมะพร้าว

coffee gah-fair กาแฟ

cup tôo-ay ถ้วย

  a cup of..., please kǒr...
  tôo-ay nèung ขอ ... ถ้วยหนึ่ง

fruit juice núm pǒn-la-mái
น้ำผลไม้

gin lâo yin เหล้ายิน

  a gin and tonic, please
  kǒr yin toh-nik ขอยินโทนิค

glass gâir-o แก้ว

milk nom นม

mineral water núm râir น้ำแร่

soda (water) núm soh-dah
น้ำโซดา

soft drink náhm kòo-ut น้ำขวด

> **Travel tip** Thais don't drink water straight from the tap, and neither should you; plastic bottles of drinking water are sold countrywide and should be used even when brushing your teeth. Cheap restaurants and hotels generally serve free jugs of boiled water, which should be fine to drink, though they are not as foolproof as bottles.

sugar núm dtahn น้ำตาล

tea núm chah น้ำชา

tonic (water) núm toh-nik
น้ำโทนิค

water náhm น้ำ

whisky lâo wít-sa-gêe เหล้าวิสกี้

wine lâo wai เหล้าไวน์

wine list rai-gahn lâo wai
รายการเหล้าไวน์

another... èek ... nèung
อีก ... หนึ่ง

Beer, spirits, wine etc

เหล้า lâo alcohol, liquor

เบียร์ bee-a beer

ขวด kòo-ut bottle

เหล้าบรั่นดี lâo brùn-dee
brandy

ค็อกเทล kórk-tayn cocktail

แก้ว gâir-o glass

เหล้ายิน lâo yin gin

ยินโทนิค yin toh-nik
gin and tonic

น้ำแข็ง núm kǎirng ice

แม่โขง mâir-kǒhng Mekhong
whisky

เบียร์สิงห์ bee-a sǐng
Singha beer

วอดก้า word-gâh vodka

เหล้าวิสกี้ lâo wít-sa-gêe
whisky, scotch

เหล้าไวน์ lâo wai wine

Coffee, tea etc

คาฟีน kah-feen caffeine

เย็น yen chilled

โกโก้ goh-gôh cocoa

กาแฟ gah-fair coffee

โอเลี้ยง oh-lée-ung
iced black coffee

กาแฟเย็น gah-fair yen
iced coffee

ชาใส่มะนาว chah sài ma-nao
lemon tea

กาแฟผง gah-fair pǒng
instant coffee

น้ำชา núm chah tea

ไม่ใส่นม mái sài nom
without milk

ไม่ใส่น้ำตาล mái sài núm
dtahn without sugar

Soft drinks

น้ำมะพร้าว **núm ma-práo**
  coconut juice

โค้ก **kóhk** Coke

เครื่องดื่ม **krêu-ung dèum**
  drinks

ซ่า **sâh** fizzy, carbonated

น้ำส้มคั้น **núm sôm kún**
  fresh orange juice

น้ำแข็ง **núm kǎirng** ice

น้ำผลไม้ **náhm pǒn-la-mái**
  juice

นม **nom** milk

น้ำมะนาว **núm ma-nao**
  lemonade

น้ำแร่ **núm râir** mineral water

น้ำส้ม **núm sôm** orange juice
  (bottled)

น้ำสับปะรด **núm sùp-bpa-rót**
  pineapple juice

น้ำโซดา **núm soh-dah**
  soda water

น้ำขวด **náhm kòo-ut** soft drink

นมกระป๋อง **nom gra-bpǒrng**
  tinned milk

น้ำมะเขือเทศ **núm ma-kěu-a**
  tâyt tomato juice

น้ำ **náhm** water

Picture credits

All maps and photos © Rough Guides.

Photography by: Martin Richardson (back cover, pp.5, 29, 32, 34, 39, 45, 48, 110, 119, 128, 139, 150, 166, 202, 207, 210, 234); Karen Trist (cover, pp.6, 22, 26, 55, 62, 72, 78, 85, 92, 101, 161, 174, 179, 195, 228, 236, 239, 246).